# Never Had a Dad

Also by Georgie Codd

*We Swim to the Shark*

# Never Had a Dad

## Adventures in Fatherlessness

### GEORGIE CODD

**WILLIAM COLLINS**

William Collins
An imprint of HarperCollins*Publishers*
1 London Bridge Street
London SE1 9GF

WilliamCollinsBooks.com

HarperCollins*Publishers*
Macken House
39/40 Mayor Street Upper
Dublin 1
D01 C9W8
Ireland

First published in Great Britain in 2024 by William Collins

1

Copyright © Georgie Codd 2024

Georgie Codd asserts the moral right to be identified as the author of this work in
accordance with the Copyright, Designs and Patents Act 1988

A catalogue record for this book is available from the British Library

ISBN 978-0-00-860302-1

All rights reserved. No part of this publication may be reproduced, stored in a retrieval
system, or transmitted, in any form or by any means, electronic, mechanical,
photocopying, recording or otherwise, without the prior permission of the publishers.

This book is sold subject to the condition that it shall not, by way of trade or otherwise,
be lent, re-sold, hired out or otherwise circulated without the publisher's prior consent
in any form of binding or cover other than that in which it is published and without a
similar condition including this condition being imposed on the subsequent purchaser.

Typeset in Adobe Garamond Pro by Jouve (UK), Milton Keynes

Printed and bound in Great Britain by CPI Group (UK) Ltd, Croydon

This book contains FSC™ certified paper and other controlled
sources to ensure responsible forest management.

For more information visit: www.harpercollins.co.uk/green

For every never-hadder.
And for Mum.

# 1

# (DIS)EMBARKING

'Ladies!' Peter's boisterous Welsh accent cut through the background noise of breakfast plates. 'How are we this morning?'

My mother – splitting two dry bread rolls for later; stuffing them with cheese oblongs – said, 'Very well, thanks.'

Peter raised an eyebrow. Then he looked down at me with a smile, awaiting my answer.

We were supposed to be in Shetland.

If we had been, I don't know what Shetland would have sparked. Possibly nothing. Possibly we would have all kept keeping on, never knowing the strange experience we had missed.

At the time, I was frustrated. Along with the offer of three buffet meals every day, plus opportunities to scan the waves for flukes and fins, Shetland had been the big hook for this cruise with my mother – the highlight of a return passage from Tilbury Docks to the North Atlantic sea.

Shetland. A rugged archipelago sitting far north of the far north of Scotland. Wild, pure, escapist Shetland, where the sky and the land and the water all merge, and sea monsters wave their tails as tourists munch through steaming bannocks.

Except the ship we were travelling on, an enormous vessel with hundreds of passengers, hundreds of staff, tens of thousands of tonnes, couldn't enter the harbour. There was too much tide and gale-force wind.

I watched from the deck as Shetland lurched away. We were diverting, the Tannoy told us, to Invergordon. Returning to the mainland two days early.

My mum and I pulled the same face.

'Inver-where?'

The next morning, as we slowed into port, our disappointment grew. The main sights around us were the hulking platforms of oil rigs, towed into the bay for repair. I pressed my forehead to the window until my jaws vibrated, the ship engines shuddering to dock. Invergordon showed itself as a small town with layers of mainland houses. Mainland cranes. I couldn't pretend we were secluded, surrounded by nothing but wilderness. Head in a straight line and we would encounter suburbia, not sea monsters.

The other passengers didn't seem to mind. They were catching coaches to shopping outlets to buy Live-Laugh-Love kitchen blackboards. Taking overpriced tours to Loch Ness and Skye. Or staying on board to read the broadsheets and work through their quota of drinks tokens.

I focused on the rest of the view. Hills. Trees. A bay that curved for miles. 'Let's find a coastal path,' I suggested.

'We'll need waterproofs,' said Mum.

'If it's shit, let's come back early. Buy a Cocktail Package.'

'Sounds good.'

I jiggled my legs, eager to leave the ship and begin. Mum began requisitioning napkins to smuggle out free cheese rolls. Apples and satsumas bulged in her pockets. Meanwhile a tall Welsh shape approached us.

And now he was awaiting my answer. How was I?

'Thrilled at our stunning surroundings?' I offered. 'Shetland eat your heart out?'

'Exactly,' he replied, emphasising the *ack*. 'That's the spirit.'

There wasn't space for Peter at our table-for-two that morning, which was okay with me. On the few times he had joined us, my mother had drawn him into at least one conversation that felt destined never to end: discussing the state of the NHS until both were shaking their heads, bound in a loop of dismay that neither knew how to exit. That day I wanted out early. I was ready for Invergordon to be better than expected and annul the anticlimactic sense that had characterised our ship's return journey south.

Taking a spot a few tables across, Peter gave us an amiable wave, then struck up a conversation with a passing Malaysian waitress. She was youthful, petite, made-up. He broke off only to glance at the chest of a wandering female passenger. Catching me looking as he was looking, he adopted a conspiratorial mock-shocked expression – *The size of those*, it said – and switched back to the waitress.

'See?' said Mum, without moving her lips, continuing a debate that had started just beyond the Thames. 'He doesn't want to hear from an old bag like me. It's you he comes over for.'

'The man's 70. He wants to be in *your* pants.'
'Don't be so naive, Georgina.'

When we were finally permitted to disembark, Mum and I turned down the offer of a free shuttle bus. We had all day to squeeze the excitement from this area. There was no point going straight to the tea rooms and blowing our one safe bet.

October gusts assaulted our ears as we trudged on a beach made of stone and grit. The nearest B-road ran parallel, cars and vans speeding along it in their rush to leave the area.

We followed signs for a footpath. They led us away from the bay and into some patchy woodland, for a different-yet-near-identical view of the traffic. Further on, we were forced to join the B-road itself. My face grew stiff and ruddy.

'It's going to get better,' I declared, as another fast car had us leaping into a thicket. 'I can sense it.'

Then the rain started.

A new route to the beach presented itself. We took it and scuffed across stones. The B-road trailed us at shoulder-height for a while, bringing car tyres beside our heads, before it jerked away towards a village. We stuck to the beach still, never far from the edge of somebody's mainland house and mainland garden, wordlessly trudging until we reached two tiny ponies stood in a field. Their manes streamed artfully in the breeze; a duo of horse-shaped Elvis impersonators. While they took turns nosing my raincoat, I tried to take pictures. My fingers were white with cold.

Mum ate wasabi peas at our friends. She looked pained.

I narrowed my range of vision, thinking, *This could almost be Shetland.*

The snarl of a motorbike broke across the white noise of the waves. There were clustered homes in front of us; oil rigs behind us. Another motorbike coughed its guts out.

This was not Shetland.

'Do you want to turn around?'

Mum crunched another handful of peas and nodded.

It was after lunch by the time we re-entered the outskirts of Invergordon. Passing the giant cruise ship – its long blue hull and towering decks – we caught sight of an official noticeboard advertising an attractive coastal walk, headed westwards. We had picked the exact wrong direction.

'Shitting path. Shitting town.'

'*Language*, Georgina.'

At least there was still the chance of a quaint Scottish tea room.

Mum and I made our way to the high street, a single road lined with mute-coloured buildings, and jointly scoured for baked goods. Metres later, a familiar voice called out, 'Ladies!'

Peter was standing solo outside the town's only museum. He looked cosy in his quilted jacket, hands tucked tightly in his jeans. 'Been exploring?'

Mum confirmed we had. I confirmed it had been crap.

'That's the spirit.'

I peered around his shoulder at the entrance. 'What's this like?'

'Not bad, not bad. Bit of the local history. This and that.' A small group of women passed by, fussing with their scarves inside the entrance. Peter lowered his voice. 'The old biddies seem to like it. All buying their souvenir postcards.'

'Biddies?' Mum protested. 'They're probably younger than you!'

'Of course, Denise, right you are.' He gave me a wink. 'How's about we all go get a coffee?'

My mother did not answer right away. She was gazing at the doors to the museum. She loved a local exhibit. To browse it, oh-so-slowly.

'We'd like to see this first. Wouldn't we, Georgina?'

I grimaced.

'Very good,' Peter said. 'Coffee after?'

'That would be lovely.'

Inside I shuffled between exhibits, trying to find weird pictures, torture devices, buttons to press; failing to get excited about the stethoscope on display, or the 'selection of items your granny would have used'. I already knew what items my granny had used: I'd watched her using them. Many of those items were now in my flat.

I did laps, weaving in and out of the cruise folk. Several exhibits behind me was Mum, reading every scrap of text she could find. Inspecting every image. In close detail.

Eventually she allowed herself to be coaxed back out. There we found Peter still waiting. By the looks of it he hadn't moved. On seeing us his face lit up. His posture straightened. 'How was that then?'

'Really interesting,' Mum enthused, as if she was the only one of us who'd been there.

'Eleven stars out of five,' I added. 'The stethoscope game was top-notch.'

'Ignore her. Uncultured swine.'

Peter's merry chuckling hit a high note.

As I patrolled the street ahead of us, I longed to find the tea room I had in mind. Warm. Quiet. Everything made by hand, fresh from the oven; shortbread that even Granny Codd would have coveted.

Instead the town seemed doomed to disappoint. Barbers, insurance brokers, a betting shop. Too many places faded and marked with 'To Let' signs. A modestly sized community café seemed to be the one half-decent option. We entered and found a table.

Not for the first time since we'd met, Peter immediately morphed into Host Mode, asking, 'What can I get you?'

'We'll do ours,' said Mum.

'No, no,' he said. 'That won't do. Sandwich? Cappuccino? Afternoon tea? Victoria sponge?'

I intervened. 'Why don't I buy this?'

'*Please*,' said Peter. 'My treat.'

Mum smirked. 'Do you find it difficult when women pay for themselves?'

Our companion's expression cracked a little. 'Stop misbehaving and let me buy you a bloody cup of coffee.'

Mum's smirk deepened.

'Okay,' I conceded. 'You can buy.'

Peter raised his hands in mock-prayer before patting me on the shoulder. 'What do you want? Anything.'

'I would like . . . a tap water, please.'

'And?'

'That's it.'

'Dear God, I'm going to strangle you in a minute.'

In the end Mum went to the counter with Peter, to try to further disrupt the paying process. They came back with three cups of tea and a couple of bars of chocolate.

'I tried to pay,' she started, 'but—'

'Bloody feminists, the pair of you.' Peter tossed a chocolate bar my way and dumped a tea beside it. 'Cake wasn't quite right, apparently.' He gave Mum the side-eye.

She leaned towards me and mouthed, 'Too dry.'

Overhead a new voice piped up. 'Is anybody sitting here?' The voice belonged to a woman, who gestured at the empty fourth chair at our table and took a polite step back.

'You're very welcome, please do,' said Peter, reanimating as host. Before she had time to pull out the chair, he added, 'I was just telling my wife and daughter it'd be lovely to have some company.'

Mum rolled her eyes and groaned.

Staring at her, I waited for more vocal protests. Peter must have sensed them coming too. 'Ex-wife,' he corrected. 'We like to go on holiday still for Georgina. Keep the family together.'

The woman sat down and tucked herself in. Peter's smile was impossible to interpret.

Our tablemate looked about her, waiting for someone to speak.

A bubble inside me grew, then threatened to burst.

'Don't mind Pops,' I said. 'He's insane.'

'What a way to talk about your father!' he retorted.

The rush of pressure escaped me as a loud laugh.

'We're very proud of our girl, aren't we, Mother?' Peter eased in to the role. 'Yes, Georgina's very clever. She's a writer. She's even publishing a book! She did really well at school.'

The compliments continued. I wondered how long he could keep it up. Surely he wouldn't be able to. Surely this random stranger wasn't buying it.

When he eventually paused I leaned forward. 'Pops worked in the fire service, you know,' I recalled. 'He's a retired firefighter. He used to go up and down the town in Swansea, asking the ladies to get on his fire truck!'

Mum snorted.

'Pass me those.' Peter reached for the sunglasses on my head. 'They need a good clean.'

Taking them before I could respond, he began to gently wipe them with the corner of his fleece, muttering, 'I don't know how you see a thing through these.' Once he was done he held them up to the overhead light for inspection, handed them back with care, and pointed to the sunglasses in Mum's hairline. 'Your turn, Mother. Hand them over.'

I could hardly bear to look at our guest, who was asking now if we were from the ship. She recognised us, she thought. She was staying on board helping to care for her elderly mother, and needed a break from it all. My own mother was quick to sympathise, instigating a conversation about the state of state-funded care homes.

A clutch of inappropriate giggles rose in my throat. I did my best to keep them down; fixed my face into a rictus.

*She must know we're fake*, I thought. *Any moment now she's going to push up from her chair in disgust and expose this weird pretence to the rest of the café. Or I'll make another*

*remark about Pops and he'll switch the whole thing off: 'That's
enough of that.' Confess to this woman, 'I never married, you
know, never had kids. Always been a free agent, thank God.'*

I waited for that to happen.

It didn't happen.

The woman finished her cup of tea, excused herself from
the care-home chat and cheerfully said goodbye; perhaps
she would see us on board again later.

Peter, Mum and I gave our own goodbyes and watched
her leave. Afterwards we sat in silence, none of us speaking
about the charade.

Eventually Peter coughed. 'Right! What next?'

'We need more seasickness pills,' said Mum.

He gathered his coat. 'Let's find you a pharmacy, shall we?'

We exited onto the high street, walking as a three along
the pavement, my mother pausing at every shop window. If
Peter spoke, I didn't hear it. Until Mum darted into Boots
in search of the next batch of Stugeron. Standing beside me
on the pavement, hands in his pockets, he chuckled. 'Big
fan of Invergordon, eh?'

'Absolutely not.'

The chuckle repeated. Adjusting his sleeves, with unchar-
acteristic solemnity – almost as if interpreting a dream – he
said, 'You know . . . I always wondered what it'd be like to
have a daughter.'

A response flashed into my head. It flashed and I didn't
say it.

That I had always wondered what it would be like to
have a dad.

*

On the cruise ship that afternoon I pretended I was cycling into the sea. So many rooms and levels, so many places to eat; only two exercise bikes. I pedalled on automatic, half observing the open deck below, where other passengers strolled, or gazed at drilling platforms, or stumbled indoors to eat more pastries and sandwiches.

Not everyone was back on board yet – presumably they were still on the road, on their day trips – and the atmosphere was a restful one. The noise in my head, however, was raging, exacerbated by three recent helpings of quince tart with double cream.

It was as if I'd won a prize that I couldn't collect. I wasn't sure what the prize was for.

For successfully pulling off a spontaneous prank?

For finding something interesting in Invergordon?

For passing as a person with a father?

I replayed the scene from the café. Moments of being praised in the third person without any sexual undertone or hint of an ulterior motive.

By a man.

Being spoken to, and about, in a tone that was proud.

*By a man.*

Peter stepped into my peripheral vision. He was down by the empty swimming pool on the foredeck where Mum and I had first met him, beginning a post-tea circuit of the ship. Every few moments he stopped to speak to another passer-by. It was near compulsive, how he gave everyone a quick word – a hello or a nod. I guessed he would be making comments about the weather, remarks about the sun and the cold; swapping notes on where we'd come from and would go next.

Peter seemed to be easy company most of the time. He had a good sense of mischief; was a keen traveller with plenty of stories to share. I liked the one about the burning casino, where he fell through the first floor, then burst through the wall of a restaurant, surprising the diners.

And the one where, as a teenage chef in the army, he took a joy ride in his boss's car and tricked the whole of the unit into saluting him.

Other tales I wasn't so sure of. Like the way he talked about his multiple trips to Thailand, where he had paid female bar workers to press pause on their jobs and go holidaying just with him. His mirth at the envy of other male tourists 'forced' to spend their meals with their more age-appropriate wives. The pranks he sometimes played, such as making one young woman choose her earnings from dollars, euros, pounds or baht, while forbidding her from looking up the exchange rate. ('My *God*, she was fretting!') He didn't mention having sex with these bar workers. Still, holed up later on in our cabin, Mum and I drew our inferences.

There was a story, too, about a young woman in Swansea. Peter would buy her coffee and meals, or drive her up the coast for scenic days out. 'She won't leave me alone,' he laughed, in a way that implied: *loser*.

Mum and I gave each other a look. 'Then why do you take her out?'

'Oh, I don't know. I suppose I feel sorry for her.'

Red flags on the mast.

The thing was, I kind of felt sorry for Peter. He wasn't too well, he had said on Day One, in a casual comment at lunch. When we pressed a little we learned that, nowadays, an incurable cancer kept him up at night and gave him pain while walking. He also claimed with a laugh that the treatment had killed his libido. 'Nothing they can do,' he said. 'You've got to stay positive, haven't you? I've no complaints. Not really.'

Peter especially seemed to have no complaints when young waitresses were leaning over him; then he'd cartoonishly smack his lips and rub his hands just out of view.

(If this was a dead libido, we thought, imagine the strength of it living.)

Now I watched him walking on, briefly solitary again, then not, as he started another conversation with another fellow passenger. He spent longer talking with women, of course. Particularly the women with no partners on their arms.

I tilted my head back and looked at the sky. When I closed my eyes I saw images bloom like cloud-swell: growing numbers and odd configurations.

There were about seven and a half billion people on this planet, if I remembered rightly; billions of males – millions over 50. And here was me.

My mind fizzed.

Let's say there were thousands – tens of thousands – of people in Peter's position. Not all of them would be suitable, of course. Yet statistically, surely, some would be just right.

All these men who always wanted a daughter.

And among them, potentially, the ideal dad.

My pedalling slowed. My heart beat faster.

Back in London, after the cruise, I found I still had an appetite for action. Working from home in the flat that my boyfriend Duncan owned – and I paid rent for – my focus wandered. In theory I was preparing a book about fear and giant sharks. As part of the process I'd spent months interviewing various people about fish, scuba diving and death. Now I wanted to shelve all the professional things in my schedule and crack on with ideal-dad-themed things exclusively. Devote myself to a project that might never be read; that might never even be readable.

Over dinner, when I told Duncan about my plan, he stopped looking into his phone, even going so far as to put it face down on the table.

'You're going to look for a father,' he echoed.

'Yes.'

'A man to, like, actually be your dad.'

'I'm going to find the best dad out there,' I clarified. 'I chose you. I chose my friends. So why can't I choose a father?'

To my surprise, he enthused, 'That's a great idea!'

More surprisingly, his phone remained untouched for the next half-hour. It was how I knew I was on to something.

There were plenty of researchers who said, over decades, that being without a father could impact a person's development in long-term ways. They said things like: 'On average, children who experience single parenthood during their childhood have poorer cognitive outcomes than those that grow up in families that remain "intact".'

And that 'being born to an unmarried mother, in a society where marriage is the norm, is associated with socioeconomic disadvantage throughout life'.

Also, that 'the well-fathered daughter is the most likely

to have relationships with men that are emotionally intimate and fulfilling'.

Even: 'Girls in homes without a biological father are
more likely to hit puberty at an earlier age.'

I had not felt warped by my lack of a dad as a child; at least,
not in a way that entirely fitted these findings. Cognition-
wise, my school grades were the joint-best in my year group,
and strong enough to get me in to a decent university.

With respect to 'socioeconomic disadvantage': sure,
Mum and I didn't have as much money as the man-inclusive
units in the family – our house was smaller and more run-
down, our neighbourhood less fancy – but she saved so I
could travel almost as much as my wealthiest cousins. Now,
with my boyfriend's salary paying the mortgage, and my
rates as a freelance writer steadily rising, I was higher on the
socioeconomic ladder than ever before.

On which note, as far as relationships went, there had
been two largely successful long-term couplings pre-Duncan.
There had also been a pretty big blip that I did my best not
to dwell on – though, when pressed, Duncan insisted he
*wasn't* a two-faced dickbag who would walk out on me.
(Helpful to know.)

Lastly, full-blooded puberty hit my body at age 11,
exactly in synch with the UK national average.

Effectively, I had grown up with two parents. There was
Mum who worked full-time to pay the bills, curated packed
lunches, organised fun days out and holidays, drove the car,
and occasionally disciplined me with a raised voice and the
threat of cake confiscation. The other parent, a few streets
away, was Granny Codd, Mum's mother – a key player in

the unit until her decline and death, aged 98 – who walked me home from school each day, taught me how to hand-write and draw, shared the various backstories of her lineage, and presented homemade treats for us to eat in front of *Neighbours*.

The thing was, neither of my parents were male – and that contrasted with every other set-up I encountered first-hand as a child.

Even my school friends and cousins whose dads no longer lived at home (dads who went solo, started new families, skipped countries, died young) had grown up knowing who their male parent was. Had grown up knowing that male parent's face. Knowing his habits. The sound of his voice.

All of which had me wondering, as I had wondered for years, if there was something fundamental I'd been missing.

Could it really be that I wasn't too late to find it?

# 2
# DADVERTS

'Well, my dad spends lots of his time in golf clubs.'

'Golf clubs!' I reached for a scrap of paper to scrawl down 'golfer'. 'I didn't think of that.'

'No, no, no.' Mabry shook her head. 'You do not want a dad who plays golf. Cross it off.'

'What?'

'It's too boring. You should hear them in their little groups, talking about handicaps and courses and club types. Honestly, don't get a golf dad. Did you say you have a proper list?'

I stepped across our empty plates to reach the desk. Returning with my laptop to my friend – a former house-mate I'd known for 15 years – I opened the latest version of my spreadsheet.

'Okay.' I clicked on the first row. 'Places to dadvertise. *Country Life* magazine.'

Mabry frowned. 'Why?'

'It's fancy. For a dad who likes the outdoors and also probably has a stately home with many acres.'

'Ah.' She nodded, satisfied.

'*Classic Boat*. For a dad with a boat. So he can take me boating.'

'Mm-hm.'

'The *London Review of Books* for a cultured dad with a decent reading list. The *Psychologist* for a dad who understands how to build healthy relationships—'

'Good angle.'

'—The Explorers Club for a dad who likes to travel and have big adventures . . .'

I paused. The man who lived in the large house opposite had begun his irregular night-time noises. At various points in the week, he would shriek in stop-starts near his open front door before marching down the street, windmilling his arms to match the outbursts.

Mabry rested her chin on my shoulder, browsing the columns in front of me. 'South Hams Today newspaper group. Like South Hams, Devon?'

My neighbour's shrieks reached the corner of the road. Faded out.

'Yeah.' I turned back to Mabry. 'For a dad who lives in Totnes. Someone who can make houses out of willow bark or something.'

'I'd like a Totnes dad.' She scrolled through the rest of the spreadsheet, picking her favourites, making occasional noises of approval and excitement; imagining how my ideal dad might turn out. 'It's like shopping, isn't it?' she beamed.

'In a way.'

Our conversation had started like many I'd had in the past few weeks: I asked Mabry the question I'd been asking everyone: 'If you could have any father you wanted, what father would you choose – and how would you find him?' At the same time I had drawn up plans for dad adverts – 'dadverts' – to go in magazines, journals and newspapers; on billboards and on noticeboards; in libraries, camping grounds, club houses. The list was growing longer by the day.

———

Things felt very different to the last time I thought a dad might enter my life, seven years earlier. My closest aunt had not long died from cancer, and I was stuck in a sorrowful kind of Fuck It Mode. When my doctor suggested therapy I readily agreed, thinking this could be an excellent way to leapfrog the grief. A few sessions in, however, my new therapist told me it wouldn't be that easy. We'd need about a year.

Later, during a monologue about Mum, he stopped me. 'I'm thinking about your dad,' he said.

'Why?'

The therapist studied my facial expression.

'Why?' I repeated, baffled. 'I wasn't talking about him.'

'It feels relevant.'

'How is that relevant?'

The man continued to look at me.

'This is about my aunt dying and my mum being extremely sad. It's not about me being fatherless.'

'Okay.'

'*Thank* you.'

The next week something similar happened. I was talking about my grandmother's age – she was approaching her mid-nineties then – and how the thought of her being dead soon was too awful.

'What does this make you think about your father?'

I halted. 'Oh my goodness. It doesn't.'

'You don't think about him?'

'No! Hardly ever.'

The subject emerged again in our next session. And the next. I would be talking about my love life, about Mum, Granny Codd, my fears, and the therapist would reintroduce my father. How his absence must have affected me deeply. How the man might be curious to meet me. How I might also be curious to meet him. And how I could set those wheels in motion, if I wanted.

Eventually losing patience, I advised him to talk to someone about his obsession. 'Get yourself on an NHS waiting list.'

———

I thought back to that first therapist, and what he would say about me being ready to share my new idea with everyone I was close to except Mum; about me making spreadsheets; putting down sharks to pick up dads; reading, researching, plotting.

I heard him say to me – not for the first time – 'I think we need more sessions.'

There was no time for more sessions. Christmas was on its way. That time when men across the UK were unwittingly being signed up for gift subscriptions to magazines and newspapers. A time when someone might think more about the family they wanted to have, or wished they didn't. My moment to press the Fuck It Button.

I sent out emails to a handful of advertising departments, requesting prices to place some words in print. In the message I copied and pasted I kept things vague, referring to my intention to publish a *201-character classified ad . . . just words, no picture . . . advertising a bit of a personal adventure (nothing sales-y)*. I added that I was a writer, suspecting it might protect me from certain accusations. *A writer. Ah, of course she'd be eccentric.*

In my initial round of queries I wrote to *New Scientist* (for a father who knew things and would appreciate an experiment), *Private Eye* (for a father who valued wit, and/ or was Ian Hislop), *The Herald Scotland* (for an excuse to go north of the border more often – just not Invergordon) and *Farmers Weekly* (for a father with practical skills, who might save a piglet or lamb for me to befriend).

The sales team at *New Scientist* – weekly readership: 360,000 – was the first to respond with a price quote, offering me a discount rate for placing the ad on a date in the new year.

It would be two weeks past Christmas then.

It would cost over £200 including VAT.

Unsettled by the price tag, I responded to say I needed time to think.

That evening, a couple of friends came round for dinner – two adventurous women I'd met during my search for big fish. Out loud, I deliberated over *New Scientist*. I had deliberated over it all afternoon. Should I do it, I asked the group, or was it unjustifiably expensive?

How much was too much to spend on a possible parent?

'Why wouldn't you?' said Greta, who was a practising mental health counsellor. Earlier she had described how much she loved her father, in spite of his lying addiction.

(How he once explained a small scratch on his face as being the result of a hammer attack from a stranger; how the evidence pointed instead to him having lost his balance when cycling; how 'he lies to make his life feel exciting' – her eyes shining with pride at each anecdote.)

'Why wouldn't I?' I scraped my plate. 'Because I'm not earning loads of money; because Duncan already says my lifestyle is "poverty"—'

'It is,' my boyfriend chipped in.

'—and because spending on dads like that will make me bankrupt.'

'Nuh-uh.' Greta shook her head. 'Two hundred pounds is nothing. You'd make that back from a father within a few Christmases.'

'That's right,' Duncan nodded. 'Good investment.'

I pictured the scene. A cheery new face at the Christmas table. Festive expressions of fatherly pride. My piglet wearing a bow tie and squealing heartily.

The following day, I gave *New Scientist* the go-ahead. All they needed was my text to submit for the editor's approval. I pasted my draft, hit send and crossed my fingers.

Not long afterwards, my phone went off. I jumped and answered, expecting someone calling from *New Scientist*. Instead I found myself talking with a gently spoken woman named Sian from *The Herald Scotland*. Sian explained that she had been given my number by her colleague; someone who, a few hours before, had requested a draft of my advert to provide the most accurate quote. Wanting the cost before showing my hand, I'd reluctantly sent through a draft. Now it seemed I was going to have to explain myself.

After completing our introductions, Sian said, 'So.' She paused. 'Er . . .'

I made myself smile – never mind that she couldn't see me.

Sian gathered herself. 'I'm a wee bit concerned that your ad might be misconstrued. I wouldn't want you to be contacted by ominous people.'

I forced myself to laugh. 'Ah.'

'I'm feeling a wee bit uncomfortable,' she said. 'I don't want to put you in this position. Maybe you could reword your advert – or look at alternative platforms . . .'

The blood rushed in my ears. And when Sian began to talk about 'unsavoury people getting in touch', I interrupted. 'Don't worry,' I said in a sprightly voice. 'I know how weird it sounds. I know I'm going to attract some weirdos. But that's okay. I mean, I'm totally okay. I'm a *writer* and—'

'Oh!' Sian's relief flooded through. 'You're writing! I see, okay.' She giggled, then confided: 'I was concerned that maybe you weren't fully aware of what the dangers may be. I wasn't sure if there'd be underlying *health issues*.'

Sian was calling me mentally unstable.

'Ha ha ha ha ha.' I shifted in my seat.

After more distraction and minimisation – 'Yeah, my first book's coming out soon'; 'Yeah, this is basically the same but the fish are dads' – I convinced Sian I was legit, and therefore ethically safe to take payments from. All

I needed to do was send her an email stating that I was aware of the dangers of placing my dadvert in a national newspaper. Me, a 31-year-old woman actively looking for strangers in the 50s–70s age bracket.

Ending the call on steady terms, I switched back to my desk and composed the message. *Hi Sian*, it began.

> *Thanks so much again for your call earlier – it's good to know someone's keeping an eye on what's what!*
>
> *As requested, here is a formal email to let you know that I am fully aware of the risks of receiving messages from potentially dangerous/unsavoury/disturbed characters as a result of placing the ad I sent earlier [i.e. 'Friendly fatherless 31yoF looking for intrepid M50s–70s who wants to try being a father figure (not sugar daddy). Personal adventure; could be long-term, who knows? Email neverhadadad87@gmail.com'] . . .*

Before I hit send I reread what I'd written.
I read 'fully aware of the risks'.
I read 'dangerous/unsavoury/disturbed'.
My finger hovered over the mouse.
I clicked send.

———

My therapist's obsession was clearly getting to me: at some point in between our early sessions, I made a secret decision to consult the internet. There I found an image of my biological father, seemingly enjoying a trip to Australia.

I had typed in what I thought was his name, wondering if the man was dead or alive, and found a tiny number of web pages that featured him. He was called Carl, the internet confirmed; he wrote songs and played bass guitar; he took black-and-white pictures for a living.

My mother had told me these things at least once before, albeit so briefly and long ago that I struggled to keep hold of them. Now those minimal statements were being made real in pixels.

I stared at Carl's face for a while, not knowing what to make of his features. A bit like mine, I supposed. In a way.

I then contemplated the whereabouts of that face, wondering at the significance of Australia. When I was a child, too young to fully grasp what I was hearing, Mum had complained a few times about Carl's pleas to the courts. 'Your father claims he's broke.' *Your father* – as if I owned him without even knowing what he was; like the premium bond of uncertain value that Granny Codd once purchased in my name.

In the court, so I heard later, Carl argued he was too hard up to contribute even the small amount of child maintenance set for him, blaming his circumstances as a jobbing photographer. Once he told them about an accident that damaged his arm; another time that his driving licence was taken away; later that he lost his primary work contract; finally that his freelancing wasn't enough. For some reason, several times, the court chose to accept these excuses, rather than suggesting he take on more work.

Yet there he was. On holiday, said the caption. Vacationing on the other side of the world when I was aged – pausing to calculate – 6 years old.

Nothing online explained that Carl had been with my mum for more than three years.

Nothing online revealed that I was conceived just before the relationship ended.

Nothing online described how the man ghosted Mum when he found out she was pregnant, then insisted – after months of silence – that she should have had an abortion.

And nothing online confirmed whether Carl still existed.

One thing did appear that I had not been prepared for, however: a brief reference to Carl having a daughter. Except that daughter was not me. That daughter had come *after* me. And, from what I could tell, that daughter was now dead.

―――――

It seemed likely that my extended family – a moderate network of aunts, uncles and cousins – would probably approve of my dadvert plans. After all, they used to enjoy asking after my childhood mission to kidnap Arnold Schwarzenegger, dispatch his wife and children, and make him the principal man in my life.

Mum's dadvert support, however, would be trickier to obtain.

Fresh from the station, I slung my backpack across the banister and fussed over her Jack Russell with his muffled, ball-stuffed growls. Mum and I cooked a cheesy pasta bake and ate it in her lounge, surrounded by her collection of pig-shaped trinkets; tokens of the porcine infatuation I had inherited from her. She filled me in on the news. My eldest cousin's three kids were looking well. Her old friend's grandchildren were adorable. Somebody's husband was leaving them. Oh, and I must check Facebook. So-and-so and Thingummy were buying a house; undoubtedly Thingummy would soon be pregnant; motherhood would suit her.

I made my excuses and carried my bag to my bedroom. On the bookshelf was my picture of Arnold's waxwork in Madame Tussauds, me wrapping my 9-year-old arms around the bulging crook of his elbow, looking as if I'd mainlined 10 sherbet straws.

Back in the lounge I stretched out on my usual spot. Mum put her feet up from hers and turned on the TV, preparing to flick through the channels. Between us the dog couldn't settle, torn by his loyalty to the woman who typically fed him (Mum) and the woman who might take him out for the earliest park walk. He gazed at me, slow-blinking, a tennis ball at his feet, then gave up, slumping equidistant from both of us.

In the corner, Mum's television stalled, struggling to load every channel. A small red circle turned and froze. Turned and froze. While the sound stayed off I seized the moment.

'I've got a new project I want to work on,' I said.

My mother swore. 'The amount I pay every month, and this bloody thing never works.' She huffed and threw the remote on the cushion beside her.

'I've got a new project I want to work on,' I repeated.

'What's that then?'

I focused on the ceiling. The bumps in the off-white wallpaper. 'I'm going to try to find an adoptive father.'

I felt the sharp attention of Mum's eyes.

She said, 'Oh, Jesus.'

I swallowed.

'Why?' she asked.

Aiming for care-free, I said, 'I think it'd be *really* interesting!'

'Right . . .'

Mum scrutinised me.

Said again, 'Oh, Jesus.'

The TV sprang to life.

# 3

# STRATEGY

Christmas arrived. Family members laughed at my plans in all the right places, while Mum stayed unusually quiet. It was one of those rare occasions when I was glad it took a while for her true thoughts to show. I felt a rare gladness, too, that Granny Codd was no longer with us. I had a feeling she would have seen through my tomfoolery.

Before new year I caught a train to see Duncan at his parents' house. In front of the fire, drinking tea, I told his mother and father about my plans, adding that the first dadverts would go out in a couple of weeks. His father looked over my head and out the window. 'You haven't asked me,' he said.

I laughed at his joke.

It wasn't a joke. Which was interesting.

'Do you want to apply?' I asked.

'You haven't asked me.'

'I'm asking now. Would you like to be my dad and apply for my project?'

Duncan's mother sat forward, putting a hand on her husband's knee. 'I did say, didn't I, a while ago, that Georgie would probably see you as a father figure given her situation?

And you were surprised when I said that, weren't you? You didn't believe me.'

I frowned. The most recent time we had met them for lunch, Duncan's dad had taken one look at my jeans and quipped, 'So you *do* have an arse.'

On the plus side, he had decent taste in music, and had almost succeeded in making me like jazz.

I cleared my throat. 'Actually, I've never had fatherly vibes from you. But if you *would* like to apply then I would be . . .'

The man was wincing. 'It's fucking weird, isn't it?'

'I suppose it is.'

'I'd fucking say so.'

'Okay.'

His wife sprang up from the chair. 'Who wants to share some yummy-scrummy choccies?'

In early January, *New Scientist* gave my dadvert the all-clear, and promised to send a copy of what it looked like before printing, in case last-minute revisions were needed.

Over the weeks I'd been trying to work out if this was the cleverest or stupidest idea I'd ever had. At night, while Duncan slipped into his enviable routine of instant unconsciousness, I veered towards stupidest, computing everything that might go wrong.

I knew I would find it hard to cope if anyone was mean. That there could be gross suggestions, written abuse, dick pics. Plus more immediate, frightening behaviours – aggressive, sexual, stalkerish – if I made it to any face-to-face encounters.

It put me on edge to imagine how I would feel if I really

liked a father who didn't like me back. Or how a person might handle *my* rejection, in case I wanted to stop against their wishes.

In those long, slow hours before morning, as the man across the road shrieked and whirled, I also noticed I'd formed a picture of what I wanted. Whenever I thought of somebody making contact, he appeared. I couldn't see his face in detail, only that he wore a Panama hat and a light linen jacket. He looked like a cross between Monty Don and the Man from Del Monte, circa 1990.

It perplexed me to reflect on why a British TV gardener and a voiceless globe-trotting magnate who devoted his fictional life to tinned fruit had fused to take up space in this part of my psyche. And why he looked so different to my blond-haired, blue-eyed biological father, Carl.

I committed to casting out this hybrid fantasy, along with any other expectations. And to buying some seeds and canned peaches for the flat.

The longer I nocturnally pondered what lay ahead, the more it became clear that I was lacking some key information. Namely, I didn't know what fathers were actually supposed to do, whenever they did more than 'father' in the DNA-sharing sense.

As a child, I had seen dads as people who offered playground fun, a pair of sturdy shoulders to ride and extra money to buy Game Boys. All the things my mother and grandmother refused to – or could not – give.

Fatherhood in reality? The ideal dad for me now? A little less clear.

For a while the idea of analysing the animal kingdom enticed me, my thinking being it could offer fundamental clues to the intrinsic nature of fathers, introducing me to 1) a cross-species overview of male-offspring relationships, and 2) the roles dads adopt when guided by natural instincts alone – rather than, say, any mission to win the most 'likes' for their family home movies on social media.

Following an investigation, I wound up with a mixed bag of examples. On the proactive side: male emperor penguins who incubate eggs for months, enduring diabolical Antarctic winds, eating nothing while their females fish at sea; male seahorses and their self-fertilising 'brood pouches', which carry up to 1,500 eggs; male South American owl monkeys, who far surpass females in the time they give to play, transport, groom and resource-share with their babies.

On the more troubling end of the spectrum: male gorillas and other male apes, who contribute nothing to child-rearing; male bears, which are known to attack and kill cubs to 'gain higher sexual opportunity'; male sand goby fish, who leave eggs unattended when their females aren't looking, and occasionally gobble up the ones that take longest to hatch – thus lightening their guard duties.

First lesson: no universal state of fatherhood exists between the species.

Second lesson: aim more for owl monkey than gorilla.

A few days before *New Scientist* went to print, I received a copy of how my dadvert would look when it hit the news-stands: simple black text on a pure white background, framed with a double-lined border. I had come up with a headline, too, which seemed to fit the house style.

I squealed to myself and the two toy pigs I kept beside my desk: plush gifts from friends who lived far away, specially bought for any work-alone days that called for something to cuddle. Now they were becoming my close confidantes.

The dadvert was just what I wanted. Proudly I read aloud to my mute, snouted audience:

*A SOCIAL EXPERIMENT FOR 2019.*
*Friendly, fatherless 31-year-old woman seeks intrepid man, 50s to 70s, who may be willing to take on the role of father figure.*
*This is a personal adventure; could be long-term, maybe not. Who knows?*
*Email: neverhadadad87@gmail.com*

I read out the dadvert again.

Something didn't sound right. Finding an earlier email request, I placed the two messages side by side and saw the difference. There was no sign of the line where I had specified *no sugar daddies*.

Within seconds I sent *New Scientist* an urgent follow-up, asking for the line to be reinstated. I was sure that if I didn't make it clear, the dadvert would attract sugar daddies exclusively. I had seen those guys in the papers. On TV. On YouTube. On websites that offered to make those relationships happen. All these blokes in my specified age range – though younger too (sometimes younger than me:

one leading site reported having hundreds of thousands of 'daddies' in their twenties, plus almost 2 million more in their thirties) – willingly offering cash, handbags, holidays, homes, even the wiping-out of entire student debts, for the dedicated attention of an amenable young person.

Websites that targeted 'sugar babies' skimmed over the notion that sex was part of the package. They talked about 'companionship', about 'elevated relationships'. Except in all the commentaries I found, people said these phrases were really code for gropes, hand jobs, full-blown sex, etcetera.

As one 27-year-old summarised: 'The oldest guy I dated was 75. We became intimate after a few dates once I trusted him. He certainly popped a Viagra.'

No thanks, Dad.

Really. I'll pass.


There was no response from *New Scientist* the next day, so I sent out a chaser.

When a reply finally came it explained that my line had not been added and that we were now past the deadline. The dadvert would go out as it was, not as I had written it.

I left a panicked phone message. The magazine's classifieds manager called back, apologising profusely for the error. He had been ill for a while, he said. He had contracted whooping cough, seen five doctors, gone to hospital three times, lost consciousness more than once. He reckoned he had caught rogue bacteria on the London Underground, and that his parents must have decided against vaccinating him in childhood.

I started issuing apologies of my own.

He stopped me. 'No. Getting whooping cough was a revelation. While I've been recovering all this time, I've been able to sit and play chess with my two young kids, done jigsaw puzzles together, all sorts.

'I'd describe it as enforced intimacy,' he added. 'It was wonderful.'

The story reminded me of a quote I'd recently found from a female anthropologist: 'fathers are a biological necessity but a social accident'. Her statement was controversial, yet this man's experience seemed to support it; as if he had stumbled onto something; as if efforts from human fathers towards their offspring were fundamentally opt-in.

'You sound like a good dad now,' I said.

From the other end of the line came an uncertain sound. 'We've gone off topic,' he said.

My dadvert would be printed free of charge. The money could go elsewhere, back into my father fund.

Feeling better, more emboldened, I asked what his readers might make of the advert.

'They're pretty engaged and attentive,' he said. 'We'll maybe get some letters. Or I might get a tap on the shoulder from my editor, asking what it's all about.'

After the call I imagined that tap. *What's this all about then?*

I couldn't imagine the answer, though. What could this man say?

The time to go live was quickly approaching. Deciding I needed more supporters on side, I made myself practise speaking to various friends about the project; testing how it sounded; seeking extra validation. Duncan would be an especially helpful ally, I thought, as he and I spent half an hour testing the privacy settings of my inbox. ('FYI that email address looks 100 per cent like spam.')

My agent for the shark book could be another. ('Remember, when your new dad invites you for a month on his yacht, it's *vital* you take me with you.')

Expanding the circle of people to whom I confided, I tested out how to express my project in ways that sounded rational, then took note of the responses.

With my old friend Safia, who discussed her father with adoring eyes: 'What are dads like? Well, mine is the most reliable person I know. He's not exciting at all. But *so* reliable.'

With a new client, over coffee: 'You want to know what dads do? I remember watching *Family Fortunes* once, when the question was: 'Who do you call in an emergency?' I spent minutes shouting, "Dad!" at the TV. Turned out the answer they wanted was the police.'

With near strangers at a housewarming party, where two boys assured me a friend of their mum had no father either. 'It's *not* weird,' they insisted, before suggesting various neighbours to match my requirements.

And with a former colleague, to whom I said, 'I'm aiming to enter into a manufactured father–daughter relationship with a stranger' – and who replied (once he'd recovered from his laughing fit): 'I take it you'd be playing the role of daughter?'

Very rarely, on the phone, Mum shared a few thoughts of her own. Like: 'It's not true that you didn't have any father figures growing up. You had two uncles. You had your boyfriends' fathers. And you had my friend Nick. You were his bridesmaid, remember?'

'Not all the boyfriends' fathers wanted me around, remember?'

'You mean the Arsehole?'

'I mean the Father of the Blip.'

'Yes, the *Arsehole*.' Her voice went up an octave. 'What a loathsome, narcissistic—'

'Forget him. The others, though – Nick, my uncles – they had children of their own.'

'And . . . ?'

'So they didn't have much headspace for me, growing up.'

'Hm.'

'I didn't ever spend one-on-one time with any of them.'

'Hm.'

'*Mum*. Stop making that noise.'

Nick, Mum's friend, could have been the ideal father figure. For years he had joined us on Sunday walks. He liked sea swims. And jokes. And well-made cakes. But above all, first and foremost, he liked to spend time with his wife and his son.

Besides, Nick was a family friend. He wasn't in the Dad Zone.

'But what *is* the difference between a man and a father?' one friend asked.

Which seemed like a question I ought to start asking too.


With a day to go before the *New Scientist* dadvert, I braced myself; upped the distractions. The South Hams papers took my spare money and prepared for publication. *Farmers*

*Weekly* was also happy to help. The Explorers Club, however, turned me down. My dadvert was *just not appropriate a communication to our members*. Not the acceptable kind of exploration.

I found my lead in the nautical world when *Classic Boat* magazine offered me space. Though as I talked through the details of the advert, their sales guy interrupted.

'I'm not sure about that line,' he said. 'It's like you're specifically asking for it.'

'But I'm specifically saying "*no* sugar daddies". I'm making it clear that *isn't* what I want.'

'It's like if you're at a dinner party, and you say, "Hi, I'm Shaun, I'm not a serial killer." Everyone there is going to think you're a serial killer for bringing it up.'

I frowned. I wasn't sure the analogy quite worked, or why I was suddenly 'Shaun'. Then again, this man *was* a man, and presumably understood how his gender functioned better than I could.

I followed his advice and kept out the reference, agreeing to a mini headline that told readers I was LOOKING FOR FRIENDSHIP. The sales guy thought that would fully desexualise things. Never mind that friendship wasn't what I sought.

'I might get jealous,' Mum warned on another call. Grateful for the flash of honesty, I asked her advice on advertisements, trying to make my quest more mother-inclusive.

'Try the *Guardian* and *Private Eye*,' she suggested after mulling it over. 'If you want to find someone most like the men I'd have dated in the eighties – if I think about my ideal partner back then, he'd be reading those.'

I assured her *Private Eye* was on the list. 'The *Guardian*'s not in the running, though. Ads in the paper start at a grand plus VAT.'

'*How* much?'

'Some dads are just out of my price range.'

Like the female cousins I spoke with, like myself at half past midnight and beyond, Mum was more preoccupied with the parts of the process the dadverts were building up to. 'What happens when it gets to meeting these men? How are you going to protect yourself?'

I took a breath and told her about the basic filtering strategy I'd been testing. It started like this:

1. Dadvert goes live.
2. Man reads dadvert.
3. Man feels intrigued and gets in touch.
4. On sending whatever man wants to send, man receives an instant bounce-back message.
5. Only once man responded to *that* would conversations begin.

This bounce-back message had been crafted and re-crafted over days, to set straight all possible misconceptions ASAP. It thanked whoever wrote for making contact, introduced me by my first name – my proper first name; the name only family and healthcare professionals used – and gave my occupation as 'writer'. It reiterated that this was an experiment.

The message then briefly described the circumstances around my biological father's absence and that he had left my mother before I was born, retelling the explanation I had received: that he didn't want a child.

*I've always wanted to know what it would be like to have a father,* I wrote.

*Maybe you've always wanted to know what it would be like to have a daughter. Maybe you've got one already and want another. Maybe you had one and lost her.*

*I was raised by a loving mother and grandmother, plus uncles, aunts and lots of cousins. My mother is still alive, and not looking for a partner (this is not an elaborate matchmaking service for her, although she is a catch).*

*I am a curious person, I like adventures, I like being outdoors, I like meeting new people and I like sharing stories. I don't have a specific type of father figure in mind; a perfect 'dad' who I hope will reply to this email.*

*I am not looking for money. I also definitely don't want any funny business (I'm very happy with my long-term boyfriend, in case you were in any doubt).*

*I have no expectations of what course this experiment might take. My only plan is to see whether a positive 'father–daughter'-style relationship might be possible for a dadless novice in her thirties. I'd like to give it my best shot. If we get on, and you're as interested as I am in making things work, this could have the potential to become a rewarding relationship. But let's not put any pressure on things (I certainly won't).*

Before the email ended, the man was set a basic task. All he needed to do was hit reply and answer five questions:

1. *Where did you see my ad?*
2. *Why did you reply?*
3. *What county/country do you live in?*
4. *What do you think you could offer a prospective 'daughter' in her thirties? Just so we're even, for my part I'd be offering a prospective 'father' my time, enthusiasm, curiosity, plus a willingness to meet and share new experiences.*
5. *What would you like to ask me?*

This was where the proper filtering began. Those who didn't want to reply could willingly deselect themselves right there. Whereas those who made the effort of writing again would be the men I would email. Whether this would then be an 'I-don't-think-so-thanks-for-writing'-style message, or an 'I'd-like-to-keep-talking-if-you-would' depended on what, and how, they'd communicated earlier. By that point, in theory, I would have a rough idea of their social skills, how far I would need to travel to say hello, and what their motivations and priorities were – or, at least, what they wanted me to think about all these things. Because no strategy I could think of could really grant me the truth of a person.

Not if they were intent on hiding it.

The night before *New Scientist* hit the shelves I lay flexing my toes under the bed sheets, unable to keep still. I had spooned Duncan to sleep hours earlier, which left endless time alone to run through everything.

If I got into an awful –

If somebody called me a –

When a man tried to –

*Oof.*

Thank goodness I was a writer, I reminded myself. Writers can turn bad events into decent stories. (At least some of the time.)

Our troubled neighbour across the road began shrieking. He was on the move in the night again, with nobody at his side.

I wondered if he had family. I wondered who was out there to protect him.

The next morning, a Saturday, there were no copies of *New Scientist* in our nearest corner shop. Agitated, pacing floors, I convinced Duncan to join me for a Tube ride to the city centre and its newsagents, sealing the deal with an offer to buy him pastries. A few steps from Warren Street station, I spotted a well-stocked paper shop and asked my boyfriend to go in on my behalf. If he could read the dadvert without combusting, I'd consider it safe to do the same.

He raised an eyebrow. 'Really?'

'Please, man! I might die!'

Moments later Duncan beckoned me in: he had the magazine and couldn't find it.

I flicked through the pages, breathing fast, unable to find it either. Until, near the back of the issue, I glimpsed a familiar double-lined border. The black on white. 'Jeebus,' I gasped. 'It's so big.'

My boyfriend and I looked at each other. There was no going back now.

I bought my copy and yanked on Duncan's arm as we exited. 'What if someone's written already? What if my dad is waiting? Oh, but what if no one writes? *What if no one writes?*

'It only takes one,' he said.

As an elderly, job-free parent, Granny Codd had taught me how to pass time without much trouble: regularly replenish both the book pile and the biscuit barrel; exchange polite words with shopkeepers, bus drivers, dogs (and, sometimes, their walkers); find comfortable spaces in public places, and try to come up with the life story of everyone in your eyeline.

As a working, reporting parent, what Mum taught me was this: ask questions; take notes; get involved.

Flipping between the two modes, crumbs of chocolate biscuit littering my desk, I found a researcher whose PhD explored the pain of 'involuntarily childless men'.

Various life circumstances had deterred Dr Robin Hadley from becoming a father: a significant break-up, spiralling mortgage costs, a partner who didn't want children herself. Yet those deterrents had not led him to a point of comfortable acceptance; quite the opposite. 'There have been times when I have ached to be a Dad,' Dr Hadley wrote. 'My reactions to my "broodiness" have included: anger, depression, elation, guilt, isolation, jealousy, relief, sadness, yearning and withdrawal.' And while many men reassure themselves that they have time to deliberate, Dr Hadley's feelings were further compounded by the discovery that, contrary to popular opinion, male fertility and sperm quality deteriorate with age. (Up to a 23 per cent decline annually in fertility from age 39; plus an increase in miscarriage rates from roughly age 45.)

Dr Hadley detailed how his experiences had spurred him on to seek out other men like him, through which he learned that other childless men could be just as broody as childless women. In a 2009 British survey, for example, he found that 59 per cent of childless males and 63 per cent of childless females wanted to be parents, while a representative German survey of childless people aged 31 to 40 found this same desire to be equal between the sexes.

The idea that this many men actually *wanted* be fathers was foreign to me, and also seemed like good news for my project. I got in touch and was thrilled when Robin agreed to an interview from his home near Manchester.

A video link took me into his sunlit office, where Robin sometimes broke off from talking to pick up a pair of binoculars and observe the birds outside his window. If he *had* been a dad, I realised, that hobby might either have passed to his child, been openly scoffed at by them or, most likely, elicited both reactions over the course of a lifetime. As for me, I promptly decided I, too, should keep binoculars within reach.

So how did it feel to research men like this, I asked?

'How does it feel to me?' Robin laughed at the question. 'It feels to me: don't research men.'

I was surprised.

'Really. There's no money there, or very little.'

In his experience, Robin explained, academia was all about money: 'If you can save certain people going into hospital at whatever-it-is a day by putting £100 worth of research-based intervention in at a local level, then that's brilliant.' For childless men, however, the links between not having children, poor health and hospital costs are not so obvious. At the very least, their childlessness means they're far less likely to receive compassionate care from relatives than their counterparts, on account of childless men *having* fewer relatives as a group, if indeed they have any at all.

Part of the problem, according to Robin, is that childless men aren't often studied as a group – even when they're of child-making age. He told me that after a birth a woman's fertility history is taken and added to medical records as standard, helping feed our national bank of statistics. The man's fertility history is not recorded, however. 'And you know that saying? If you're not counted, you don't count.'

Another element male childlessness lacked as a cause was a poster boy. 'You need a big-hitter,' Robin said, 'you need a high-achieving professor in academia who can highlight your issue to other academics and influence "the powers that be". Otherwise, it's not going to go through for funding.' Having a champion outside academia could be crucial too, Robin thought; someone who holds sway over the general public's outlook.

Pausing to think which popular figures could be star names for the issue, my brain instinctively went the other way. All I could see were men past their fifties who still made babies, sperm quality be damned: the Simon Cowells (first-time father at 54), Donald Trumps (latest son at 59) and Mick Jaggers (eighth child at the tender age of 73).

While in the work Robin was doing to make this issue better recognised, audience reactions were speaking volumes.

'The international response is good,' he said. 'When I give a talk there's a silence after I finish. It shocks people because they don't expect it, which says a lot about what people expect of men, and not really knowing how to cope when it's something emotional and fundamental.'

At a British fertility conference, however, Robin had met with a more disturbing reaction. After informing me that he is often the only man in the room at such things, he described his general approach to these events. 'I used to go to the front, and to the side, so that I'm visible and all that sort of thing.' At this particular conference – again as the only man – 'I was listening to somebody else's talk, and the speaker, she pointed at me and went "and the paedophile in the corner—"'

I gasped, then checked myself, not sure I'd processed his words right. Was Robin saying he'd been called a paedophile during an academic discussion, simply for being a man interested in fertility?

'Yeah!' he nodded. 'Yeah. I wrote to the organisers the next morning and said, "Look, I really enjoyed the conference, but this was wrong." Then I wrote to the regulatory body. And absolutely nothing happened.

'I think some feminists are protective of that reproductive

element. Feminist scholars say feminists hold the spotlight on reproduction. The narratives all reflect the general story of: "It's all around women. And actually, men don't need to be involved."'

Except when men were not involved, it meant that women, by default, were carrying the burden on their own. And I, for one, wasn't sold on that approach.

After a couple more days of biscuits and books, I decided enough time had passed. Peering through my eyelashes, I clicked to open the inbox. Slowly, the loading bar filled to completion. There, unmistakable and unread, were responses from two different men.

Two.

I shot up from my desk and circled the room. When I was calm enough to sit down again I saw that only one of the respondents had sent a second message: he had already answered my bounce-back. I took a deep breath and started with the other guy.

*Hi, Please tell me more. Cheers.*

That was it.

The alternative man wrote at length, introducing himself as Roland. He was in his mid-sixties and married, with a daughter a few years older than me. He lived in Surrey.

*I'm not sure I can meet your 'intrepid' requirement, but I would be delighted to hear more about what you're trying to do/achieve and then take it from there.*

Answering my bounce-back message, Roland said he had made contact because he was intrigued by my words and wanted to know more, including why I chose to run my advert in *New Scientist*. He could offer *over 60 years of life experience, more than 30 years 'fathering' experience, empathy and friendship*, and restated that he would like to know my objectives.

*P.S.*, he added, *I hope that you haven't been deluged with middle-aged men looking for a sexual relationship – it would be very easy to read your ad as 'looking for a sugar daddy!'*

# 4

# NEW SCIENCE

Dear Roland,

Thank you very much for getting in touch, and then answering my questions. It's great to hear from you! Funnily enough, the advert that was supposed to go in New Scientist had a line to specifically clarify that I didn't want a sugar daddy, but unfortunately that was overlooked in the final cut. On the plus side, New Scientist's ad team felt so bad about leaving it off that they decided not to charge me for the space. Also on the plus side, no sugar-daddy deluge has occurred (or not yet, at least) . . .

Anyway, thank you for asking about my objectives – that's an important question. I feel like many scenarios could come out of something like this, some positive, some negative. Obviously, I'm most keen on the positives: to find someone (or possibly more than one person) of father age who wants to make a connection, and see whether it's possible to create a happy relationship over time with him/them; to learn about what father figures can offer; to see if having a platonic relationship with an older man might make me feel less like I've missed out, not having any real father figure in my life so far.

The chance of reaching that point with anyone is potentially slim though, I feel, and could be a very long time in the making, which is why I'm staying very open-minded. My main objective for now is to gain more of an insight into fatherhood from a variety of different people I wouldn't otherwise speak to, or meet.

The reason I picked New Scientist as a way of placing the advert is that I hoped it would appeal to male readers who are as interested as I am to try something a little bit different. I think of New Scientist readers as being curious people, with a sense of adventure. It seems that you don't think of yourself as 'intrepid', but I'm not so sure – I think you're very brave to get in touch! Did you have a father when you were growing up? Do you still have a father? What is/was he like?

I was really interested to read in your emails that you already have a daughter – and that she's not so far off my own age. I am an only child, too, as you may have gathered. Have you spoken to her, or your wife, about sending a response to my ad? If so, what did she/they think?

I have lots more questions bubbling up but will leave them for now. I don't want to bombard you, and it may be that, having read this latest email, your curiosity is satisfied, and you don't feel the need to take this *exchange any further. If that is the case I understand. If it isn't, it would be lovely to hear from you again. Feel free to bombard me with questions if you like.*

*With warmest wishes,*

*G*

Roland seemed to be open for it all. Within a few messages we were flying. I learned about his health issues, about the trust and respect he had for his mother, about the difficulties he felt around not having a second child, about his love of fatherhood.

*On reflection, I can truly say that our daughter's existence in my life has been 90% sheer joy and 10% tedious annoyance and upheaval. Her gift has been more delight, pleasure and total contentment than ANYone or anything else could give me – and that goes for other relations, my wife, significant events, work, and so on.*

I could feel myself getting excited.

*My wife and I have discussed this,* he told me another time.

*She gave her support for whatever appealed to me while requesting and suggesting I stay wary of any possible scams.*

*My daughter and I have not yet spoken, just because the opportunity has not presented itself. But she will be staying here for a few days from the weekend and I'll speak about it with her then – afterwards I'll let you know what her reaction is (here we go: my first proper commitment to you).*

He finished the message with, *I believe this can 'work' between us and look forward to setting aside the time and effort to make it happen – let's at least aim for a solid platonic friendship and take it from there – what say you?*

As I reached his signature I was beaming.

In the days that followed, other dadverts went live in other places. A few more potential fathers trickled through. Among them was: *I am in the right age range and, having never had children, feel that there is a big hole in my life where a daughter should be, so I felt I had to respond.*

And: *I am single, 51, fairly fit, solvent, average-looking . . .*

Hooked to the screen, I scrutinised tone and word choice, trying to glean every clue as to who they were. I wanted to know if anyone really needs their dad to be at least average-looking. I wanted to know what 'big hole' in a life could only ever be filled by a daughter.

And how to describe the 'hole' that existed for me.

––––––

A few weeks after that first internet search for my biological father, back in my mid-twenties, I managed to find contact details for Carl's mother. If online parish updates were any-thing to go by, my paternal grandmother was an active churchwarden. What's more, her stomping ground was less than 30 miles away from Mum's house; a quick drive from where I had grown up. And now I could reach her for church-based queries with a single phone call.

The process seemed so simple. I couldn't believe it.

Deliberating over how best to introduce myself, I waited several evenings to dial the number. I did not consult Mum or Granny Codd – the idea seemed like betrayal, to be wanting a meeting with Carl in spite of their care. I did, however, raise it with my therapist.

He leaned forward, growing larger inside his grey jacket. 'How are you feeling about it?'

'Sick. Angry. Intrigued.'

'Tell me about the anger.'

I told him about knowing that my paternal grandmother knew I existed. How I knew she'd been told Mum was pregnant. How I knew Carl's parents initially offered to give their support and later retracted that offer, hiring a lawyer to demand I be DNA-tested. (I was. The test proved I was Carl's.) 'All these years she couldn't be arsed to make contact, and neither could her husband – he's dead now, apparently; I found an obituary. And they were both teachers. Church-goers. Upstanding members of the community. Yuck.'

'Yuck?'

'They lived a short train ride away. They never came to meet me. Actually, the grandfather did, apparently, just after I was born. He held me, then gave me back and made it clear they'd be offering nothing to Mum, financial or otherwise. Very fucking Christian, don't you think?'

My therapist announced that it made sense to be angry.

'But I can't be angry, can I? I have to be nice and all "water under the bridge".'

Aside from anything else, I needed the woman's cooperation. Needed to know whether Carl was still around and might be willing to meet.

To look me in the eyes.

To acknowledge my existence to my face.

To give me a decent reason for leaving me fatherless.

At the end of that week, I shut myself inside my bedroom and entered the woman's number on my phone. It rang for a while, until – 'Hello?' Her voice was hard. Assertive. Not a speck like Granny Codd's.

I caught my breath. Imagined myself as up for Best Actor in the Cold Calling Awards. 'Um . . .' I cracked a smile and laughed a little. 'This is a bit of a strange one,' I said, 'but I'm Denise Codd's daughter.'

My paternal grandmother's voice turned instantly frosty. It said a crisp 'Ah.' And a 'Yes.'

I pressed on. 'I found your number on your church website, and . . . This is strange, isn't it?' I laughed again. 'Anyway, I wanted to introduce myself. My mother's sister died a little while ago – it was pretty awful, and it's got me thinking about hereditary things. I realised I didn't know anything about the health of my father's side; I don't really know anything about Carl or you, or . . . I thought I'd better try to find out. See if there's anything to be cautious about.'

'Carl won't want to talk to you.'

My insides deflated. At the same time I heard the present tense: *he's alive.*

'He hasn't got much money,' the woman said, with extra ice.

I fixed a smile. Kept going. 'I'm actually not interested in his money. Not at all. I'm actually fine for money. That's not what this is about.'

There was no response.

'I can see why you might think it might be,' I continued. 'If there's some way I can assure you – uh . . . I don't actually know how I could do that, though, short of sending you some bank statements?!'

She didn't laugh.

'Is there anything . . . health-wise . . . Actually, I did find an obituary for your husband. I'm sorry. Cancer, wasn't it? Did he go into a hospice? My mum's sister didn't have time for that in the end. God, it's an awful disease.' I stopped suddenly, caught off-guard by a flashback to my aunt's last day alive.

When Carl's mother spoke again, there seemed to be a thawing in her voice. Her late husband had died from stomach cancer, yes. As for Carl . . . She hesitated. 'He's not been in a good way.'

Over the next few minutes I learned more about my father than months of searching through websites could tell me. The narrative was tragedy after tragedy. And it started with the death of an infant born years after me.

I had indeed had a half-sister. My half-sister's name was Caroline. And unlike me, she had been, as his mother described her, 'Carl's baby'.

———

When I thought about Roland, my mind came back to siblings.

Envisaging a meeting with Roland's daughter, I could picture the outcome being either completely glorious – two only children teaming up to gain the full-grown sister they never had – or prickly and abrasive. Of course I could never be the favourite. The position of 'Roland's baby' was already taken.

My thought experiments continued. This time, I imagined Mum telling me that a total stranger coveted her as a parent; that she was thinking about meeting up with that stranger, and seeing how it went. My feelings would be . . .

Suspicious, I thought. Bewildered.

Also, perhaps, understanding.

For his part, Roland was behaving optimistically. Our correspondence had not yet stretched to seven days, and he was already angling to meet. It panicked me. *Maybe we should leave it for another few weeks,* I wrote. *What do you think? I've rushed into things in the past before, and later wished I'd taken more time about them. I am prone to getting overexcited and then afterwards often feel like I've been a bit of an idiot.*

As my boyfriend prepared his bag for work, he asked about the man I had been writing to. Duncan had approved of the serendipitous snippets I'd told him so far. How Roland could scuba dive – like me. How he had a boat – which we could visit. A charming, smiling picture Roland had shared of him with his wife had also received a thumbs up. So when I told Duncan about my latest note he was concerned. 'Why are you putting him off meeting you? You should be capitalising on his excitement.'

'Because . . .' I paused to think. 'I don't feel ready yet.'

My boyfriend wore a warning look. 'Roland's been giving you so much of himself. He's really friendly and really interested. If he thinks you've gone cold, he might give up.'

'Do you think he would?'

'He might.'

'Hang on.' I pulled on my dressing gown and hurried to my laptop. 'He's probably responded already,' I called back. 'He's fast and I wrote last night.'

I loaded up the inbox. There was nothing.

'Well?' Duncan walked in.

'Maybe he's cross with me,' I said. 'Is that possible?'

'That's what dads do,' said my boyfriend. 'They get upset.'

I told myself not to keep refreshing my emails that morning, and to create some distance from this early bump of rejection. Using dating apps to find a boyfriend years before had been exhausting. Using a similar concept to find a dad was *situation: unknown*. Still, best to keep the plates spinning. If one dropped away or flung itself off, there would be others to reach for.

I opened my spreadsheet of places to dadvertise. Colourcoded each row to show which so far had said yes, which had said no, which I could afford, which I must chase. I channelled visions and added ideas: *National Trust Magazine*, *Soldier Magazine*, *Veterinary Practice*. I remembered to add in *MOJO*, which one cousin described as 'where cool dads who dug good music would hang out'.

Cool dads, good music; it sounded appealing. I called *MOJO* and received an information pack for professional advertisers. Less than a fifth of the magazine's readers were over 55, the pack told me. The majority would be far too young for my purposes.

At lunchtime, I lay face down on the sofa.

After lunch, I checked my emails.

Roland had replied!

*I would like our meeting to be relatively soon,* he wrote, *BUT I do not want to push you out of your comfort zone and it will not do me any harm to wait a few weeks.*

A shock of relief passed through me. The long message ended with Roland wishing me and my boyfriend a nice weekend. That Sunday, his daughter would arrive with him for her stay. Then, if he kept to his commitment, he would discuss me and ask her opinion.

My spreadsheet grew. The Arts Club in London said they had neither a noticeboard nor a newsletter, so were sadly unable to help. *Rolling Stone* magazine would go no lower than $700.

My agent suggested I visit every branch of Waitrose in every town I liked and place my dadverts there.

I added his idea to my list.

A man called Jerry entered my inbox to introduce himself, then responded to my bounce-back:

*I reside in sunny Blackpool.*

*I wrote because my gut instructed it.*

*I am working through a divorce, so meeting you, among other current life projects, will give me further perspective. I'm a believer in flourishing through problems, and this quandary will elevate me to the next*

*level. I love Blackpool, and am in love with an amazing
lioness of a woman, so no 'funny business'.*

Jerry proudly shared his plan to become Blackpool's *most
subversive mayor*. He also offered to take me and my *Plus One*
out on the town – most especially to drink at the top of the
tower, where a rooftop bar would give us miles of views to
Blackpool and beyond. *Perhaps you could offer counsel re the
lioness as I have yet to share my feelings. FYI I fell for her after
the start of the divorcing process, so not the inciting event.*

On Monday I wrote to Roland – a friendly, checking-in
email wondering how things had gone with his daughter.

He did not write back that day.

Replying to Jerry, I asked about his family life; his own
parents. Both had now died, he said, and he was bereft.

The next day came. Roland did not write.

I sent my ad to *Private Eye* and checked my savings.
Rearranged the budget. When I logged in to my inbox
again I found that a small batch of new emails had arrived,
including one from –

'Roland!'

I saved his message for last.

Jerry expressed gratitude for my continued correspondence and wanted to know more about my writing.

An earlier applicant reappeared to say that he had
thought about things and *concluded that having now satisfied my initial curiosity I should bow out at this point*.

Someone else messaged twice en route to his choir
practice:

*I feel some mystery around my full motivations for contacting you. In part I admire that someone could be so liberated from any social fears to make such a bold request. It must, too, be partly that I did not come to learn until three children entered my life (all are grandchildren of an ex!) that an inherent fatherly-ness lay within me, if that makes sense . . .*

*Another thought strikes me now: that what you need from any father-type figure you encounter is pure, unconditional love. Could such a thing be generated? I have no idea. Life clearly has lessons to teach us.*

The suggestion seemed both hopeful and terrifying. Tensing up, I switched to Roland, both eager and dreading to hear the news about his daughter's reaction.

It was difficult to properly read his words and not skip through. Forcing myself to slow down, I reached the key details. *Her reaction*, he wrote,

*at first (after approx. half an hour) was, on reading your ad and our first few emails: 'This is very strange!'*

*She told me she'd like some time to think about it and I replied that she could/should of course do that, and since she was obviously feeling awkward about it I'd hold off on the emails until she had come to a firm decision, and promised I would not do anything to 'risk' the connection she and I have together.*

*She did ask if my reason for doing this was to address 'shortcomings or gaps' I sensed in the relationship between me and herself. I responded, truthfully, 'It isn't, but I would like us to spend more time together.'*

*All this is why it has taken me until now to reply – she went home after lunchtime today.*

I took a deep breath.

*Over last night's dinner, my daughter shocked me. She told me she'd thought very deeply about this over the past week and had reached a firm decision: that she felt extremely uncomfortable with what I'd been doing and also felt (surprising herself!) that if I continued working towards a 'father-figure role' with you she was likely to get jealous.*

*She requested that I re-confirm what I said to her last week, which was that I'd now 'step back' from our communication so far (and from working towards a father–daughter-style relationship) – and I confirmed this to her.*

*Georgina, Georgina, Georgina. I'm so very disappointed and so sorry!*

*It's been so enjoyable to get to know you up to now and I was seriously looking forward to us meeting, but I truthfully feel as if I have no other alternative. There is a tiny number of people in my life who I love dearly. My late mother, my wife and my daughter makes just three – and I can't put our relationship in jeopardy, or risk causing her any hurt.*

*I have therefore given my commitment that I won't
carry on in pursuit of a father–daughter-style
relationship with you.*

As I typed a reply my fingers felt constricted. Tired.
Unwilling.

Wanting to look on the bright side, while feeling not-at-
all-bright, I said:

*Roland, what I feel you have shown me is that there are
people out there who would like a platonic relationship,
and who are willing and enthusiastic to make a platonic
connection. I was worried that might not be the case
when starting out. You have very much boosted my
faith in human nature, so thank you!*

*I do hope that you start to get more and more joy in
your life. Indeed, it seems to me that you are exactly
the kind of person who not only deserves joy, but also
that you have just the right levels of curiosity to fill your
time with the good stuff.*

*If your daughter ever tells you that she feels more
secure about the idea of us meeting, perhaps that is
something we could work out between us. Perhaps she
could come too. Otherwise, yes, we had best not put
her happiness at risk. Thank you again, though. Thank
you hugely.*

I signed off my email and cried.
*It only takes one.*

# 5

# NICE PEOPLE

Helpful factions were forming around me. In the Cousins Team were seven viewpoints to draw from. Next was the Undergraduate Team: a small bunch of people I'd studied with years ago. My Creative Writers Team stretched across the UK in different subgroups, while small islands of school friends were also on hand. In quieter times, two Ex-Colleague Teams could be called upon. Their members included a no-nonsense receptionist (a former air stewardess who'd worked for years in first class and on private jets) to whom I presented the latest classifieds section of *Private Eye*.

She mouthed the words of the dadvert to herself and then looked up. 'Tell me this isn't you. It isn't you. It's not you.'

I assured her it was definitely me.

'There is *no* man between his fifties and seventies who wants anything platonic with someone your age.'

'But—'

'No, Codd. No, no, no.'

Though telling myself her views must have been jaded by years of entitled, jet-setting businessmen, I started to research gay newspapers and magazines, looking for men who wouldn't want anything sexual from me at *any* age. A couple of friends recommended the *GAY TIMES*. When I made contact I learned it would cost £1,990 to put the dadvert in print.

I spent a little more time face down on the sofa.

During a phone call, Mum let me know that one of her male friends had set up a bank account in my name soon after my birth. She had no idea where the account was now, or what happened to the money. 'Could you find out?' I asked.

'I doubt it.'

My sofa imprint deepened.

Then the man who had not long declared he was going to *bow out* re-emerged to send me a Valentine's Day message. His e-card was decorated with pink tulips. *Happy Valentine's, Daughter*, it said. Beneath it he described a scene in which he was part of the audience as I collected the Nobel Prize for Literature.

*I'd love to be there, heart bursting with pride: 'That's my daughter!'*

I spent the rest of that day contemplating the line between sweet and stalkerish.

Increasingly hunched at the shoulders, I opted to book myself in for a massage. The masseuse I used had hands that could reshape bricks, plus a father who absconded to Italy when she was a teenager, leaving her, her mother and siblings behind in England.

What were fathers for? I croaked, as she kneaded more

air from my lungs. Please: what *was* the difference between a dad and a man?

The masseuse paused for a moment, then said: 'Dads are shit.'

I wheeze-laughed so hard that I dribbled.

Thankfully, Dr Frank L'Engle Williams, a biological anthropologist based in Atlanta, had more academic answers to those questions. His book, *Fathers and Their Children in the First Three Years of Life*, precisely covered that period in which men transition to dads. Its existence was inspired by his realisation that there was so little literature out there for men who – like him at the time he began his research – were about to make the leap with pregnant partners.

Over a video call made patchy by my internet connection, Frank introduced himself as a 'divorced dad now, unfortunately'. He had just finished dropping his three kids at school.

I explained in brief what had led me his way: the cruise, the search, my ignorance. Soon we were bonding over a shared lack of fathers.

'My mum was a single mum,' I said. 'My dad wasn't interested and – it's a bit like a Thomas Hardy novel, when I think about the details.'

I was thinking, partly, of that time my father's father visited Mum soon after I was born. The devout Anglican man who felt compelled to let her know, as she recovered at home with her baby – recovered with his first grandchild – that, 'In the eyes of the church, this child does not exist.'

There were other things, more Hardy-esque, that I pushed out of my mind.

Frank nodded with enthusiasm. 'Part of the motivation for my book is that I'm also in some ways fatherless. My father left when I was 4. I saw him, like, once a year. When I was 18, he sent me a ticket to visit him in California. It was really weird because I didn't know him very well, so I was there like an older friend. At that time, I felt closer to my grandfather than my father. We remained estranged for most of my life. He died a couple of years ago.'

Frank went on. 'In many cases, humans can develop relatively normally without a father. In other cases, humans can't. We have to compensate for the lack of the father: so mothers can step in, older siblings can step in, grandparents, uncles, aunts, and help to fill that gap as best as possible. But there's still that loss that can never be repaired.

'I've tried to repair it myself through having children and becoming a very doting father, probably to the children's detriment. I can't help it. It led to divorce, I'm certain of it. I was more invested in the children than my wife.'

Frank explained that he felt there had been a lot written around fatherlessness, and its negative social outcomes. For active fathering, however, 'There's a dearth of inquiry about it – on the scholarly level, as well as the popular.'

Why?

'Childbirth changes women's lives in a fundamental physiological way, obviously; that's a huge part of it. And not only is there the birth, but then there's the breastfeeding afterwards. Fathers *have* to be second. They are immediately . . . In my book I argue that this is how we evolved. But it's the pair bonding between two parents that ropes males in to taking *care* of these helpless children for the next two decades. Because in my view being a father is not just about impregnating the woman, like what happened to your mom. That's a genitor or a pater. It's someone who contributed to your genetic make-up, but that's not what makes up a father. What makes him a father is his pair bond with the mother and the child.'

In other words, from the anthropological standpoint, not all men who father become fathers.

According to Frank, Carl could basically never be my real dad, not without fully committing to Mum and me. Here the anthropological knowledge became more compelling still: Frank revealed how the transition from man to father is more complex than simply deciding not to leg it when a female partner gets pregnant; sticking around comes with proven biological consequences.

'A male's testosterone goes down when they're actively with a child,' he said, 'when they're basically constantly being with them, or are actively participating in parenting in other ways. And in the care-taking father the prolactin goes up – which is part of the breastfeeding hormone. It goes higher than in women who are not mothers.'

I squeaked.

'You have these hormonal effects, and you have to wonder. This is an evolved system! If your father had maybe been around for the first few years of your life, he might have stuck around for the rest of your growth and development. But missing that initial window was critical. When males miss that window, or it's interrupted by active service duty, or status – the drive for status interrupts that window.'

Essentially, the cycle was self-fulfilling: put in the time to father, and men could hormonally become the caring fathers that families needed.

--------

Whether Carl put in the time with his second child, Caroline, before she died, I wasn't sure. At the end of my phone call with his mother, I agreed I would not ring him. The man was not in a good way, that was clear.

His baby, Caroline, had died before her first birthday – cot death, I was told.

Her mother, Carl's long-term partner, had died only months before I rang – of an aggressive and gruelling tongue cancer.

As for Carl, he was currently in remission – from a cancer of the throat.

'He's getting better,' his mother told me. 'But he's not himself.'

Instead we agreed I would send Carl a letter. After that I would wait.

And wait.

--------

I found out more about hormones and dads through the work of a British evolutionary anthropologist, Dr Anna Machin. Like Frank's book, Dr Machin's *The Life of Dad* takes a close look at the fundamental make-up of our genders. She describes how essential neurochemicals that help parent–child bonding (oxytocin and dopamine) are generated in fathers *even during pregnancy*, as long as the man spends enough time with his pregnant partner. Machin also reveals that levels of testosterone – what she calls the 'sex hormone' – have not only been shown to drop among men who are present parents, but that they drop most sharply among males who have the highest female-attracting levels of testosterone to begin with.

Once the sex hormone has done its work in males by attracting a mate and reproducing, it synchronises with the levels of the pregnant partner, and permanently eases off to facilitate caring, fatherly behaviour, regardless of whether the man later lives with his children or not.

'And we know,' says Dr Machin, 'that men with lower levels of testosterone are more responsive to a child's cry, are more likely to wish to co-parent their child and show more empathy and affection towards their children than men with higher testosterone levels.'

I closed Dr Machin's book, grabbed a toy pig and threw it from one hand to the other. For a moment it seemed the odds were stacked against me: if I could go back to the embryo stage and somehow bind Carl to my mother for nine months, perhaps the hormones would have done their thing. (Then again, forcibly binding people to each other probably wasn't, I suspected, the greatest route to a happy family.)

In the absence of a time machine and the means of long-term physical entrapment where did that leave me? Looking for men with naturally low testosterone, perhaps? Hoping that might make them more suitable for my requirements?

There had to be a way around this. After all, I'd read somewhere that the average age of children adopted in Britain was 3.5 years – meaning plenty of adoptive families missed the earliest window. I also knew from a few friends' experiences that forming familial bonds with a non-infant adoptee was not only possible, but could be deeply, richly rewarding for parent and child.

Locating an involved dad through my search seemed like the way ahead. And perhaps not only for me.

I allowed myself to be swept into a new fantasy, wondering what would happen if every office in the land had a dedicated batch of pregnant women working in it. Or if jobs in toxic workplaces were expanded to include daily child-rearing duties. Would the uncaring folk in those buildings gradually soften?

And what would happen if all the baddies out there – the dictators, the warmongers, their scheming allies – were secretly pumped with super-strength testosterone inhibitors?

It couldn't be that simple.

Could it?

'Fuck it! Why the hell not!'

It suddenly seemed as if working out how to form strong, sexless father–child bonds later in life could benefit not only me, but the fundamental ways men and women interact with the world.

In jubilation, I threw my pig into the air. It hit the edge of the ceiling light, dislodged a raft of dust and bounced to a lifeless halt beside the footstool.

The thing was, my own body wasn't chemically prepared for that kind of task. And could it not be argued that the hormones I was emitting were instead evolutionarily crafted to get me reproducing a child of my own; to be knocked up by men like those who were now responding to my dadverts?

For a week I wrote to new respondents, thinking often of Roland, already perceiving our exchange as 'the good old days'. The pickings since then had been slim. Some vague one-liners from farmers saying hello. A few back-stories about daughters and second marriages. And a theme: people who didn't ask questions beyond the bare minimum. Of which I was suspicious.

Jerry seemed mostly to want to talk about his campaign to run Blackpool, while Mr Pink Tulips wanted something more professional of mine to read. When I let him know that the only easily accessible things I had out then were PR-style blogs, he said, *Even if it is marketing bits and pieces, to me it would be very special. I could read it, my heart bursting with pride, and think 'my daughter wrote this!'*

By this point we had exchanged about ten short messages.

I drummed my desk with my fingers, summoning optimism. *I can appreciate the urge to feel some pride*, I wrote, *and that you really feel you've missed out on having a daughter in your life. I still don't know much about you yet though – nor you me, really! What was your own father like, for instance? And why do you think that a daughter is so important for you? What events in your life have brought you to write to me now?*

Days later he wrote back, not replying to my questions, but letting me know he was married, and that he understood my wishes were platonic.

He added:

*Although in the past I have fantasised about the idea
that I might find a young woman, and run away together
somewhere where neither of us is known, so that we
could live together as father and daughter, I recognise
this as just a fantasy! I do think, however, that perhaps I
am more inclined to think of the father figure – daughter
figure relationship as a role-playing exercise than you are.
Park this thought for a while. I'll come back to it.*

*Okay,* I replied. *Let's park it and come back.*
He never did come back.

Aside from Roland, few men seemed to want to know
who I was. As far as they knew I could have been anyone.
Planning anything. Sharpening the points on my knuckle-
duster between hourly doses of steroids.

In fact, I had noticed my mood was more tempestuous
than normal. With my boobs feeling tender, I took a pregnancy test, wondering if my contraception had somehow
failed. The plastic stick processed my pee as a negative.

'That's good,' said Duncan on hearing the news.

'Okay,' I replied. 'Then it's definitely good.'

Back in the inbox, a new person made himself known. A
short initial message shared his intrigue and asked for more.
Responding to the bounce-back, the man then wrote again
just half an hour later. *Hi Georgina,* he began.

*OK, you asked for a second email and here it is.*

# NICE PEOPLE

*I'm single at this point in my life but didn't make contact seeking 'funny business', instead because your advert ignited something in me I couldn't define. I lost my dad at an early age, so I know what being fatherless is like. Grieving as a child in the 70s was challenging. No psychological help was offered to me or my brother, or seemingly available. My mother couldn't handle the situation so we received no support or acknowledgment of what was happening for us. In that very traditional way of British families, nobody ever mentioned my dad again. Being shy didn't help things. My romantic relationships have usually faded to nothing. Today I see how intensely affected I was by my loss and trauma, and that sticks to me still. I am certain those I love will suddenly, unexpectedly vanish, and no matter how deeply I want to stay with someone I quickly enter self-preservation mode, pushing them away. Having children has never been my plan for a variety of reasons but the urge does take me sometimes when I get to thinking how nice it would be to spend time with a now grown-up child.*

1. *Advert found:* Private Eye.
2. *Responding because: see my rambles above.*
3. *My home county: Suffolk, UK.*
4. *Offering to you: I think I can give openness, decency and my own type of curiosity.*
5. *My question: Want a cuppa?!*

*Very best,*
*Grant*

I read it out to my boyfriend, who approved. 'He writes like you talk.'

'Hm.' I pulled the screen closer.

Hi Grant,

Thank you very much for taking the time to get in touch – and then to answer my follow-up questions. It really was great to hear from you, and learn about your own experience of fathers and bereavement.

One line you wrote struck a major chord with me: 'I am certain those I love will suddenly, unexpectedly vanish, and no matter how deeply I want to stay with someone I quickly enter self-preservation mode, pushing them away.' I've found myself doing the same thing before – it's been a real issue at times in my past relationships. There have been some major deaths in my family over the years, and they've all left me feeling pretty anxious about the future. I am trying to use that as a motivation to get out there and not put things off. Fear of death and of losing my loved ones was actually one of the reasons I decided to place my ad. I feel like death could appear at almost any moment, so am desperate to do what I want while I have the chance.

Anyway, I see your cup of tea – and raise you a piece of cake! Let me know if, having read this reply, that is something you'd still like to do at some point. As I alluded to in my auto-response message, this is a potentially 'nerve-racking' prospect, and not only for me. Perhaps we could exchange a few more emails *first. Perhaps you have more questions you'd like to ask me? Or perhaps this reply I'm sending today will have satisfied your curiosity, and you'll no longer want to correspond. If that is the case I understand, and wish you all the best.*

*Thank you again for writing to me, whatever you choose to do next.*

*Very warmest wishes,*

*Georgina*

To stop myself getting carried away I immediately vacated the inbox and started browsing recipe books. Granny Codd's famous Eccles cakes would be perfectly time-consuming. When Grant ghosted me I could then stuff my face and tell myself it was okay, because they were mostly fruit, because of all the currants. I thanked her spirit out loud for the legacy and hurried to the fridge to find butter.

The next day:

*Hi Georgina,*

*Thank you for your reply. Although it's possible I'm projecting my own issues on to you, I think I get what you did just there. I think you 'gave me permission' not to email to help yourself feel better in case I didn't. That's something I do a great deal myself. Never mind that it's rationally counterproductive. When I properly think about it, I think that even if a correspondent had the intention of replying they might feel doubtful after seeing that kind of prompt. And if they were already doubtful, it might just seal the deal. Anyway . . . I am back!*

*Communication is everything for me. My family barely communicated (well, not in a way I see as communication). When there are reality shows on TV showing families sat with each other, speaking and joking together like old pals, I feel jealous. Cheated too. My brother and I hardly see each other. He only lives in the next county but we've not swapped a word since Christmas. I take my mum to lunch every six weeks or so, which just about suits us. For years I felt things were all her fault, and was a furious young man at times. I would hold things in and then erupt, and still she didn't try to understand. As an adult I've been able to remind myself that she's a flawed human being like all of us. Like her own parents too.*

*You are of course correct to write that death can rear its head without any warning. That's the same for everyone, only some of us dwell and make copious plans because we're primed. Are you an organiser? Are you keen on schedules and lists? Though my house is sometimes a bit messy I am always on time. And if anyone tells me they'll do something and don't do it, I find that seriously hard to handle.*

*I get your nervousness. That feeling has always been with me and has always held me back. People say 'feel the fear and do it anyway'. That doesn't work for me with most things. For years I have been on dating apps. They don't suit me at all but there doesn't seem to be anything else. Dating is a terribly nervous thing for me.*

*I'm not pleased to admit that I have stood girls up because of those nerves. At the moment I am on a new dating website and cancelled a meeting a few weeks ago. The fear seems to trump my yearning (what I might call my desperation) to not stay single. For me, the idea of us meeting for tea and cake is far less of an issue as neither of us is trying to wow each other, or measure each other up. The two of us know 'the lay of the land'.*

*The ever-dwelling sceptic in me wants to ask: is this a purely personal venture or are you writing about it?*

*Very best,*

*Grant*

Now I was too pumped up to eat Eccles cakes. Too excited to do anything but reply.

*Hi Grant,*

*Me again – I was really pleased to see your message in my inbox.*

*It feels very weird hearing someone pinpoint certain key aspects of your character, despite them knowing relatively little about you. I've had various helpful bouts of therapy over the years – mostly in my efforts to deal with bereavement – and like to think I'm pretty self-aware. Still, I'd never properly associated my obsessions with lists, schedules and timeliness with my experiences of death. Or maybe I had not framed it in that way. If I ever get in a real tizz over someone being late, or wasting my time (as I perceive it), I have occasionally had the lucidity to relate that to my deeper feeling of: things have to be perfect because everything I want might disappear at any moment.*

*What I hadn't thought about was how this relates to promise-keeping! Yes: I find it extremely difficult to cope with broken promises. With change in general, actually, if I'm honest. I am trying to work very hard on this, but it doesn't come easy.*

*You've given me some major things to ponder there.*

Pause. More pondering. Then:

*Thank you for putting your 'ever-dwelling sceptic' hat on! I can't believe you're the first person who's properly asked me about writing this. It would have been one of my earliest questions too. As you might imagine, this 'venture', or whatever it should be called, is a very personal thing for me, and is driven by my desire to make a meaningful connection (or possibly connections) with someone (or more than one person) who is as interested as I am in exploring whether a platonic father–daughter-style relationship can be created in later life. I feel deeply sad sometimes about not having had a father, and hope that there could be something positive to come out of it; that I will learn more about my feelings on what I've missed; and more about other people's attitudes and experiences too.*

*I have written creative fiction and non-fiction in the past (my first book to be published, which has nothing to do with fathers, is going to come out next year) and I have thought that, depending on how this goes, I would also like to write about this journey one day. Maybe I can publish something on the subject down the line. I believe that the possibility of putting this into a book could be quite a way off, if it is possible at all. My priority is to try and make this project work first somehow – for my own benefit; not for the benefit of any readers.*

*In my life to date, I have found writing to be a really helpful tool in protecting my feelings. When something goes wrong, or someone behaves badly towards me, I tell myself, 'That's OK, maybe I can write about it one day.' More often than not, I don't. Still, I'm not sure I'd feel strong enough to embark on something like this if I didn't have that notion behind me. Putting my 'writer hat' on is the best way I've found to try and override my anxieties.*

*I don't know how you will react to what I've written, or if this truly conveys my sincerity as I want it to. Being honest is very important to me. It may be that this information puts you off writing to me further. I really hope not. I would like to find out more about you, and am really grateful for what you have shared so far about your family and experiences. I feel like there's a lot more we could talk about. But will leave things for now, just in case.*

*Hoping to hear from you again,*
*Georgina*

Against the backdrop of my now-speeding exchanges with Grant, Duncan's mother came to stay. I set aside an afternoon to take her out on a chocolate binge – a treat I'd bought her for Christmas – and during our second tray of truffles, noticed I was hiding behind my mug. 'I'm just not very happy about this, Georgie?' my sort-of-mother-in-law repeated, her raised voice turning statements into questions. 'I don't think you'll be safe?'

I insisted there were nice people around. 'I know there are. They're not all bad.' I took a gulp of hot chocolate.

She shook her head. 'They've only got one thing in mind, these guys. We're talking about men in my generation. You probably don't realise it, but they've been brought up with *massive* problems relating to women. Lots of them went to boarding school, and they don't know how to talk, be, act around someone like you without wanting, well . . . *you* know.'

Her husband, Duncan's dad, had gone to boarding school. The two of them had been together for decades. 'Is there something you're trying to tell me?' I probed.

Carefully, she tucked her hair behind her ear. 'Well, it's a Pandora's box, isn't it? I just think, considering your mental health, you're opening up a massive can of worms.'

'Eh? My mental health?' I stuffed a truffle into my mouth. '*My mental health is okay*,' I managed through a glob of ganache.

She rolled up her sleeves. 'What does Duncan think of all this?'

'Cautiously supportive, I'd say.'

'Really?'

'Mm-hm. Yep. Absolutely.'

After the chocolate was gone we returned to the flat. Still stuck on the subject, my mother-of-sorts asked her son the same question in the exact same tone. 'What do you think of all this?'

'There's a lot that could go wrong,' he said at once. 'A lot.'

I waited for a positive follow-up comment. Something beginning with 'But'.

It didn't come.

My arms folded. 'You've not put it like that before,' I said.

'I mean, it's obvious, isn't it?'

'I'm afraid I'm doing this project whether you like it or not, so I'd appreciate your support.'

'I *support* you . . .' said his mother. There was a long pause. 'But.'

The two of them shared a look.

Hi Georgina,

OK, here's a deal. Let's agree there's no need to give each other permission as a way of protecting ourselves. I'm not going to vanish. If I decide I need to stop I'll tell you. The same goes for you to me. We don't need to give reasons but we can communicate at least. We/you can relax on this small thing if on nothing else. What do you think?

While you're considering that please let me put forward another challenging thought. It's really quite challenging, so take it slow. It's from my personal experience. It's about being in control. The final ultimate control when nothing else is going to plan.

*The idea of suicide has been part of me ever since I can remember, and my most recent effort happened twelve months ago. Depression is a dark old friend. I'm sometimes up, sometimes down, but have been feeling optimistic for a decent length of time. I don't take meds for it because I still haven't found a doctor who is really willing to hear what I'm saying. I probably do too much complaining about things being wrong. Unfairness and injustices hit me quite hard.*

*Once upon a time I imagined writing books, but it seems to be beyond me. I don't think I have the patience. Even with emails I get caught up with refining and refining what I'm saying, although the emails I'm writing to you feel much easier and spontaneous.*

*What has your week been like?*

*I crave openness and honesty, by the way. Better brutal honesty than anything else. I think that's come from being told my dad would be coming home soon, but that didn't happen. You can't be too truthful with me.*

*This is a short note since I'm going out to play tennis in a moment. Take care of yourself.*

*Best wishes,*

*Grant*

Long breaths. *Quite challenging* was right.

I had no idea how best to respond. All I knew was that I did not want to stop.

Writing back to Grant, I thanked him for his thoughts; shared that I'd had my own struggles in the past, relating

them back to grief. *I found it really helpful then to know that
the way I was feeling was common, I said. I'm glad to hear
you're feeling mostly optimistic at the moment. Me too.*

Gently, I followed him onto steadier ground.

*My week is going alright, thanks – I'm trying to keep
busy at the moment (it's a quiet time of year for work;
slightly unnerving) so I really like having emails to write
back to. Yours have stopped me in my tracks a few
times!*

*If you did still want to think about arranging tea (and
possibly cake) at some point, it would be nice to meet
you in person. But no pressure. I'm nervous about
it – though I also think it'd be a very positive thing to
do. I imagine you might feel similarly, but I don't know.
Thoughts?*

*Warmest wishes,*

*G*

*P.S. Roger that on the brutal honesty front. I'm with
you there.*

Grant was willing to meet. He suggested that Sunday, and
sent through a photograph of himself. He had dark hair
and dark eyes. His face was unsmiling and calm. The picture had been taken as part of his work for a local union.

'He looks like you,' said Duncan, stealing a glimpse. 'I
think you might have found your actual dad.'

'Are you saying I look like a fifty-something-year-old man?'

'Same nose, same eyes, same forehead.'

'Stop.'

That morning I plotted a day out in Colchester – roughly midway between Grant's home and ours. In the evening I bribed Duncan to travel with me, by offering to buy all his drinks and food that day. By the end he sounded excited.

'But . . . I thought you weren't on board with this project,' I said.

He looked puzzled.

'Because of what you said when your mum was staying.'

'Lots *could* go wrong,' he insisted. 'But the idea is excellent. You can do it.'

I paused to take in his words. 'Do you really think so?'

'Absolutely.'

Mum rang to give me her news and ask for mine. Tentatively, I revealed my plans for the weekend, expecting an unfavourable reaction, or a swerve away from the topic. Instead she acted interested. 'A union man,' she said. 'Which union?'

I told her.

'Oh, so he's got principles.'

As she reminisced about her own union experiences over the years, it occurred to me that I may have found my mother's ideal partner.

'He's very open about his mental health,' I explained. 'And self-aware. Sounds like he's had a tough time in the past, though.'

'Who hasn't. And you said he liked cake?'

Suddenly I felt like I'd done a decent job. A feeling that I realised, even as it bloomed inside me, might not last.

# 6

# FIRST MEETING

Sunday morning arrived. I ground into consciousness, wanting the day to be over before it started. Too much was at stake.

'We're going to have a proper fun adventure,' effused my boyfriend.

Groaning, I rolled from the bed. My body was uncomfortable and sore. I took a new pregnancy test to the bathroom. Like the first, it showed a negative. 'Thank God for that,' I muttered.

It was time for me to get practical and scour the wardrobe for outfits. I needed something that said, 'I'm not a maniac.' And, more importantly, 'Not vying for any sexual interest.' In the end I settled for jeans, a loose overshirt patterned with zigzags that I borrowed from Duncan's cast-offs, and zero jewellery or make-up. In our latest round of emails, since I had decided against sending a picture, I told Grant I'd be wearing my fingerless gloves. I made sure they were safely on before we left.

Duncan listened to my briefing as we walked to the

Underground. The prospective dad and I would meet at a hotel café. There we would have tea and talk.

'A *hotel!*' repeated my boyfriend. 'I mean, that screams of sex to me.'

I advised him I might strangle him.

The morning was frosty, the sky shining blue. We made our way south to the station, there catching a train that was scheduled to arrive three hours early – I was building in time for a walk that might settle my nerves. Overnight, something had happened in my brain, some kind of faulty rewiring. I'd started to associate the picture of Grant with the actor Daniel Day-Lewis. Every now and again I would realise I was thinking of him as Daniel. Referring to him as Daniel out loud. The more I tried to correct it, the more it persisted.

'Ask me his name,' I pleaded. 'Keep asking and don't stop.'

Duncan picked up a newspaper. 'What's his name?'

'Grant.'

'What's his name?'

'Dan – Grant.'

Long pause.

'*Duncan.*'

'Yeah? Oh. What's his name?'

'Grant . . . Grant, Grant, Grant, Grant, Grant.'

As my boyfriend tackled yesterday's sudoku – part of what I assumed was an unspoken plan to calm me down by proxy – I imagined what it would feel like to be en route to my biological father instead. Carl, my pater or genitor. Or rather, I *tried* to imagine it, since when I told myself, 'This is it. I'm going to meet my dad. It's really happening. It's happening', my mind wouldn't let me go there. It chose to play instead with *Grant, Grant, Daniel, Grant, Daniel, Grant, Grant.*

At Colchester we tottered off the train. The air was part-frozen, the pavements dusted with snow. Solitary men in their fifties seemed to be everywhere. Sitting in parked cars, buying Sunday papers, possibly asking themselves why I kept throwing them nervous glances. Concerned that Grant might be one of these men – might pass by and see me early, before I was ready – I removed my gloves and stuffed them into my pockets. Such was my belief in the awesome power of this disguise.

'I'm worried we've picked the wrong venue,' I fretted. 'Should I suggest changing it?'

'If this guy changed it last minute, you'd shit yourself.'

'Okay. Fair. I would.'

We navigated to the country park, me keeping my head down all the way. My fear of being stalked and bundled into a van was increasing. Alongside that was a mightier fear that Grant and I would run out of things to say. As we walked I pulled out my phone, revising notes from our emails, picking out possible topics of conversation. At no point in our park explorations did I feel calm.

All too soon, we were heading back into town. There was now half an hour to go.

I trailed Duncan to a pub near the hotel. We were about to step in when he came to a halt and barred the way with his arm. '*I think that's him.*'

I stopped dead. 'For real?'

'He just went past us in the opposite direction.'

Cautiously, I turned my head. A hunched man in slouching grey joggers shuffled and chain-smoked in the street. His backside was almost totally exposed.

'I don't think that's him.'

My boyfriend frowned. 'Are you sure?'

'I fucking well hope not.'

Inside the pub, Duncan ordered himself a pint, brought out some work from his backpack and gazed at the log fire.

My legs pistoned under the table. 'I want to stay here,' I said. 'I don't want to do this anymore. I'm going to be sick.'

'It won't be that bad,' said Duncan. 'Probably.'

'How can you be so chilled?'

He shrugged.

'If I don't get back in a couple of hours you need to call the police, remember? Same if I don't text you within the first 30 minutes.'

'Okay.' The pint arrived. Duncan held it to his lips.

'He'll be scared too, won't he? Maybe worse than me. Grant. Grant. Grant.'

My boyfriend said, 'Mm, that's tasty.'

Time had already run out. I was nowhere near ready.


I power-walked out of the pub and up the street, trying to convince myself I was confident; to convince my insides that everything was fine. From 50 metres away I saw a man standing alone outside the hotel. He was wearing glasses and staring down at his phone. It was as if his eyes were glued in position, so wilful was his attention. The will of somebody fighting off nerves.

It wasn't until I got to within 10 metres that this person raised his head. I held up both of my now-gloved hands.

'Georgina!'

'Grant!'

It was a warm and friendly greeting. A tight hug. The two of us grinned, then stepped back. Grant was shorter than me.

'The hotel's shut for some work by the looks of it,' he said.

'Dang it. I need cake.'

We resolved to go searching for somewhere else, making fast small talk as we went. Grant's tone of voice was not shy. When he revealed that he used to be a local tour guide I could see it clearly: him chatting from the front seat of a coach to all his passengers.

We criss-crossed town from place to place. The first café: too full. The second: too quiet. The third: too closed. 'I'd prefer somewhere independent,' said Grant.

'Me too! I love independent!'

Colchester had other ideas. Five minutes later we were in the queue for hot drinks at one of the nation's 2,400-plus branches of Costa Coffee. 'I bet you're the soya-milk-drinking type,' joked Grant, noticing the pattern of my shirt. The server looked at me.

'One decaf latte with *normal* milk, please,' I told him.

Grant smiled. 'Did you avoid the soya milk because I just said that?'

'No, actually,' I lied. 'Soya milk tastes crap in coffee.'

It kept me occupied to ponder what it said about him that he ordered a piece of lemon meringue pie. Me, I asked for a chocolate chip cookie (regression, I noted; shades of *Sesame Street*), then insisted I pay for us both.

Grant bagged a table for two that had a ring of spare tables around it. It was in the middle of the room, buffered by peripheral chatter on all sides. Making an excuse to visit the loo, I texted Duncan to say things were okay, updating him with my location.

On my return I made myself ask: 'So am I about what you expected so far?' hoping for a better idea of how I came across in words alone.

'More or less.' Grant nodded. 'Slim, tall, brownish hair, attractive, nicely spoken.'

I flinched at the 'a' word; tried not to show it.

'Not sure about that hippy shirt, though,' he teased. Changing tack, he asked if I was a journalist.

I shook my head. 'Just a writer.' In the next instant I debated whether or not to expand that answer as I would in a normal conversation. Doing so would reveal details that could help Grant identify me further. I wasn't sure I wanted that yet. Then I considered how much we knew about each other already. For instance, I knew where *he* worked – had verified that with an online search before meeting. Plus I knew his surname. And his hometown.

I cleared my throat. 'My mum worked as a journalist for our local newspaper,' I said. 'She retired recently. She thoroughly put me off the career.'

'Ah.'

Grant had a kind smile. Making myself breathe more slowly, I broke off a chunk of cookie to chew. 'This is a bit strange, isn't it?'

'Yep,' he said. 'I'm kind of drawn to strange things,

though. I once proposed to someone on a first date. Not long after my first divorce.'

My mouth sprang open. 'Like, actually proposed? Like, down on one knee?'

'I'm afraid so.'

Grant described how they'd met online. The woman had accepted his offer, then agreed to go on a weekend break with him. As he spoke, he shook his head in disbelief. His new fiancée moved in to his house right after the trip was over. Within six weeks they were married.

'I knew it was the wrong decision. I knew she didn't like me. I was in a very bad place and she was too. I once asked her to say she loved me. She said, "I have grown accustomed to you."'

'Oof.'

'In the end it got so bad that I used bailiffs to serve the divorce papers.'

Before I could fully process this, Grant then began speaking about a woman he had liked from Fiji – again, found via the internet.

'We got on so well, we made plans for me to fly over. On my way to the airport that Icelandic volcano erupted; I couldn't travel. I rebooked and then *that* was cancelled because of a staff strike at Heathrow.' He swallowed a mouthful of tea. 'I didn't feel like she reacted strongly enough to the news I wasn't coming, so I broke things off. I regret that. She married someone else.'

Our conversation continued. I worked on letting my guard down, just as Grant seemed to be letting down his.

We talked about the writing I was doing. About bereavements. About therapists. About my current relationship.

We talked about children, and not having children.

'I've got no idea what to do,' I complained. 'If I pop one out and decide I don't want it, it's not like I can properly change my mind. Having kids seems like the world's most high-stakes bet.'

Grant agreed. 'I don't regret not having children. You never know what you're going to get. And it can go so wrong.'

For a while we swapped tales of friends who had kids, and later confided that they wished they hadn't. Men and women who believed their lives could have been better off without that endless, all-consuming slog.

'The only thing is,' I wondered, 'perhaps when things go right with kids they go *really* right?'

I dabbed at my plate. Grant and I had somehow talked for two hours. Duncan might be wondering where I was.

We said our goodbyes on the pavement, sharing another big hug. 'Let's do this again?' I suggested.

'I'd love to.'

My chest swelled.

Back at the pub I moulded the length of myself into a chair. Duncan finished his emails and latest pint, requesting anecdotes.

'So, he's pretty adventurous,' he summarised. 'Which is what you wanted.'

'Seems it.'

'A nice guy.'

'I think so, if you can say things like that after just one—'

'Good dad material then.'

I rested my palms on the table. 'That's just it: how would I know?'

The following day I wrote to Grant, thanking him for the meeting. Duncan had a point: the man was clearly intrepid. He seemed to have time and the headspace for commitment. He was good at conversation, showed interest and compassion, and had interesting stories to share. Before we parted ways he had also asked for my help: he wanted to write an advert that might attract a partner. Seeing as I was now pretty much a professional people-finder, that ought to be right up my street. I raised the subject in my message, thinking it could be an adventurous task for us to bond over.

His response came about an hour later, beginning perfectly as ever, characteristically putting my feelings first, and giving me ample space. *Thank you for getting in touch,* he wrote. *I wanted to wait for your email before writing, in case that felt like pressure. I genuinely had a wonderful time in your company and hoped you felt the same, but was keen to give you an exit if you wanted that.*

He then offered his observations:

*I suspect most people in your life think you've got it all sorted. Friendly, talkative, spirited, bright, self-aware, attractive, nice boyfriend with decent prospects, a good home in London, pursuing her dream career, etc. I reckon modesty would stop you from saying/thinking the same.*

All round, the email was lovely. However, I was snagged afresh by the 'a' word.

Then again, his paternalism would take time to grow. Possibly years. In the meantime, more information was needed: my knowledge of Grant was promising, yet inconclusive. I suggested we plan a game of tennis for next time.

My friend Mabry – she of the anti-golf-dad strategy – came over that night for dinner. She was on form, excited, giggling. 'I've become obsessed with serial killers,' she confessed. 'Like, addicted.' A programme about Ted Bundy had set her off, that sadistic American murderer with his tens – perhaps hundreds – of crimes. 'He seemed so charming to everyone,' Mabry recounted. 'He had proper long-term girlfriends and was enrolled in law school. But *also*, he bludgeoned women to death, and raped them, and did terrible things to their corpses, and escaped from jail more than once, and there's apparently a *gene*, a serial killer *gene*, that can get activated in certain people depending on their childhood. Then you see Ted Bundy on film, like in documentaries, and mostly he looks *normal*.'

'Are you telling me I'm going to meet a serial killer?'

'It's possible.'

She asked me about Colchester and Grant. 'I don't *think* he's a serial killer,' I said.

'He could be. But you don't think so?'

'I'm probably more likely to be the murderer out of both of us,' I said.

'Okay.'

The two of us started looking up Ted Bundy facts on our phones. 'Shit!' I cried.

Mabry leaned over. 'What?'

'Bundy never had a dad.'

My friend sat back on the sofa. After a few moments, she asked, 'Did he have a paternal feel about him?'

'What did the show say?'

'No. Grant. Did you feel like he was paternal?'

I sucked the air through my teeth. 'He said he thought I was attractive.'

'Oh.'

'He mentioned it again in his latest email. I feel like . . . It's tough.' I paused. 'I feel like the word "attractive" implies attrac*tion*.'

She asked if he had been giving off those vibes.

'Not really. Although if I'd started flirting, it might have been returned.'

'You think?'

'Maybe not. I just think he wants a partner more than a daughter.'

The topic continued to bother me. I couldn't decide if I was overthinking things. In my message to Grant the next day I tried to find out. *Can I ask*, I wrote, *did our meeting bring out any paternal feelings in you, whatever that means? My sense is that we were talking more like pals than anything else. Perhaps you interpreted things differently.*

Grant came back with: *Yes, you hit it right, it did feel a lot like pals meeting up but I suppose that's largely what I had envisioned if I'd gone straight to the adult children option having bypassed the noisy smelly stage.*

I thought about Mum's friend Nick: the man for whom I'd been bridesmaid, long ago; he who most closely fitted my mould of the ideal father figure. There had never been any hint of attraction in that dynamic, as far as I could recall. The only comments on appearance he'd made had come when I was much younger. All were along the lines of: 'Your face is glowing, Georgina. You look sickeningly healthy.' And, 'Where *do* you put all that cake, child? You ought to be obese by now.'

Researching more about dads, daughters and attraction, I heard about a memoir called *The Kiss*. Written by US author Kathryn Harrison, it detailed her reunion with her estranged father. At that point she was 20, he was 38. Aside from two brief visits when Harrison was aged 5 and 10, the man hadn't been in her life since she was a baby. I ordered a copy and nestled down with both pigs tucked in my waistband.

'My father is an absence,' wrote Harrison, 'a hole like one of those my grandmother cuts out of family portraits.'

Chapters later, she described the moment of their reunion as adults:

> My father looks at me, then, as no one has ever looked at me before. His hot eyes consume me – eyes that I will discover are always just this bloodshot. I almost feel their touch. He takes my hands, one in each of his, and turns them over, stares at my palms. He does not actually kiss them, but his look is one that ravishes.

At the end of that visit, her father asks, 'How can a daughter of mine be this beautiful?' adding, 'When I look at you, I wonder if I, too, must not be handsome.' When he kisses her goodbye, he pushes his tongue into her mouth. The moment begins a sexual affair.

Gripped, I read to the end of the book in one sitting. When I finished, I told the pigs, 'I do not want this.'

Harrison's father was not alone in equating offspring with sexual property. A number of unnerving respondents were creeping in to the inbox. In time, I would come to think of them as a specific genre of man and quickly close myself off to them, or anyone remotely like them. Before that, one writer stole first place in the League of Surprising Emails.

*Dear Madame,*

[A chivalrous start.]

*Now there's a spectacular advert – I can't say I've seen anything of its ilk before, so consider me most thoroughly intrigued.*
    *In short: I'm Devon-based and frequent my home in the north of Spain every summer. My spouse joins me there near the season's end; while at the beginning I host a variety of lady friends your age and above, who join me on their own as a break for them and exclusively platonic company for myself.*

[*Okay*, I thought. *Where is this going?*]

*There is one thing that unites them, that being a shared love of the naturist lifestyle: the villa is perfectly suited for full-body sunbathing and rejuvenating nude dips in the pool.*

*[Ah.]*

*Should you be amenable to joining me there this July, we could perhaps meet for refreshments in the capital soon, and proceed from there. Which may lead to the style of relationship you seek*

*[Um . . . ]*

*– and then again, may not!!*

*[!!]*

The man did not reply to my bounce-back. By that measure he should not have been someone I contacted in return. Yet I found it impossible not to ask after his story, marvelling at this bare-skinned interpretation of 'family'.

*Dear _____*
    *Thank you for your email. As you might imagine, your reply was not quite what I'd expected when I placed my ad! I've never been a naturist, or ever received that sort of invitation. But I would like to know more. For instance, how did you meet the other women who join you out in Spain? Is this something you've been doing for a while? Could you talk me through a typical day?*
    *I look forward to hearing from you soon.*
    *Warm wishes,*
    *G*

# FIRST MEETING

Two days later:

*Dear G,*

*How marvellous to hear from you.*

*The 'other women' of which you enquire have various links: they are, for a few examples, acquaintances of my wife, neighbours and, sometimes, other contacts' daughters and female co-workers: you would probably be astonished to learn how many people show an interest when one finds the opportune moment to raise the topic. My wife and I took up ownership of the property in Spain around a decade ago, but naturism has been an active part of my life since my earliest recollections. While my parents didn't practise the hobby as such, my family, siblings and I would frequently be naked around each other at home, even when passing to and from the bathroom of a morning, so nothing about it seemed at all unnatural. Quite the opposite. Moreover, my mother dealt in figurative art, meaning nudes were a prominent feature of our daily lives.*

*As for a typical 24 hours in the north of Spain? I can't say I believe that exists, but I suppose it could well feature:*

- *Resting beside the pool and in the house: on many occasions, no one has wished to wear clothes for two or three days.*
- *Suiting up for shopping or local sightseeing – we do wear clothes sometimes!! Guests adore being*

*shown the surrounding countryside and its exquisite villages.*

- *Paying a visit to the nearest naturist beach (about 10 minutes' by car, and considered by some to be one of the best in Europe).*

*Now, back to you – what do YOU hope to achieve through your advertisement? I have a lovely son but no daughters, alas; and while my ex-wife did have a daughter who shared our home for many a year, I don't believe it's ever quite the same. I therefore viewed your advertisement as a chance to potentially create a father–daughter relationship that could truly be mine – whatever such a thing entails. But let's see how we go.*

*With the warmest of wishes.*

Curiosity pulled at me. I was one wiry pube away from agreeing to have that drink in the city. Perhaps, yes, normally fathers *would* see their children nude often. And northern Spain did sound appealing. A pool, the countryside, seeing the sights . . .

Except: attraction.

Except: *The Kiss.*

Except: the daily sight would be my host's genitals.

# 7

# PUSH

When in doubt – and feeling bewildered – try statistics.

Like this one: 80 per cent of men in the world become fathers, in a gene-sharing sense, meaning 20 per cent of men in the world do not.

On the other side of the gender divide, the proportion of women becoming mothers is generally higher. While 78 per cent of British women were genetically parents by age 40 in 2010 (a figure excluding those who have their first child *in* their forties – an age group for which pregnancy rates are on the rise in the UK – not to mention those women who adopt or use egg donors), the same can be said for 82 per cent of women by aged 40 in the US, around 87 per cent of women in Spain, Norway, Denmark, Belgium and Sweden, and around 91 per cent in several Eastern European countries and Iceland.

More recent figures for sub-Saharan Africa found that an average of just 2.9 per cent of women have no children, compared to 3.5 per cent of men. Of course the overall picture in the region is far more nuanced (this admittedly being one downside of statistics), with 'female childlessness levels' at approximately 16 per cent in some regions, and 'male childlessness levels' ranging from 16 to 33 per cent in others.

It took me a while to envisage what these figures looked like in reality; what it meant to have higher numbers of mums alongside lower numbers of dads. Fewer biological fathers to go around was what it looked like, I decided. Plus a bunch of men for whom, voluntarily or not, their own sperm was out of the game.

Digging deeper, sharing occasional snippets with the pigs, I found plenty of reasons to account for different child-making rates worldwide. They include: the availability and acceptability of contraception (fewer rubber johnnies meaning more baby John and Joanies); the impact of education ('Got kids?' a very drunk man – a father of two – asked me on a morning bus. I shook my head. 'Of *course* you don't. I can tell from your voice: you're an *intellectual*'); plus the rise of autonomous, self-sustaining female adults – a 'process [that] may increasingly leave men childless by circumstance, as they are left behind on the mating market'. (A quote evoking the world's most galling, debauched shopping experience.)

There is also the impact of cultural 'norms' to consider. These norms could include the social stigma and pressures of being childless. In Ghana infertility can provoke hostility and name-calling; in Kuwait it is linked to 'evil spirits, witchcraft and God's retribution'. In the US, men are less likely to seek reproductive support than women for fear in part of emasculation (and this in spite of the global average sperm count dropping by *51.6 per cent* over the last 50 years). Conversely, those norms can encompass the perceived encumbrance of having kids. One study I found, for example, argued that greater exposure to the lifestyle of high-income countries through global media has helped disseminate an alternative version of adulthood in lower-income countries, 'whereby desires for recreational and luxurious opportunities can be met without the burden of children'.

That said, whichever way I looked – and wherever I chose to start looking – the numbers of adults who would not be parents seemed universally in the minority.

So who were the haves and have-nots on either side? Was it those who *have* a hole in their life, where they feel a child should be, or those who *have-not* got as much time, money, agency because of parenthood?

Should the phrase be 'childless', I wondered, or 'child-free'?

Had Carl missed out by not parenting me, or was it a reprieve?

If he'd been able to raise Caroline past infancy, would his life have been greatly improved?

I wondered these things again at a weekend wedding, as I was being asked about my work and free time by Neil, a friend of a friend: a lovely man with a lovely wife, and some lovely puppy pictures on his phone.

Parenting was also on Neil's mind. 'My wife and I were thinking about the idea of "home" recently,' he said, 'thinking about how home is somewhere you can be yourself and can feel sheltered.'

We were in the early reception stage of the wedding: the

couple had been hitched and were being photographed in different poses, as the odd guest speculated on how soon the bride would 'get one in the oven'. Neil and I both reached for a passing tray of canapés.

'For us,' he continued, nibbling, 'parents are home; parents make a home. And for us, being Christians, God is the ultimate parent.'

I brushed a smear of cheese from my lip. 'I don't know if God exists, but I always imagined he would be like my Uncle Jeff. Formidable with rude jokes, sometimes irritable, and Jew-*ish*.'

Neil conceded this might be possible.

After telling him about my project, I asked if he thought I should look for men who were God-like. He wasn't sure. 'You could think about fatherly forces, though. Or parental forces. Universal forces. That's something.'

Another waiter passed by with a canapé pile. This was the kind of universal force I could get used to: father as almighty food-provider.

Our conversation enlarged across more rounds of tiny snacks. Eventually Neil told me he and his wife had recently experienced a miscarriage.

'Oh no.' I stopped chewing. 'I'm so sorry.'

'I felt so much grief around it. We both did. Of course, Sarah had that extra physical layer of things to deal with, which was especially awful. But as a man I've found it so difficult. Sarah's grief for that loss is recognisable in society. It's easier to place than mine. I've also lost something, but it's like I'm not there when it comes to the doctors, the midwife. I understand why, and also: it hurts.

'I really want to be a father. I love children. But instinctively other women pass their babies to Sarah to hold, never to me. It's difficult. It seems there aren't really any outlets for men who feel like I do. So at the moment I'm focused on being a good father to our dog.'

That night I caught Duncan before he slept, telling him Neil's story. 'It's sad, isn't it? How some people really crave babies and can't have them, and others shoot them out and don't even care.'

My boyfriend closed his eyes. 'Yeah, must be.'

'Neil and Sarah would be great parents. Do you think we'd be great parents?'

Duncan's breathing deepened.

I poked his arm to rouse him. 'Hey. What if I gave birth,' I asked, 'and our baby wouldn't stop crying, and you had to stay up instead of getting your standard eight to nine hours a night?'

'Urgh. That's disgusting.'

I wedged myself close to his side. 'You have said you want children one day.'

'Silent children who don't cry.'

'Good luck with that.' I tested him with another angle. 'What if the baby came out really ill, and needed lots more care and attention than usual?'

Duncan smiled, eyes closed again. 'Throw it in the bin.'

'I'd laugh except I think you're not actually joking.'

'I'm not joking.'

'Listen. I'm a woman. Statistically speaking – biologically speaking – I'll probably have to make these decisions before you do. Which means, if we stay together, you making them with me.'

The smile faded. 'I'm not ready.'

'No shit, dude. Neither am I. I don't even know if I want them.'

He murmured, 'Spoon me.'

'What?'

His warm legs twitched. For a second he looked so vulnerable. I nestled to his back and stroked his hip.

'Hmph.' He grunted. Gone.

Sighing, I returned to my pillow, and thought about ways a person could experience having a child with minimal hassle; minimal risk of being left holding the baby as Mum had been with me. I didn't want to rely on her like she'd been forced to do with Granny Codd. I didn't want to rely on anybody.

Perhaps I could donate some eggs to an infertile couple and see if any embryos emerged to make contact later. Or maybe I could make an advert:

*Friendly, childless 51yo looking for intrepid young person who may be willing to take on the role of son/ daughter.*

Grant told me he was up for the tennis, then went quiet. He must be busy, I decided, engaging in important activity for the union. Meanwhile a new style of message briefly came and went: *A friend showed me this ad for a father figure. Intrigued and somewhat sad that you advertise. Surely this can't be right. Right?* ☹ *Signed, a father.*

And:

*Your ad crossed my desk today. I wanted to express that I felt quite a pang to read it, mainly because I'm lucky enough to be a happy father already. This isn't some kind of scam, is it? If it isn't, I sincerely hope you find an appropriate father figure to make up for the dad you 'never had'. I don't want to be a parent to anyone else at this stage in my life, so if you are indeed authentic I wish you all the success and fortuity the world has to offer . . .*

And:

*This is no doubt an obvious comment, but do please take care of yourself and pick very wisely – this world may be filled with marvellous people, but it is also filled with many who are not. I'm certain you will be swamped with replies and I hope you find what you're searching for, but I fear that a significant number of people who write to you will be doing so for the wrong reasons.*

 *Crossing everything that you track down your perfect 'dad'* ☺

At a noodle restaurant in the city we met with Duncan's parents. His mother wanted an update, so I told her about the naturist. She held her hands to her mouth and laughed, incredulous.

Through her laughter I heard a murmur from Duncan's dad. 'She hasn't asked me.'

I turned to face him, confused. 'I *have* asked you. At Christmas.'

'No, you didn't.'

'I did and you didn't seem interested.'

'How would you know? You haven't asked.'

'Would you like to apply?'

He speared a tempura nugget with a chopstick.

'The invitation is there,' I said. 'Should you want it. I would feel surprised and privileged.'

'This is awkward.' He snorted and left the table for the bathroom.

'Have you found any *suitable* fathers, Georgie?' asked his wife. 'Ones that keep their clothes on?' There was an *I-doubt-it*-ness to her voice, which I pretended not to hear.

'Actually, yes,' I replied. 'Well, maybe.'

'Oh?'

I told her about Grant, carefully omitting the details of his first-date proposal and two divorces. 'We're going to play tennis next month,' I finished.

'That's not the man who drinks champagne?'

'Er . . .'

Duncan's mum had heard of the Man Who Drank Champagne on her last visit, after conducting the chocolate-shop intervention, after the talking-to with Duncan at the flat, and after her 'I *support* you . . . but.'

Shortly afterwards I'd been staring at the kitchen counter, discombobulated, when she called me back to the lounge to read the emails I'd had so far. 'I'd love to hear them.'

'Really? But—'

'I know it's important to you.'

'It's just—'

'Some of them are mental,' Duncan said. 'Want another cocktail, Mum?'

She faux-groaned. 'Oh *God*. I'm such a – what is it? Lightweight?'

'*I'll* have one, please,' I said.

His mum patted the soft blue of our sofa, then pulled me in for a hug. It was long. It was lovely. She still had her arms around me several emails later. By then my cheeks felt as pink as her lipstick; my glass was smeared and empty.

'I like the sound of the chief executive,' she decided, in reference to someone who wrote via *Private Eye*; someone I was ready to discount. I hadn't been sold on the passing mention he made to sipping champagne at an airport while writing. Or the details he then shared of his relationship.

*I'm happily married with no children*, I read aloud.

*And one reason my marriage is such a success is that my partner understands me totally – as I understand her. My wife has always known, and warmly accepted, that I thrive in the company of younger women and that we get on well. In fact, I've had two longish relationships with women about your age (my wife got on really well with them too – we're not your usual couple).*

My boyfriend's mother pulled a face.

*At first, those relationships were entirely about physicality, but became increasingly about the mentoring as they progressed, building on the supportive father figure element. That process was deeply rewarding for me. To be honest (which is an extraordinarily useless phrase, on reflection, yet here I am using it) I'd be open to a relationship (an adventurous one, perhaps) with a younger woman that lands anywhere on the spectrum of a father figure wagging his finger about her going vegan for January to an intense physical relationship, or anything in between. Come to think of it, I reckon that one which evolves and adapts over time would be my top choice.*

'He does write well, at least,' she had concluded. 'Maybe don't rule him out.'

In the restaurant, back in the now, Duncan's dad returned from the toilet; returned to his bowl of broth.

'It's not Champagne Man, no,' I told his wife.

'But he plays tennis. That's encouraging. I didn't know you played.'

'I don't.'

She leaned forward. 'Champagne Man, though; he's worth investigating. Didn't he run businesses?'

'Maybe.'

'Have you tried any skiing magazines yet? And how about *Forbes*?'

'Ooh, *yeah*,' said Duncan, 'Mon-*ay*!' Sweeping one palm fast over the other, he fired out invisible banknotes to the room.

The next day: an alarming turn from Grant.

In my latest message to him, I had asked if I could borrow a racket, chuntered about my week and weekend, asked after his. Four days on, his reply appeared.

*The more you think*, it said, after a brief introduction,

*the more it becomes obvious that suicide is the only rational choice because life is inherently meaningless and if you've always been at a loss to (truly) find joy through life it's a big issue. Add to that the rationale which says all the good people are attached, I'm single, so I'm not good. Couple that with the belief that others just tolerate me. Plus my complete dearth of responses via dating apps. Plus never knowing what it's like to not feel totally alone.*

*I know myself. I understand better than anyone that I'm a challenge to be around and I don't want to burden you with that.*

*Take care of Duncan and make sure he takes care of you. Don't put up with any bullshit from anyone and follow your dreams with all your heart while youth is on your side. Explore the 'what ifs' today, not when it's too late.*

*With my dearest wishes,*
*Grant*

My guts went into freefall. Straight away, I responded. It sounded like he was saying goodbye, I wrote:

*For the record, I don't feel like you've burdened me, or as if I've had to tolerate you. I feel like we have been building a positive connection, but perhaps it hasn't been heading in the direction you were expecting it to? I don't know. I can only guess. For what it's worth, I feel like I am mostly good at getting distance when I need it, and at telling people if I'm not comfortable with them. But this communication is as much about you as it is me, and if you're not comfortable then I will respect that.*

*I just hope you are okay. Whether you write to me again or not, I only hope you can prioritise yourself, look after yourself, and reassure yourself that you are a good person, who still has opportunities coming his way.*

# 8

# LOST

The freefalling sensation persisted all week. No answer from Grant came back.

A man purporting to be a 'practising psychotherapist' began sending cryptic messages, each one signing off with a kiss.

*Do you know who you are, Georgina?* he asked. And: *If you were to walk alone past a slightly open door in a darkened building, would you go through the door, or would you pass by?*

'Ugh,' I said to the screen.

I thought of Grant constantly, trying to unlock what happened and why. Retracing his words, I found the line: *Here's a deal . . . I'm not going to vanish.*

And: *No matter how deeply I want to stay with someone I quickly enter self-preservation mode, pushing them away.*

I closed my eyes and saw him, clenched and crying. Then his face turned grey and expressionless.

Online, I searched for his name, bringing up the same work picture he had sent. I searched his hometown's local news. I searched his hometown and 'death'. My fingers typed 'body discovered'.

Each time the page reloaded, my chest prickled.

Perhaps, if he had killed himself, whatever remained of him had not been found. Perhaps I was the only person with whom he'd shared his state of mind.

On a government page, I read that 'Males accounted for three-quarters of suicides registered in 2017 (4,382 deaths), which has been the case since the mid-1990s.'

I clicked off the page.

Each new day Grant did not write, the situation grew heavier. My only option seemed to be calling his work – if only to establish whether or not he had been seen there. Then, perhaps, I could let myself step back.

I shared the conundrum with people I trusted in case they had better ideas. Nobody did. 'It's interesting,' said one. 'He's done what he said his father did to him: suddenly disappeared, never to be contacted again.'

Multiple times I reread Grant's last email – both over the phone for advice and in silence to myself for clarity. In one way, it seemed like a cry for help. In another, it seemed disconnected.

Repeatedly I asked Duncan what to do.

'Call his work,' he answered for the umpteenth time.

'What if he picks up instead of a colleague?'

'Put down the phone. There's your answer.'

'What if they say he hasn't been in for a while? I can't say I'm worried about him, can I?'

'I don't know.'

Holding a sofa cushion over my face, I said, in the smallest voice I had, 'I want someone else to call for me.'

Duncan left the room. 'You need to do it.'

'I know. I know.' I breathed into the cushion.

In the shower, I tested accents. Glaswegian. Mancunian. Irish. Straining my tongue and throat muscles.

Dried and dressed, I called the only person I knew would answer at eight in the morning; a person always primed for something serious to occur. 'Mum, I need your help.' After sharing the whole story, I asked if she thought that ringing his work was a sensible plan or ripe for disaster.

'Well . . .' she deliberated. 'At the paper, when there was someone I was worried about, I let the police know. They assured me they would look into it and be discreet.'

I reminded her how few people associated the police with discretion.

'*I* trust them,' she said.

'I'm not saying I don't trust them, it's just . . .'

I remembered a 999 call I had made to help my shrieking neighbour on a night when he sounded more distressed than ever. The police showed up three hours later, long after he had retreated, knocking brutally hard on his door while the rest of the block was fast asleep. When he answered they spent all of one minute with him.

'Actually, maybe I don't trust them. Not for something this sensitive. What if they go to his work and he's humiliated in front of his colleagues – and that pushes him over the edge?'

Mum didn't answer.

'Also, I keep thinking he might have killed himself after that email anyway, and if he killed himself last

Friday, he's definitely dead by now. No one would be able to help him.'

'Yes.'

'I don't know what I want from the call.'

'No.'

'Peace of mind. I want peace of mind. Except I might not be able to get it. Is your mobile on?'

We spent the next few minutes establishing if I could ring Mum without her phone logging my number, and therefore place a truly anonymous call. After a few misfires she answered, sounding unsure. 'Is that Georgina?'

'Right. I'm going to try the switchboard at his work. Get this over with.'

She wished me luck.

Stiff, I dialled the number. It rang a few times before a woman picked up. Only then did it occur to me that I hadn't selected an accent for my disguise. A booming, resonant Burnley voice escaped before I could stop it. 'Hellur,' it said.

The woman hesitated. 'Um, yes?'

'Could yer put me through to yer union rep? Puh-lease?'

There was a pause. It was long.

I panicked. 'Hellur?'

'One minute.'

A string quartet of holding music started. Gnawing my lip, I prepared to end the call.

Instead another woman's voice answered, announcing her name and department. I rushed my lines. 'Hellur there, do you work with a man named Grant, I've been tryin' to get hold of 'im for a while now to speak.'

'He's in this department but not in this office,' she said. 'I can put you through?'

My heartbeat hammered. 'I've been tryin' to get 'old of 'im for a few days for a meeting,' I said, stalling for time. 'I've not been 'avin' much luck. D'you know if he's been in?'

'He's not in this office,' she repeated. 'Do you want me to put you through?'

My throat went dry. 'Okay.'

The holding music returned. I kept my finger millimetres away from the 'end call' button. Yet the waiting time only extended. I wondered if the woman was speaking to Grant now. What she might be saying.

Abruptly, the music ceased. A robotic recorded statement invited me to leave a message. I cut the call before the beep, then took refuge on the floor.

Mum answered. 'Was he there?'

I gave my report.

'Inconclusive, then.'

Again, I thought about calling the police. Except, 'It just seems so extreme.'

From somewhere in her vicinity, Mum's dog grumbled.

I cast my mind around for alternative plans. 'Maybe I could call the Samaritans . . .'

'That's an idea.'

As I waited to be connected to the UK's leading suicide reduction charity, I remembered something I'd learned about the hotline during a day for prospective volunteers: that Samaritans exist to listen; nothing else. Their ethos meant not ever giving advice.

'*Shit.*'

A breathy, well-spoken man picked up the phone.

I said: 'I was calling to ask your advice and I just remembered you can't give any.'

'No,' he confirmed.

I sighed. 'I guess I'll just talk it through then?'

'Go ahead.'

Loosely, I sketched out events without details: some research I was doing; new contacts; sensitive topics. I recounted Grant saying he had no friends and no one he talked to, explaining I didn't want to cause a fuss at his work, and how even leaving a message might be intrusive.

The Samaritans Man sympathised like a pro. 'That sounds really tricky.'

'I don't know what to do. I can't force him to call me, and I don't want to force him. I know if he's made up his mind to do this, I can't change it. I don't know him well, but he seems like a good person, for whom things haven't gone like they should.' My throat tightened. 'I want him to know he left a good impression.'

The man told me I'd done the right thing to write back. 'He's lucky to have someone who cares.'

'But my worry is he'll never know that. And I'm scared. If he is okay, I don't want to set up this dynamic between us: where, if he feels lonely or desperate, he only tells me.'

My Samaritans friend agreed. 'You could try writing again,' he offered – a line that sounded almost like a soft, sugared seed of advice.

Then he attempted to ask about the impact of all this on

me. I brought the call to a close with thanks and reached for my laptop.

*Hi Grant,* I typed.

*I'm so sorry for the further communication – I hope it's not unwelcome. I'm just very worried about you and hope you are okay.*
    *I'd be really grateful if you could send me a short message and if you want to be left alone I'll respect that.*
    *With warmest wishes,*
    *Georgina*

It was reassuring to think that I had done as much as I could. Even if I never heard from Grant again, I could find comfort in that.

Maybe.

Within an hour of sending my message, Grant replied. *It's not unwelcome, far from it,* he wrote. *I just know I'm hard work for others because I'm hard work for me! It would be lovely to keep in touch.*

His tone as he wrapped up seemed more light than dark, almost breezy. It was disconcerting.

What had I set in motion?

Another near-sleepless night followed. The next morning I shared my worries with Grant in writing. I told him what had happened between his messages – the call to his work; the distress; my experience of real and imagined events. *I don't feel like I'm the right kind of friend for you to have in your armoury at the moment,* I said.

> *Perhaps you feel that way too. Perhaps that's why you made the decision to cut contact last week.*
> *I would love to imagine you feeling able to track down some support when you're feeling a bit more stable, or perhaps just treating yourself to a nice slice of cake in the sunshine while you work out what to do next.*

Wishing him well, still uncertain, I pressed send.

# 9

# DISTRACTIONS

Once, I had seen Carl as a child. Once, when I was aged 4. Mum and I were at the local arts centre, watching a stage production of *Postman Pat*, when somehow I became aware that the man in the row in front of us was my father. He was sitting with a woman and a blonde toddler.

I could still picture the outline of his head.

Later, much later, Mum told me I couldn't have known who he was; besides, he had been sitting behind us, not in front. The woman was a friend of his and the child was that friend's granddaughter.

She said Carl did not approach her until the interval, and that I would not have heard their conversation. In the foyer Carl told her he wanted to visit, to start getting to know me. My mother decided not to stand in his way, offering him the option of dealing with just Granny Codd; not her. He insisted he wanted to reconnect with Mum too.

They spoke more at length in a follow-up meeting. My biological father reassured Mum that he was keen to proceed; that she could even go ahead and tell me he wanted to meet me. Together they picked a date to discuss the next steps.

Arrangements were carefully made. That evening, Mum would collect him from the train station. Beforehand, neither she nor Granny Codd would reveal where she was going or why. Which was sensible. Because when Mum went to the station, Carl did not turn up.

Thinking he might have missed his train, she waited for the next one, and the next. There was no sign. After worrying on the platform in the dark, thinking he might be ill or worse, she called both his work and the number he'd given her. Nothing.

'He did that twice,' Mum said. 'Made plans to come and didn't. Then reappeared, no apology. He was saying things like, "I *really* want to be involved. I want to see you. Both of you." After the second time I said, "No more." I couldn't have him disappointing you.'

I nodded. 'Good thinking,' I told her.

It was still so disappointing.

Grant's reply, when it came, was a sad one.

*In this life all the brilliant people, you included, are with someone (because they are brilliant). I will always be lonely and alone because there is something repugnant or revolting at the core of me. No one brilliant has ever shown a romantic interest in me and that really hurts sometimes.*

*I hear exactly what you're telling me so I'll say*
*goodbye here. I will scrap this inbox and email address*
*as soon as I press send.*


I stared at his words, feeling guilty.
Low.
Disappointed.
And not at all brilliant.

If Granny Codd had been alive, I might have sought refuge in her living room. Instead a friend called Claire, one of Duncan's housemates from university, joined me for chunks of cake at the flat. Claire was a radio journalist and gifted at questions, questions, questions. When I finally let out the Grant tale, she asked, 'How will you know when your project is over?'

The question startled me. 'I've no idea,' I said. 'It might be over already.'

'Nah. It's too important! Keep it going.'

I sat straighter. Asked for details about Claire's own father. 'He doesn't act excited much,' she said. 'When I told him I was buying a house with my boyfriend I got basically no reaction, and I'm his eldest! I did complain, though. He said: "I don't know what I'm supposed to say." '

I nodded into my cup. 'Makes sense. Who does?'

Before she left, Claire agreed to be a kind of mentor. She wouldn't be able to do lots, she said – she was quite busy making a podcast. But she could teach me how to record and archive important thoughts and conversations on a

Dictaphone so I could keep track of them. She could also suggest new avenues of father-finding, should the dadverts dry up.

Even then, it took a while for my body to feel less like an outline, and more like a person; more like I was someone who could do this, who could make their wishes visible in this way. During the adjustment phase, I eased back in to the inbox.

I decided to pass on advertising in the *The Herald Scotland*; it seemed too far for meet-ups, plus I'd save £80. Besides, after my first burst of multiple dadverts, I was starting to get decent numbers: a steady stream from *Private Eye* and the south-western papers. On the downside, they included more men who wanted to share their physical and financial credentials. One of them was the guy who had kicked things off by saying, *I am single, 51, fairly fit, solvent, average-looking* – and who, by this point, had addressed my bounce-back:

> *Why did I respond? The advert ultimately piqued my curiosity – was it a mere cry for paternal support? Could it be a new approach to dating, or perhaps it was sexual? The entire father/daughter dynamic inspires many stories and more right across the internet, both physical and emotional.*

I grimaced, wary to see the subject so prominent for him. Yet I had pledged to stay open-minded. Holding down my protest reflex, I took in the rest. Perhaps more context would change things.

DISTRACTIONS

The man wrote that:

*I never had a daughter, or a son come to mention it,
and I guess I am simply offering my life experience, my
time and with any luck some guidance that may
prompt her to find some happiness in herself, only led
by my own personal happiness and contentment with
'my lot in life'.*

There were no issues with that, surely.

Before he signed off, he asked what, ultimately, I was looking for. Since he had taken the time to write twice – and since both of us were essentially making the rules up as we went – I began to draft a response, reiterating: *I am not looking for anything sexual.*

Figuring extra clarity could only help both of us, I added:

*In your email, you brought up the subject of physical/
emotional father–daughter relationships online. Could
I ask what you mean exactly? Even if a physical aspect
is not what I'm angling for in this search, I am still
intrigued to know more (in an interested, non-
judgemental way).*

Maybe there was something I'd missed. Maybe he hadn't meant for his words to sound horny. *I am also keen to pose your last question for me back to you,* I finished. *What are you searching for ultimately, do you think?*

His next message was friendly. Conversational. It also gave me reason to know we were radically non-aligned.

*What am I searching for?* he echoed.

*I suppose it's something and nothing, in truth. I am currently unattached and have been for a while now. I do have feelings for someone special, but unfortunately she is engaged and I think her intentions to marry are sincere and I should attempt to move on without her . . .*

*I was intrigued by your advert, primarily as a hint of titillation as reading into it more deeply I wondered if you could be like an ex of mine who was very aroused by the father/daughter dynamic particularly in bed. Her 'thing' was to be treated with some roughness, provocative spanking, etc. and to finish by crying, 'No Daddy no,' and so on. Fairly dark and not a thing I feel too concerned to repeat in all honesty, but curious nonetheless. Your response has ultimately satisfied me that you aren't searching for something similarly physical.*

Titillation. Spanking. Mock-incest. This man was testing the water. Flicking some droplets towards me to see if I flinched.

It was the first email thread I decisively marked as 'Horny', sending it off to a sub-folder all on its own. It would not be the last.

I thanked him for his time. Wished him luck in finding what he wanted. Opened less troubling messages.

Three new men had started up conversations: Car-Boot Harold, Draughts-Player Lenny and Clear-Headed Clive. All wrote in ways that seemed gentle and good-humoured.

Harold was a bargain-hunting enthusiast committed to weekend car boot sales, whose eldest of three daughters had died as a child. *Maybe that's my impulse for writing, I don't know.* He explained that he had been like a dad to other friends' children whose fathers were absent. He felt this could be his calling.

Lenny joked that he was *reasonably normal*, and explained that he had raised his son solo since birth. *What could I offer you?* he wrote. *Ye Gods. Who knows?* He asked if I had ever played draughts or wanted to learn.

Clive was retired and lived in the mountains, a few train rides from London. He was a recovering alcoholic, a statement that rang an alarm bell in a largely disconnected part of me. Then again, he had not drunk for years, and was now an eager proponent of honesty, openness and compassion. He had six kids from multiple marriages and was estranged from one of them. Another had died a long time ago. *I am only just beginning to understand what it is to be a father,* he wrote.

I warmed to their willingness to share themselves, and the ways in which each one expressed his trepidation.

Then I thought about whether I would hurt them. And hurt myself.

The father–daughter sex thing continued to bother me. Over the years, on sporadic trips to the land of online porn, I had noticed more and more videos describing performers as being related: often step-brothers or step-fathers getting it on with step-sisters or step-daughters. A *VICE* article about incest-themed videos reported a 178 per cent increase in 'family role-play porn' from 2014 to 2015. Commentators unpicking the situation cited various possible causes. The fact that 'fauxcest' porn could be shot anywhere and was easy to brand. The tyranny of algorithms, which sometimes fabricated trends that few people actively asked for, at least to begin with. The appeal of imagining one of life's greatest taboos. Even the incest storyline in *Game of Thrones*, which had been watched by tens of millions of viewers worldwide.

Meanwhile, of the 20 most common female roles appearing in porn-film titles in 2013 – the year of a beguiling report called *Deep Inside: A Study of 1,000 Porn Stars and Their Careers* – 'daughter' came in at number six on the list, after teen, MILF, wife, cheerleader and nurse.*

I did a quick search on PornHub, the world's leading free porn site. The word 'father' brought up just over 3,000 videos; 'daddy' over 9,000; 'daughter' summoned up 10,000-plus movies; 'son' a staggering 135,500.

It made me wonder who was leading the movement to make fathers and offspring synonymous with sex. The porn viewers? The directors of these films? Or the small cohort of people running sites like PornHub every day?

More importantly for my project: how deeply might these trends affect the behaviours of men making contact?

*

* For anyone pleased to see 'wife' score so highly, and feel all is right with the world, the author was compelled to point out that 'on further investigation, I discovered that without exception every film title containing the word wife revolved around the concept of a man having sex with a spouse who wasn't his own. Never mind.'

In a parallel universe, Car-Boot Harold and I were realising we had plenty in common. We both liked Sunday markets and haggling; ghosts and storytelling; writing, words, music. Harold composed his own melodies from time to time, he said. Occasionally I dreamed my own and forgot them in the morning.

Early on, I broached the subject of how we might not be what the other expected. Rather than mentioning Grant I referenced my biological father, letting out bits and pieces about Carl where it felt relevant, mainly the basic facts around his departure before I was born. Harold responded with great consideration.

*Oh, and before I forget. You described that your biological father didn't want you as his daughter. That's very telling. The rejection seems palpable and that can't be easy. But your father didn't not want you, because the man did not know you.*

It was an interesting idea to contemplate.
There was more.

*I recognise what you are saying when you say you might not match the picture I'm creating of you – and, of course, I might not match the picture you have. It would be damaging for your sense of self if you came up against rejection again. There's no guaranteed way I can think of to avoid that but I'm mindful that it's important you don't end up worse off emotionally from this experience. Perhaps one potential solution could be for me to promise now that I'll meet you two times at least – so, for instance, if our first meet-up is uncomfortable then instead of ending things there I promise that I'll give it another go, if you're amenable, when the preliminary oddness of things has diminished. It's a suggestion, that's all, and to repeat: completely up to you.*

After Peter's prank in the Invergordon café, I had thought I most wanted a dad who hadn't had the opportunity to be one; for both parties to be in a similar boat. Now, reflecting on Harold's responses, I wondered if dads who had already fathered would be a better bet. (At the very least – in theory – their testosterone ought to be lower.)

Our emails grew warmer in tone. I heard about Harold's failing windscreen washer. I told him about fitting 14 friends in the flat for Duncan's birthday. He explained how his surviving daughters sold their own handmade pottery online, and that their latest commission was for a pig enthusiast. My stomach flipped.

*I think you and they would get on like a house on fire,* he wrote.

We made plans to meet in a few weeks' time, in London.

Lenny, the guy who had mentioned draughts, was also keeping regular contact. I knew all about his late-night reading habits, and his impression that his son was a *silly young fool* for not liking books. I knew about the new job he was starting, at the Department for Work and Pensions. I knew that he didn't think much of social media, and yet liked using *LOL* at least once per email.

We swapped messages about school reunions, about games and cars, about the mother to his son, who was *like a firework going off* and would *be dead by now without me*; about his own mother who was in the early stages of dementia.

*My dad passed in 1996, so my brother and I share the load.*

Lenny, like Harold, seemed able to convey a strong sense of who he was through his messaging. Playful, bright, talkative. Not asking as much of me as I asked of him, which allowed me to hide a little.

His recurrent idea was teaching a four-player version of draughts, the highly tactical board game that was apparently millennia old. Granny Codd had enjoyed draughts, I knew, and a few times after Lenny first brought it up, I started to think, *Why not?*

Maybe Lenny could be Dad for Board Games, and Harold could be Dad for Deals.

Instead of settling for just one, I could keep a dad for every pastime.

As for Clive, the Dad for New Starts, there were all sorts of interesting brackets he fell into. Now in his seventh decade of what had undeniably been a colourful life – not least in becoming a parent several times over – he lived in solitude with a small pack of old deerhounds, practised Buddhist teachings and carved out abundant time to share his thoughts.

In his second email he wrote:

*I've felt achievements and failures in my role as a father, as I have in my role as a human. On seeing your request I first felt compelled to ask: Why? Meaning, why should you want a father? What does your life lack that a 'fantasy' dad could make up for? That's the stark and pressing question (I don't intend cruelty here, only honesty). Almost immediately, I then reflected on what I had provided my children. The more I contemplated, the more I began to admire the act of you asking. And felt curious to understand why, and if I could assist . . .*

*What am I able to offer? I can't be your dad, of course, but I can offer the life lessons I've learnt so far as an additional perspective for you to channel. If you have any questions, whether they be personal or more broad, I could listen to those and share my thoughts, using truth and openness as my guide. I'm a tolerant person, fascinated (always!) about life and others' experiences. I cannot reassure you that anything I do will necessarily bring you comfort or support, but I doubt any of it would hinder your fatherless situation.*

Okay, so apparently he *couldn't* be my dad. Yet I was willing to overlook that for now. Clive had my attention.

At last, I felt I was really making progress. Until the time arrived for my next meeting: my day with Harold.

# 10
# MIXED

Situation: frantic.

It had started when Harold wrote to suggest he would be able to offer a daughter *unconditional love*.

*This is what it means to be a parent – or what it should mean. And if your response to that is 'Hold on, that's too intense, I'm a complete stranger,' consider that every new-born child is also a stranger to their parents, at least to start with. My relationship with a near neighbour, a young man who has an awful and unavailable father, has shown me that having committed paternal feelings for someone who is not naturally related to you is more than possible (though any evolutionary biologist worth their salt will insist that all of us are related really!).*

That evening, Duncan and I went out to sample 'retro' bingo with a crowd of drinking millennials. We had never played before. As our fried snacks arrived, and the slips and tiny pens went to the masses, I tried to articulate how I was feeling. 'Harold wrote something kind today,' I shouted over a 1970s boogie soundtrack. 'It's freaking me out. I don't think I deserve it from a stranger.'

Stuffing fries into his face and speaking through them, Duncan asked what exactly had been said.

I explained the gist, and held out for a small moment of reassurance.

My boyfriend mulled it over. 'Yeah, he shouldn't offer that. He might meet you a couple of times and reject you.'

I stared at him, open-mouthed.

Thinking I hadn't heard, Duncan raised his voice. 'When he meets you he'll probably reject you.'

My heart twisted, sharp, like a Rubik's cube. 'I don't need you to give me the worst-case scenario,' I snapped. 'I can generate enough criticism and pessimism on my own, without you topping it up.'

'Okay.' He grabbed more fries, chewed and swallowed; washed his mouth with beer. Asked what tiles I wanted in the bathroom.

The ceiling throbbed.

The bingo caller's patter quickly overtook our topic. After a couple of hours toiling, winning nothing, we emerged onto the pavement, speed-walking, heading home.

My wish was to remain graceful. Honest and yet calm. 'I found it hard when you said I'd be rejected,' I told him, out of breath.

'That's where I had my last haircut,' Duncan replied. 'That barber shop there.'

My fists clenched. We turned a corner.

'Love is all about luck,' he proclaimed.

'*No, it isn't!*' I snapped again. 'I worked *hard* to find you,

I work *hard* to keep you, and I work *hard* to be the kind of person someone like you is attracted to!'

He blinked at me. Did not reply.

A few streets later, as the locus of my anger slipped from him and back to myself, I thought: *This is exactly the kind of ugly scene that demonstrates why I do not deserve unconditional love.*

The next morning was Harold Day.

I tried to be fun and lovable by making breakfast. Giving Duncan a long hug in the hallway. As we ate together, I asked him for some guidance on my hair. My original aim had been to look exactly the same as I had when I met Grant, maintaining test conditions. Except, in a recent moment of boredom, I'd remodelled my fringe.

Duncan told me I should use gel and sweep it back. 'Your fringe is . . . pretty short,' he said. 'Like, intensely short.'

'Like . . . I've overdone it?'

He stopped talking and went to make coffee.

After he left for work, I scooped out tracks of hair gel, trying to soothe myself. This fringe thing didn't matter. Conditions were always going to be different. Harold was different. Our meeting place was different. Everything was different. Except for my jeans, baggy jumper, patterned shirt and trusty fingerless gloves.

*Plus he said he'd love me unconditionally. Ha ha.*

No, not ha ha.

The idea made me want to vomit.

Since Harold and I had decided to meet in the city,

I decided it was okay to go alone, bargaining that the volume of people around us would keep me safe. Repressing my internal archive of crime-and-the-city-style reports – abductions, assaults and murders that took place in daylight in populous spaces – I reached Waterloo train station with 30 minutes to spare. On an empty bench I attempted to read a newspaper, wishing I had some scissors to cut eye holes in it. From somewhere in the chamber of the station, a pianist played a plinky-plonky 'Hotel California'.

When there were just three minutes left to go, I gathered my things and walked to the point beneath the clock: our agreed meeting place. The first man I saw there was a washed-out bloke rocking a pram. *A pram!* My eyes widened. A few metres beyond him, I spotted the person who surely had to be Harold. I flashed a fingerless glove at him. He smiled.

First impressions were promising. Harold looked gentle and pleased to be there. Though still on edge, I opened my arms for a hug. It was reciprocated. I noted the spicy smell of his cologne.

'How was your trip?' – 'How was yours?' – 'Thank good-ness *some* trains run on time.' We headed over the river together. Quickly we found a place for drinks and a sit-down. Quickly I reached for my credit card, insisting I would get them. 'The thing is with fathers and daughters,' Harold countered, 'the dad always pays.' He urged me to put the card back where it came from.

Our conversation roved. To flea markets around the world. Swiss engineering. Favourite cinemas. I listened more than I spoke, which helped. Then, once our first round of hot drinks was consumed, we wandered towards the next stop: the

British Museum. 'Did you tell your wife you were coming to meet me today?' I asked, as we slowed for a crossing.

'I said I was going to meet some friends in London. I do that quite a bit.'

'Oh.' I pulled back a little.

'Actually, I don't know how to tell her.'

Harold brought up the trepidation he had initially felt about writing, treading around the fact that my ad was . . . it was –

'It's odd,' I interrupted.

'Yes,' he said. 'It's odd.' We crossed another street. 'And when I read your first emails – don't take this the wrong way – I felt sorry for you. I wanted to give you love, but I knew it was too soon.'

The 'l' word ignited my face. I turned away and focused on a run of iron railings.

'Where do you see this going?' Harold asked. 'In, say, five years' time.'

I paused, unsure; not having allowed myself to think that far ahead. 'I just want a father figure,' I mumbled.

Harold made no comment. Instead he began discussing an elderly couple he'd known as a child. They had no children of their own and treated him as their son. 'I often thought how lovely it would be if they were my parents.'

His words released a locked memory: child-me in my aunt's kitchen, watching as my cousins opened gifts from their father's parents. Observing the scene from the doorway, as the elderly couple retrieved another wrapped box, I wondered why *I* couldn't have extra gifts. 'Will you be my grandparents too?' I asked.

After their laughter subsided, they said yes.

Something was in the air. Seconds later Harold said, 'I had two sets of grandparents, and neither of them ever gave me presents. I was their only grandchild – isn't that weird?'

'Extremely weird.'

'My father was also distant. Not at all how I've been with my daughters.'

We entered the museum and made our way to the medieval section. Harold began telling me about the bargains he had gathered over the years. Vintage bottles and packaging that fetched high prices at auction. Rare movie memorabilia. Discarded polaroids and amateur portraits of unknown people. 'It's not always the value I'm interested in. It's the stories too. When I think about the connections . . . Who kept these things, what their lives were like. It's fascinating.'

As a joke I asked if he had good contents insurance.

Harold gave me a look. He said he had heard of burglars who worked in league with insurance companies. 'So no one knows about my stash apart from me. And now, you.' We stopped in front of a case of plates. Harold studied me with an arched eyebrow. 'So if I have a burglary now—'

'I don't know where you live!'

My companion smirked.

We resumed our steady explorations, soon distracted by a display of ornate cogs that were twitching and throwing the gleam of a spotlight. After one revolution, I asked if it was time for cake.

'Could be.'

Back on the street, Harold asked what my friends and family thought about this.

'Mixed,' I said. 'Mostly good, some confused, a few concerned, a few against it.' I fished in my coat for my phone and scrolled through the messages. 'I had a new comment yesterday from a writer friend, actually: "How are you?? I've just heard about your dad project. It sounds awesome and interesting and also super dangerous and depression inducing. I hope you are being v careful! Kiss, kiss, kiss."'

'She's right. It could be quite dangerous.'

'Lots of people know where I am at the moment. We're in public. I'm taking precautions.'

'So I'm going to be in trouble if you go missing on the way home.'

'Yep.'

'In that case, I hope that doesn't happen.' Harold paused, then added, quickly, 'Obviously I hope nothing bad happens to you on the way home anyway.'

Now I was the one smirking.

A few hours later I returned home with a belly full of pastry, plus gifts of a 'G' made from driftwood that Harold had found in a jumble sale and a specially made USB of his music. I also had a text message: *It was wonderful to meet you. Really enjoyed it. Will look forward to our next meeting. H x*

I was about to load the device on my computer when suddenly it occurred to me: this seemed to be too easy. Perhaps I was letting my guard down too soon; the device could be bugged with a virus or tracker. Frowning at the gadget's metal end, I put it aside. Checked my inbox. Reread the latest email from Lenny:

*If you're ever in the mood for an evening of laughs, how easily can you reach Basingstoke? My pal Gordon is a top teacher. Some plonk, a circular table, 4 chairs, 1 draughts board . . . ! And bring your boyf too. That'd be the best set up – though be warned. Competing in 4-handed draughts is like preparing a partner for their driving test. Steer clear! Your boyf and you should partner me and Gordon – best play against (not with) each other.*

Harold's USB stayed on my desk until night-time. Duncan was suspicious of it too. I contemplated listening to it on someone else's computer, shifting the risk.

'You're not putting it on mine,' said my boyfriend. 'You can fuck off with that idea.'

Instead we watched the documentary Mabry had recommended.

(Passing through the portal to the website that was streaming it.)

(Bypassing the separate portal for 'Children', the platform offered by default.)

(As if every viewer should have, or aspire to, a child.)

(As if every man should be a dad one day.)

(All women mothers.)

The programme was long and intense, telling the story of Ted Bundy and his slippery, sinister ways. In quotes, the killer described how easy it was to go unseen and unaccounted for. I paused the frame, scrabbled for my notebook and wrote it down.

'We want to be able to say we can identify these dangerous people,' said Bundy. 'People don't realise there are potential killers among them. How could anyone live in a society where people they liked, loved, lived with, worked with and admired could the next day turn out to be the most demonic people imaginable?'

The episode ended.

In the night my uncertainty spiralled.

What if Harold was a murderer?

What if I was unleashing demons?

My gaze fell on the sleeping form of Duncan.

How could I know or trust anyone but myself?

The next day, an email from Harold:

*It was great yesterday. It occurred to me that you and I couldn't have got on better. On the way home I thought how, in many ways, you and my daughters are quite similar. They all would have enjoyed what we found and discussed together.*

*I actually believe that if a casual bystander had observed us interacting throughout the day, they would almost certainly have assumed you ARE my daughter. What an utterly lovely thought.*

*I'm signing off with 'love' here because 1) since we've met I hope it won't seem at all creepy and 2) it feels very appropriate! So, here we are,*

*Love,*

*Harold x*

I tested my feelings. Couldn't pinpoint if I felt creeped out or thrilled.

Packing the USB in my bag, I loaded up his collection of music files on a shared library computer. There was no apparent virus or sign of anything suspicious.

As part of the listening experience, Harold had challenged me to decide what one of the tracks was really about. I closed my eyes and listened. The notes rose to crescendos and stopped. Crescendos and stopped. Sunrise? Labour? Death?

Back at home, more messages came through.

Jerry – Blackpool's mayor in waiting – had fallen in love with a new lioness.

Clive – the Clear-Headed Dad in the mountains – had almost been run over by a log.

Lenny – he of the board games – was listing book recommendations.

And Champagne Man – otherwise known as Kit, Duncan's mother's frontrunner – was asking me questions. As I dug in and replied to them all, I struggled to remember who already knew what about me. It seemed unfathomable that anyone could ever successfully conduct a long-term affair, or commit bigamy, with so many details at play. Unless –

In a flash of inspiration, I created a new spreadsheet: *What the Dads Know.*

Along the top, I made titles:

- *Book coming out (Y/N)*
- *Subject of book (Y/N)*
- *Location of flat (Y/N)*
- *Duncan's name (Y/N)*
- *My surname (Y/N)*

I filled in the first row for Kit: *knows a book is coming; knows it's about fear; does not know flat location; don't* think *he knows boyf name; NO to surname.*

Then I contemplated completing rows for everyone so far. The idea alone exhausted me. Most of them knew most things now anyway. Apart from the title of the shark book, and my surname. (Nobody knew those. Too exposing.)

Abandoning the spreadsheet, I checked Facebook. Ever since the cruise I'd been online 'friends' with Peter – the man who had instigated everything – and infrequently he sent me updates about his globe-trotting life, avoiding all mention of illness and decline. There he was sailing through Saint Helena. And here he was in Thailand. Now he was asking after my work and letting me know about an upcoming cruise to Mauritius, where he could *maybe find another mother and daughter – let's hope they're as nice as you and mam.* I laughed, rolled my eyes and sent my own imprecise update, mentioning nothing of the strangeness he had sparked – concerned he might campaign to have me certified, or become convinced-then-repulsed that I might want him to play 'Pops' on a permanent basis.

It would never work. He was too real as Peter already.

I switched back to the inbox.

My emails with Harold lengthened. He revealed that the track I'd heard was about a funeral. He also revealed he had still not told his wife anything about me. He had mentioned me to his daughters, however – with some success.

I read the news to the pigs.

'They were totally positive and found the idea as intriguing as I did. They agreed they would like to meet you at some point. I'll get one or both of them to email you, but all the signs are very good so far.'

I could barely believe it. Neither could the pigs. The three of us were speechless for some time.

For our second meeting, Harold returned to the city, apparently glad of another excuse to ride the train. There was a nip in the air as I walked into town. Trafalgar Square heaved with people. I waited on the steps outside the National Gallery, watching a handful of children try to climb the giant bronze lions beneath Nelson's Column. The adults around them exhibited various states and styles of parenting: warmth, presence, concern, excitement, detachment, simmering frustration.

I caught a glimpse of someone in the crowd who looked like Harold. He was shorter than I remembered and looked lost. The man paused, squinting into the sunshine. It *was* Harold.

I came over – 'Harold!' – and walked into a hug. He made a little noise of pleasure and gave me a kiss on the cheek.

*This is what nice dads must do*, I told myself, doing my best not to fixate on his little noise.

We walked around the square for a while, which helped, and I joined him in speculating about where all the famous Trafalgar pigeons had gone. 'Probably culled,' I said. 'Or fed up with having their feet rotted to stumps by their own poo.'

'Funny, isn't it?' said Harold, as if he hadn't heard. 'I remember coming to this place as a kid, and now I'm here with *you*.' At the final word his voice went up an octave. He clutched my arm and nuzzled my shoulder. The intensity caught me off-guard.

'I'm not a pigeon,' I said inanely.

Patting him on the back, I pulled away. As I did, a wave of sadness overcame me. Immediately it was followed by a garbled kind of confusion. Taking a breath, I made myself recall the feelings I'd had so far with our emails.

That Harold was harmless.

Kind.

Considerate.

Grieving a lost daughter and wanting another.

My companion was already walking ahead, making a beeline for the Portrait Gallery. I caught up. Produced a smile. By the time we reached the entrance I was almost calm again.

Together we wandered slowly around the pictures. Harold said, 'Ah, yes,' in front of many of them, explaining to me where various people were from and what they had done. I noticed after a couple of rooms that I started to do the same, trying to prove myself; that I had knowledge too.

I made a few jokes about people's facial expressions and pointed out weird details. Harold didn't laugh. I disliked not being able to make him laugh and resolved to adjust my tone.

Another wave came over me.

*Be yourself or else what's the point?*

*No, you can't be yourself all at once, it won't work!*

We arrived at an area of author portraits. I looked into the eyes of the Brontë sisters as painted by their brother Branwell, then focused on the ghostly shape that showed a missing figure. It was something Mum had pointed out when she and I stood on the same spot years before: a space the brother had occupied in his own artwork, then erased. An almost-family. Nearly-but-not-quite fitting.

I was about to bring up Branwell as our next topic when Harold asked if I'd ever thought of writing a novel myself.

I had been waiting for a question from him and leapt on it. 'I've written three that haven't gone anywhere,' I said. 'That's why I started with that non-fiction proposal. The one about the fear and sharks? See, with non-fiction—'

Harold was staring at me. 'You're publishing a book?'

I froze. 'Has this not come up?'

'It's the first I've heard of it.'

His confusion sounded genuine. My thoughts slingshotted. No longer convinced we had covered the topic, I cursed myself for not doing more with the spreadsheet.

'Are you going to write about this?' he asked.

'You mean, looking for a dad?'

'Yes.'

'I think so. I don't know. I probably will, even if it's just for myself.'

Harold turned back to the wall. 'Hm.'

I held my breath, trying to anticipate what might come next.

'Dickens,' he said. 'Thoughts?'

We took a turn into the twentieth century. I had not been rejected or shouted at. We were both still in the gallery. This was still a thing.

Audibly, Harold recoiled at some of the modern, abstract works. Again, I started to copy him. In no time at all I was rubbishing things before he had even reached them: work I might have coveted otherwise. The level of approval-seeking alarmed me. At the same time, I could not stop it.

I spied through a window that, outside, the day was now beautiful. *That* was what I wanted: the outdoors. Air. Free movement.

Aiming for autonomous action, I suggested we go for a walk. A flicker of hesitation in Harold's voice indicated he was not keen. Instantly, apologetically, I retracted my idea and asked what *he* wanted to do. Which was how, 10 minutes later, we ended up not in the open air but down in the crypt of St Martin-in-the-Fields, queuing for two cups of tea.

We sat at a table side by side. My suggestion. 'My granny used to love people-watching,' I explained. Since our backs were to the wall, we could see everyone and anyone as they filed past. In that moment, I wished very hard that Granny Codd was there too.

Perhaps it was the tiny act of making a choice for me, and sticking to it, which shifted some of the dankness in my chest. The conversation that followed felt better. More equal. I even became energised enough to probe Harold for details of his daughters' reactions on hearing about me. 'What did they say first – *really*?'

'They said . . . uh, "That's . . . very interesting."'

I hooted.

'That's what they meant to say,' he elaborated.

'What they *meant* to say?'

He moved the conversation on, showing me pictures. An image of his youngest daughter with her husband. Of the middle daughter beside a kiln. Of them all together. I looked on, intrigued: his family was authentic; the daughters were definitely real. It did seem like Harold was who he claimed to be.

Above the crypt a choir sang, practising harmonies in a public rehearsal. We finished our drinks and watched them before stepping back outside. On our return to the station, Harold said, 'I think I'll tell my wife about you this evening.' He paused. 'But I won't tell her about the advert.'

I took a misstep and almost stumbled. 'What if she finds out about it later?'

'She won't. It's long gone in the bin now.'

I started to think about the other dadverts I had been placing. About his daughters' involvement. About maybe writing a book. The woman would find out then.

My ability to talk freely tailed away. I focused on the buildings around us. The bricks, the windows, the spikes. The sensation of walking on slabs.

A fancy antiques shop caught Harold's attention. 'I think I sold a bracelet to these chaps years ago,' he said. 'My friend found it in his vegetable patch and didn't know where to take it. It only made us a bit of beer money, but better than nothing.'

'Do you want to go in? Do you have enough time?'

He pushed open the door. A guy with what seemed like a Kazakh accent, his bleached hair slicked-back, his blazer and shoes all shining, greeted us from behind the counter. He was surrounded by ancient Greek tiaras, gold Celtic jewellery, massive Chinese urns; seemingly priceless artefacts on every shelf. I must have made the right kind of noises: he soon started handing me rings that were labelled as being millennia old, insisting I wear them.

'But how can you tell if you have a fake?' I asked.

The man puffed out his cheeks. 'You just know.'

Harold and I shared a look. I asked how long he'd been in the industry.

The salesman adjusted his blazer. 'Two years.' He rolled his shoulders. 'I'm often asked to the houses of the dying, you know. I will make offers for their whole collection. I will just buy it, even if I don't want to.'

Harold wandered away to inspect an urn, while the salesman emphasised the importance of getting a *British* certificate; how you could then use that certificate to sell less legitimate items.

Harold caught my eye again. We began to leave.

'I'll remember to call you when I'm rich and dying!' I shouted from the front door.

'Fantastic!' said the seller.

'Then bludgeon you with my walking frame,' I added underneath my breath.

On the final leg of our walk, Harold seemed distracted. Eventually he said, 'I can't work out if they duped me, or I duped them. That bracelet wasn't ancient. My friend found a matching ring afterwards and thought he'd struck gold, but the local museum told him it was '50s costume jewellery. He was hugely disappointed.'

I laughed. 'If the fakes do the trick, though, aren't they as good as the originals? I mean, if they give people that same feeling and sense of connection.'

Harold shook his head. It was not a response that seemed to bode well for my project. Yet, when we arrived at the station, the man became enthused once more. He proffered a CD with more self-made music on it and declared: 'I would *love* to be your dad.'

My face flushed. I took the CD. 'Thank you.'

'I still don't know your name, though.'

'It's Georgina.'

'No,' he said. 'Your *whole* name.'

A petrifying panic spread from the roots of my hair.

Harold stared. Smiled.

Was this a trap? Disarmament by affection? My scalp contracted.

Harold did not blink.

When I said 'Codd' all the moisture in my mouth evaporated.

'Like the fish?'

My soul shrivelled. 'With an extra "d",' I confirmed.

'I went to school with a Coddington.'

He asked after my name's origins. I tried my best to keep the answer flowing, except I felt brittle and dreadful. I resented the man for engineering this. I resented myself for not being able to stop him. We hugged. Harold was enveloping me, emitting the kind of 'mmm' you hear on adverts for luxury yoghurts. I pulled away.

That lip-smacking 'mmm' echoed in my ears all the way home.

# 11

# FUNDAMENTALLY FLAWED

I was miserable.

'What's the problem?' said Duncan.

Miserable.

'So he knows your name. That's okay.'

'It's not okay. I've lost a boundary. It's gone.'

'Nah.'

Miserable.

I played Harold's CD.

The music was brisk.

'And the noise he made,' I said.

'What noise?' said Duncan.

'I can't repeat it.'

'I'm sure it's nothing.'

'It's not nothing.'

The CD started to skip.

Miserable.

Research, research, research. I looked in my notebook for things that fathers can give. There were so many quotes to go through.

Gender.

'Fathers, even more than mothers, seem to have a critical part in the development of children's gender roles . . .'

Empathy.

'The most powerful predictor of empathy in adulthood was paternal child-rearing involvement at age five . . .'

Absence.

'There is no doubt that there is a tiny minority of fathers, as there are mothers, who are defined by their absence . . .'

*Tiny?*

I chucked the notebook. Went online. There I discovered the phrase 'father deserts'; discovered that, across England and Wales, there are 237 areas in which at least *50 per cent of local households* consist of families with no father present.

'Hmph.'

Picking the notebook back up, I smoothed the pages.

'. . . but there is a much, much larger contingent of fathers who stick around and do their best, and they also deserve to be recognised and understood.'

'Okay.'

I sighed.

So I met Harold a third time. We roamed the streets of London again. Agreed the Charles Dickens Museum could be a good fit.

(Dickens, whose father was sent to debtors' prison, forcing Charles into working at a shoe polish factory at age 12.)

(Dickens, who had 10 'legitimate' children along with a 'bastard' daughter who died in infancy.)

(My sighs lengthened.)

In the café – a dark, wood-floored room at the rear of the author's extravagant, five-storeyed house – Harold casually mentioned that he had once had a crush on a playwright. 'She was a psychopath,' he said, 'and possibly involved in a semi-incestuous relationship with her son.' He took a bite out of his sandwich. 'Still, she was also a wonderful visionary.'

He went on to say that he still hadn't told his wife about me. Then, when we said goodbye, there was that yoghurt-sucking sound.

My mum called in the evening to say hello. She didn't ask after any dads, and both of us acted as if we had never discussed it. I was glad to hear about beach huts instead. Better that than share Harold's sound with her. I already knew what she'd say about it, and afterwards might finally come her *real* thoughts about my project.

Instead I described the noise to a visiting cousin the following day. She said plainly, 'That's a sex noise.'

Duncan overheard from the next room and burst into high-pitched laughter. 'That's the noise?' he yelled. 'That's disgusting. The man's a fucking paedophile.'

'Shut up,' I told them. I slumped onto the floor and covered my face with my hands.

It wasn't long before we were back at my boyfriend's parents' house. His mum had asked for our help to prepare for a party.

When she and I were alone in the kitchen, I asked how she might write a letter to a dad she wasn't sure she wanted anymore.

'Er . . .' She stepped around me. 'Let me think about that.'

In silence, I chopped up a heap of vegetables for crudités, getting caught in loops around what was right and what was wrong, arguing with myself that I was being oversensitive.

*Wasn't.*

*Was.*

*Wasn't.*

*Was.*

Later, by the hob, I repeated my question for Duncan's mother: how to write to a dad in this situation.

'It's a tricky one,' she said.

Duncan's father entered the room from his office. 'What's tricky?'

'Georgie's new dad has been making sex noises,' Duncan called out from the sofa. 'He's a paedo.'

'He's not a paedo,' I said. 'I'm in my thirties, remember? And he's not my dad. Really. I don't know. I think it's probably just a normal noise that some fathers make, and I'm not used to it at all. He does *have* daughters . . .' I wiped my hands. 'Anyway, it's not just that. I feel like there are other alarm bells, and—'

'What's the noise?' Duncan's dad asked his son, not me. Duncan mimicked me making it.

His dad snorted. 'That's not a noise fathers make,' he said. 'It's fucking disgusting.'

'He's a nice man,' I protested. 'I just—'

'Make the noise again,' he said.

Duncan pulled out a chair and repeated the show. His

dad sniggered so hard his face changed colour. Duncan's mother started chuckling too.

'It's not like that.'

'What's it like then?' said Duncan's dad. 'You make the noise.'

I wrinkled my nose. The group watched me, expectantly. 'Um . . .' I shut my eyes and imagined myself at the station, saying goodbye to Harold.

I made the noise.

Now they were all in stitches, Duncan's dad parroting me, engorging the sound with lust. 'Mmm, *daughter*,' he mocked. '*Mmmmm*.'

I crossed my arms. 'Is that definitely not a sound fathers make?'

'*Fuck* no,' said the dad, at the same time his wife said, 'Well . . .'

Speaking over the men I echoed, 'Well . . . ?'

'It might be,' she said. 'It is a loving noise.'

'So you're breaking it off with this man?' said Duncan's dad, no longer laughing. 'Is that it?'

'I don't know.' I fiddled with the edge of the kitchen counter. 'I'm not sure. I might see him again.'

His face became a picture of disdain. 'Why bother?'

'Because he's nice, and kind, and might actually be what I set out to find in the first place. Plus I might be misinterpreting things. I mean, maybe that noise – out of context . . .'

Duncan's mother put her hand on my shoulder. 'I think you have to take full responsibility for this. You have to apologise for leading him on. You need to take the blame.'

'Leading him on?'

Her husband walked off, muttering under his breath. Duncan went back to his phone.

My heartbeat raced.

During the party, I felt out of sorts. By brunch-time the next day I was still queasy, barely picking at leftovers. Of all the family structures I'd known in my life, Duncan's was the most traditional. His father provided their income and discipline. His mother made the bulk of the meals, wrote the cards, bought the gifts, hugged the friends, did the washing, ironed the bedsheets and even ironed the underwear.

Man's work. Woman's work.

'It might seem very old-fashioned to you,' she had acknowledged many times. 'But women and men are different. Biologically. You can see it from when they're babies. Girls want pink and boys want to hit each other. Men can't give children what women can give. There's no getting around it.'

And: 'You won't understand it, Georgie, until you have kids of your own.'

Instinctively I bristled – but was the set-up so different for me? Duncan had the full-time dependable income while my freelance work was erratic. I often made the bulk of the meals, mostly wrote the cards, always hugged the friends and did the washing. The only difference was that both of us balked at ironing, plus Duncan reached for the sewing kit whenever a button fell off.

As for discipline: any time I got annoying or wore any less-than-flattering clothes my boyfriend would let me know, insisting it was my job to return the favour.

Duncan's work. Georgie's work.

(A worry: were we 'traditional'?)

(A thought: I did not want that.)

(Did I want that?)

I was staring out at the garden when Duncan's dad broke my silence. He wanted to know what I would do about Harold. I told him, again, that I wasn't sure.

'You have to go with your gut,' he instructed. 'Your gut's telling me this situation is wrong.'

'Is it?' I turned to him. 'I don't know what my gut's telling me. Maybe he's exactly the right type of dad.'

The man slammed down his mug of tea. 'This project is fundamentally flawed. There's no need for it.'

'There's a need for me.'

'You can't force emotions like these. You can't fabricate that kind of relationship.'

'How can you be so sure?' My voice rose. 'Have you tried this yourself? Besides, I'm not trying to force anything. I'm not pretending this could happen overnight. I'm learning as I go.'

He narrowed his eyes.

Duncan's mother spoke up. She wanted to share her story about the father of a friend she'd known as a child. How he had been so kind and caring that she had thought of him as like her father too. Especially when –

'But he wasn't consciously presenting that to you,' her husband interrupted. 'He wasn't like a father. That's fucking absurd.'

'How do you know?' My voice was too loud. 'How could you possibly know what was in that man's head? Perhaps he did think of himself in those terms.'

'I heard that this Harold bloke doesn't ask you many questions.'

'He could probably ask more. But maybe I don't always let him.'

'That's what parents do. They ask questions.'

'I do have a parent,' I said. 'I understand the concept of "parent". And some of the other men I've been talking to for this ask me loads of questions.'

He shook his head. '*Fuck's sake.*'

'The project isn't flawed,' I said. 'Relationships take work, whoever you are and however they start.'

'That's absolute bollocks.'

The two of us glared at each other. '*Are you serious?*'

His lips sealed shut. Disdain again.

Realising that I was about to start shouting, I stood up to clear my plate.

'I don't understand,' Duncan said to his dad. 'How is the concept different from a couple meeting each other and getting to know each other, and building something from there? That's not forcing emotions. Or is it?'

My boyfriend's father pushed back his chair. 'What *she's* doing is causing pain and hurt. It's selfish, totally thoughtless, and absolutely no good can come of it.' A fleck of his spittle landed on the table. 'Georgie needs to get real, grow up and stop fucking about.'

I reached the sink. Twisted on the hot tap. In my head I counted from ten to one. Twenty to one. Thirty.

By then Duncan's dad was back inside his office.

My boyfriend's mother made a melodic sound. 'Very tasty lunch,' she trilled. 'I love that lentil salad, Georgie, don't you? Do you think it had enough spring onion this time?'

Duncan keenly joined her in conversation, talking about spring onions more generally. When he ran out of material, he began to discuss a work colleague who was being investigated for sexual misconduct; a man in his late forties who'd harassed a female junior. His mother gasped and cooed. I scrubbed the dishes and tried to tune them out. My eyes were swimming in heat.

'What's the noise Harold makes when he hugs you?' his mother asked. She was standing right behind me.

'I don't—'

'Go on,' she smiled, 'make the noise.'

I couldn't stop blinking.

'Oh, go on,' she urged, more softly.

I made the noise.

'That's the noise I make when I hug my son,' she said. 'It's not sexual, it's loving.' She lowered her voice in a confiding way. 'You know, *I* think the father you find is going to be someone you don't expect.'

Saying nothing, I plunged my hands into the suds, more determined than ever to make this work.


My apprehension around the nuclear family model – 'a social unit of two parents and their children' – was ballooning. Researching the subject, I learned that the phrase 'nuclear family' came out of reference to the *nucleus*, or the core. As if the grouping was atomically – fundamentally – intrinsic to existence; that even if it disintegrated, you had done what you were supposed to, what science dictated as 'right'.

You could only be born into it, I suspected. And if you weren't, you would be stuck outside, forever looking in. Until you and a partner attempted to recreate the model yourselves.

I carried on reading.

Tied in to historic imaginings of the nuclear family model was the idea that men were the rulers of these things. That they could not be supplanted. 'For a time, it all seemed to work,' the conservative US commentator David Brooks wrote on the subject.

> From 1950 to 1965, divorce rates dropped, fertility rates rose, and the American nuclear family seemed to be in wonderful shape. And most people seemed prosperous and happy. In these years, a kind of cult formed around this type of family – what *McCall's*, the leading women's magazine of the day, called 'togetherness'. Healthy people lived in two-parent families. In a 1957 survey, more than half of the respondents said that unmarried people were 'sick', 'immoral', or 'neurotic'.

I tried again to pin down what Duncan's dad hated. Perhaps that a child could select and mould their idea of a father, rather than the other way around.

Could that be it?

I was also caught by lines in a book called *Daddy Issues*, by Katherine Angel. 'A father, historically, protects a daughter,' she wrote, 'and to the extent that he protects her, it's her value that he is protecting, as a piece of property to transfer.'

She wrote, too, that, 'You can, at least in principle, leave a husband, but you can't leave a father.'

I chewed the end of my pen. Perhaps that was the issue. Perhaps, in thinking of fathers as commodities for *me*, I was somehow going against the social order.

Except, it didn't take much to see that this order was man-made.

And that it often didn't work.


A friend of mine, who was having long-term issues with her parents – issues that had led to her blocking communication with both of them – sent me in the direction of the British writer-philosopher Dr Sophie Lewis. 'Look her up,' she insisted. 'It might be relevant.'

When Lewis's book *Full Surrogacy Now* arrived on the doormat, I could see why my friend thought I'd be interested.

Lewis had taken issue with the way in which certain babies have more social value than others – meaning those born 'naturally', into biologically linked units that other children cannot penetrate. She argued that many of these babies are essentially (and possessively) owned by the parents who made them, writing that 'the *natural* way clearly privileges making babies in the shape of personal mascots, psychic crutches, heirs, scapegoats and fetishes, not forgetting avatars of binary sex'. And that 'it is not nature but love, in all its contingency, that is the source of the real stability to which all children have a right'.

At the same time, Lewis had written how so-called stable familial homes 'are very often far from the utopias they are supposed to be', listing experiences of 'discomfort, coercion, molestation, abuse, humiliation, depression, battery, murder, mutilation, loneliness, blackmail, exhaustion, psychosis, gender-straitjacketing, racial programming and embourgeoisement'. She added: 'The private family is the headquarters of all of these.'

Children, adults and communities deserve better, argued Lewis. And achieving better could start with open, collaborative care.

Later, Lewis would write the manifesto *Abolish the Family*, which caused controversy almost everywhere it was received. She would explain then that,

> I've noticed that a lot of people have the '*but I love my family*' reaction with the most startling vehemence immediately after they've spent a long time talking freely to me about the strain, tragedy, blackmail, and care-starved frustration that characterised their 'biological' upbringing. Angry opposition to the idea that *things could be different* comes, I've found, right after we have voiced the wish that relatives of ours could have been less alone, less burdened by caring responsibilities, less trapped. Those people are quite another matter, this defensive spasm seems to say: I, myself, don't need any family abolition, thank you very much. Sure, it may be a disciplinary, scarcity-based trauma-machine: but it's MY disciplinary, scarcity-based trauma-machine.

Instead of writing to any new publications for the moment, I wrote to Sophie, pondering the motivations behind her philosophy, asking if she would talk to me about how father-hood fitted into this picture.

Apparently, she would. While we made plans to talk between London and her home in North America, she sent me some then-unpublished work that referenced her own dad. Sophie had been trying to 'break up' with him for years.

When we spoke I found myself looking through the computer screen straight into Sophie's spare room. A poster of lobsters kept catching my eye, as did her prowling rescue cat. The cat had been rejected by its birth mother, I heard, and seized every chance to leap onto Sophie's lap.

I told her what I'd been doing with dadverts. It seemed to fire her up. 'That's so fucking fascinating,' she said. 'I talk sometimes about the limitations of the chosen family. I often sort of feel like saying: the whole chosen family thing is not super great for those who don't get chosen, you know? It's not a scalable solution. Even the biggest asshole needs to be cared for.'

Which brought us on to the subject of her dad, and the reasons why she wanted to break up with him.

'Apparently, he started fighting me – or conceivably, vice versa, we started fighting each other – when I was five . . . We had this video cassette of an opera. *The Magic Flute*. In it, there's the Queen of the Night. My brother and I would dress up and be her. We thought she was pretty cool, even though it turns out by the end that she's done some bad things. (My brother and I clearly didn't care for the end, or even watch that far into the movie.) And the story is, Dad got jealous that I was identified with the Queen of the Night. He was like, "Why do you like her? She's evil, she got cast out of the kingdom by the king." But it's not that simple. She's not evil. She's helpful too.'

'Which your dad must have known, surely?'

'I swear to God, he wanted to have an argument with a five-year-old about whether the king was justified in throwing her out. Mum remembers this argument where I'm just screaming, and he's yelling at me. And he backed me up against a wall and was like, "Be reasonable!" And I was screaming and screaming. So we've been fighting on a feminist basis since. That's literally been the fight of my life.'

In the essay Sophie had shared about her father, I'd read that:

> Apparently, Dad once told Mum that he had married her because he thought marrying an older woman would spare him sexual jealousy down the road: other men would not desire his wife. It might have been shortly after this that my (gay) brother and I informed Dad that we did not intend to have children. 'Well, then, if you two aren't going to give me grandchildren,' he replied, 'I'll have to find some fertile young popsy to impregnate myself.'

More alarming was her father's steadfast resistance to acknowledging Sophie's experience of being raped as a child. To that trauma, he responded with 'essentially a decades-long campaign to refute and refuse my claim. In 2015, he sided with the Stanford rapist Brock Turner [the 19-year-old athlete who sexually assaulted a 22-year-old student while she was unconscious]. In 2017, he wrote an email to my partner noting I'd probably spun her a yarn about having been raped at thirteen; this was a fabrication, he said; "rape is good for the feminist cv".'

I hadn't thought much about dads as antagonists. Tormentors. Nemeses. And yet, of course, it happens.

Sophie was now essentially estranged from her father, much like my friend who had recommended her book.

(Should the phrase be 'fatherless', I wondered, or 'father-free'?)

Detailed estrangement statistics were hard to come by, it turned out, when I tried looking. Research from the past decade by UK charity Stand Alone revealed that one in five British families was affected by familial estrangement and its consequences. More recently, a separate poll in the US indicated that 27 per cent of adults were currently involved in an estrangement from a relative. Within this figure, 24 per cent were estranged from a parent, i.e. 6 per cent of everyone surveyed.

Described as a 'silent epidemic' by some, and a 'powerful taboo' by others, researchers seemed to agree that the number of estrangements was on the rise, in part because of the public's 'growing awareness of mental health, and how toxic or abusive family relationships can affect our wellbeing'.

There was more to discuss with Sophie. More about the dysfunctional, and sometimes hazardous, realities of family relationships. First, I needed to deal with one of my own realities.

The Harold situation was unnerving me. The knowledge

that he was lying to his wife. The way he had elicited my surname. The noise, which could be love or could be lust.

Altogether it made me squirm. And while I didn't necessarily want to cut him off, I also didn't feel a clear compulsion to continue.

In a painful message constructed over days, I expressed my concern that he had been able to access his emotions unreservedly, in a way that I felt incapable of matching.

The message hung in my draft folder, unsent.

*You seem to have been able to embrace the father-figure concept much more quickly, and easily, than I feel able to take on the role of the daughter-figure*, I had written.

*Despite our many emails, I still feel there is a lot I don't know about you, and possibly even more that you don't know about me. I don't feel like I've done anything to earn the loving feelings you seem to be showing me already. Of course, you did promise to give it unconditionally! I know that, but am still tying myself in knots over the mismatch.*

*Another thing I find tricky is that you have not felt able to talk to your wife about our meetings. After our conversations, I gained the impression that there are a few things you haven't felt able to tell her over the years, for one reason or another. Those events are in the past, and were nothing to do with me. But this friendship is going on right now, and is to do with me. Being a person you secretly visit in London makes me feel uncomfortable, despite your daughters being in the know.*

*I've been trying to avoid thinking about these things, and carry on regardless, but after some serious thinking I've been forced to accept that a) I don't feel right about this situation, and b) it is almost entirely of my own making.*

The toy pigs heard me read it out loud for about the eleventh time.

Now, looking into their faces, I sent it off.

When Harold's reply came through the next day I was too on edge to read it, anticipating some variation of grief that would sting me and keep stinging. I'd already had too much of that.

Duncan was out at a work meal celebrating the end of a project, no doubt belted in for many a course of expensive, social-media-friendly dishes. In his absence, I invited Mabry for dinner and cooked us too much rice.

'Could you possibly maybe do me a really weird favour?' I asked, plating up.

To my great relief, my friend accepted the job of clicking open Harold's message, then scanning through it on my behalf. After we'd eaten, she held the mouse, absorbing what was there. I blocked my face and ears with a stack of sofa cushions. A minute later, the silence remained, and my mind had decided to fill it with all the worst things. It was over-whelming. 'What's he saying?' I asked. 'Actually, no. Don't read it to me, please, just give me a summary. One word.'

Mabry hesitated.

'How upset is he? Does he hate me? Oh God.'

'It's very nice,' said Mabry. 'Do you want me to say what he's written?'

I moaned into the sofa. 'I'm not ready.'

'That's okay. No rush.'

'Fuck.' I threw off the cushions and pressed my fingers into my eyelids. 'Have I made a mistake? I've made a mistake. Oh, fuck.'

'I don't think so. It didn't feel right for you and that's fine.'

'Should I read it? Is it safe?'

Mabry giggled. 'I think it's safe.'

My eyes scrunched closed as I came to the laptop, afraid of what they might see. They needn't have been. Mabry was right. Harold's response was suffused with affection. He assured me he didn't feel bad and that I must not take any blame. He also included an offer: *I will leave the door open. If you want to contact me in any way, at any time, I will happily accept that; but, recognising that you have legitimate concerns, I will leave that decision entirely to you.*

I was grateful for the open door. An open door was okay. Sad and okay.

When I was on my own again I wrote to Harold to thank him. I wondered if our paths would cross again. I wondered if I wanted that.

# 12

# (NO) SUGAR DADDIES

A small stash of pictures gathered in the inbox. Some respondents thought it was a good idea to send them before we properly got to know each other. Each face looked white and English, like variations of Cotswold lecturers. Only one message so far had come from a foreign address and it was spammily cryptic: *I've no agenda. I'll send you best emails from my good freindz across the world I also hope to receive same from you, this is my only aim.*

While all printed versions of the dadvert specified a wish for a purely platonic relationship, a significant minority still chose to overlook this part of my request. Or, like Mr *No-Daddy-No*, took time to circuitously explain what they *definitely did not want* in a way that sounded like a masturbatory game of Opposites.

I was learning.

Any reference to being 'solvent' was a giveaway; an early and indirect glimpse of finance-focused sugar-daddy-style vocabulary. The immediate sending of selfies, too, was generally an indicator that physical bodies – theirs and mine – were their primary interest.

Evidence of speed and urgency were also helpful signals. The briefer the message, the less thought it involved. The less thought it involved, the less likely the writer was to be my ideal. These were the men, not the dads – and the key differences between them started to become more apparent.

Purely platonic father figures probably wouldn't write things like:

*Where are you? I'm in London, 64 and greyish.*

*I like the idea of becoming a dad to a lady . . . Here is my photo.*

*I search a lovely lady to be in my life. I am single, childless, land, horses and not enough fun . . . I hope you are also curious.*

*I'm 6' tall, white, widowed and British. Ideally, I hope to find a companion, friend, muse, lover . . . x*

The perhaps-inevitable Married Man With Highly Questionable Morals made his own conspicuous cameo:

*Taking time out in bed earlier, I flicked through my magazine to find your notice. After just a moment's hesitation, I've grabbed my phone to write you this message.*

*I have a wife and two offspring. I'm cheerful, self-sure, grounded, daring, open and naturally adept at mentoring the young.*

*I would love to be considered as your father figure. Your request speaks to me, so eloquent and direct. To avoid any doubt, I've taken on a similar position before and so truly comprehend the difference between what both of us seek and the sugar daddy role that others look for.*

*I am certain you've been flooded with responses, but very much hope you reflect on this offer I've made and write back soon. You fascinate me, I hope I might fascinate you too x*

More than even his specially chosen scene-setting of *Bed: Horizontal*, it was the notion of this person thinking he knew so clearly what I sought that put me off. In any case, he did not reply to my bounce-back message. I was glad. I was also concerned for his spouse and 'offspring', these apparently real-life people with him as their husband and dad, described in passing with such a cool and clinical tone of voice.

I wondered if they had seen this side of the man.

One morning, Draughts-Player Lenny sent his own photo-graph to my email address: him on a mountain during a hiking trip. It was the first time I'd seen his face. (Or most of it. Sunglasses hid his eyes.)

Our discussions about a draughts night were accelerat-ing. He really wanted it to happen. I was fairly sure I did too. It was just . . .

What if . . .

Ted Bundy . . .

No.

I rapped my skull with my knuckles.

'Knock, knock, who's there? Georgie who's thinking too much.'

It was draughts. Just a board game.

As I worked out my next move, cruise-going Peter sent me a new message on Facebook; his latest in our loose chain of online small talk. *Just having a coffee in Mumbles glorious day in paradise.*

That morning I decided to strike up a protracted conversation. Shared the state of the London weather. Gave him the latest updates about the shark book and my freelancing clients.

His response to that came later, and was crowned with the question: *How's Mother?*

When I saw it the next day, I laughed. How was *he* doing, I asked?

He had terrible pains, he told me, the day after that. Wasn't sleeping right. Or walking so easy. Pins and needles that wouldn't let up. *But fine really Georgie. Can't complain. One of the lucky ones really.*

We reached the weekend. Peter invited me to visit Mumbles when I fancied a change of scene. To enjoy one of *Pete's Tours.*

It was an intriguing idea – and I was reluctant. The man wasn't well; he could be at death's door. That wasn't a threshold I felt strong enough to return to.

'Lenny wants to teach us draughts,' I told Duncan. The two of us milled in the kitchen, making dinner.

'Is Lenny one of the dads?'

'We're invited to Basingstoke.'

'Hm.'

'There'll be wine,' I continued. 'We'll do it at his friend's house. They're going to be our draughts gurus.'

Duncan considered it. 'I don't think so. What if they murder me?'

'What if they murder *me*?'

'That's your choice. It's your project.'

I chewed the inside of my mouth. 'Please.'

'No.'

'I'm pretty sure he's not a murderer.'

Silence.

'If you make me go alone and *I* get murdered,' I said, 'won't that ruin the rest of your life?'

'I'll get over it.'

I pursed my lips; pushed forward. 'Draughts is supposed to be really cool,' I tried. 'Everyone's talking about it. It's apparently one of the most interesting, intellectual board games around.'

Now Duncan was firing out WhatsApp messages.

I stared into the saucepan steam. When he put his phone down I said, 'It's really tactical. Takes a while to master, apparently.' I darted out of the room and came back with my laptop. 'Lenny says: "for people with a brain, the depth of subtlety, the reasoning, logic and inferences you can reach are staggering". You have a brain, I have a brain – let's be staggered! And drink some nice booze.'

Eventually, my boyfriend seemed to succumb, or at least stopped resisting.

As Lenny and I finalised the arrangements by email, I suggested he and I team up to be draughts partners.

Lenny's reply: *I thought you'd never ask.*

It took plenty of extra effort to reassure Duncan that neither of us would be at risk with Lenny, or with his friend Gordon. I read out email highlights. Shared phone numbers I'd been given. Downloaded the hiking picture. I sensed my boyfriend's reservations softening. That we could be a proactive team on this one.

Then my eldest cousin and his girlfriend came for dinner.

We finished our starter and were on the mains when Clo asked how my dad project was going.

I swallowed my mouthful. 'On Friday we're off to learn draughts with someone – both of us meeting a dad! That hasn't happened yet.'

'Draughts?' said Nicholas. 'Isn't that a game for old people?'

'That's very ageist of you, dear cousin.'

'Sorry, what's happening?' Clo asked.

I went through the plan: how we were catching the train, being collected from the station in Lenny's car, going to Lenny's friend's house where we –

I stopped. Nicholas and Clo looked horrified. 'Oh my God, you'll be *murdered*!' said Clo. 'A stranger's house, you've never met, in a car away from *everyone*?'

On the other side of the table, Duncan's forehead divided into an intricate grid of lines.

'I have the guy's phone number,' I said, with confidence.

'What about the address? What if someone needs to find you? Have you checked it on Street View?'

'I can't remember if I have that yet . . .'

Nicholas laughed. 'You'd better have that.'

'Aren't you going to a public place?' Clo continued. 'Not at all?'

'Maybe we should go to a bar or something,' said Duncan.

Nicholas nodded. 'I mean, if you get in the car, that's it. No escape.'

'But we won't have time to learn draughts if we do that,' I said. 'We have to go straight to his house. And, like, we're not staying over, so . . .'

Clo gaped at me. 'I'm really worried about you guys.'

'Me too,' said Duncan.

'Why are *you* worried? We've gone through this. You don't need to be worried.' I turned back to Clo. 'We'll be fine. Strength in numbers.'

'Yeah, but—' Clo waved her fork in Duncan's direction. 'No offence, he is not a muscle man.'

The three of them got into it. We would be hacked to pieces. Both of us molested. Lenny would stalk us home. He would be bugging the car, the walls, the bathroom; he would film us on the toilet with a camera under the seat. Their pessimism expanded above the table, forming a single mushroom cloud of Total-Mega-Disaster.

My body tightened. Draughts must work. It would work. 'There is *no way* any harm is going to come to us on Friday,' I insisted, with more conviction than I felt. 'Not *one chance.*'

Nicholas knocked back his last splash of wine. 'You're going to die in Basingstoke.'

Before leaving, the pair insisted we find ways to let them know where we were throughout our encounter.

'But we'll be *playing draughts*.'

'It's that or death, cuz.' Nicholas winked. 'Make the right choice.'

At my desk I re-read Lenny's latest messages. He *had* sent his friend's address, and it checked out as real online. I clicked through the route as if I was travelling there. I would know if we were in the right part of town when we ought to be. He had also given me the car licence plate details. We could be sure we were getting into the right vehicle.

Duncan heard me out. Threatened again not to come.

The next day I created a WhatsApp group, *Murder Avoid-ance Strategy*, inviting Duncan, Nicholas and Clo. I screenshotted emails, the address, phone numbers. 'So much information,' I sang to myself. 'How could anyone possibly get murdered?' There was a *thuck* from my phone as each piece uploaded. 'That's one for justice, and . . .' The last *thuck* sounded. I scanned through what I'd shared. 'Maybe zero for Duncan and Georgie.'

Nicholas thanked me shortly afterwards. *We have plenty of evidence for the murder trial now.*

The night before our expedition, I interviewed Duncan, pretending we were in our own private podcast. Holding a Dictaphone near his face, I tried to suss out his true feel-ings. 'What's your understanding about what's going to happen tomorrow?'

'We're going to get to play draughts with some people we've never met before.'

I asked how he felt about that.

'I'm sure it's interesting, but I've heard it can take a long time, and it might require quite a bit of investment in knowing the rules. And combining that with meeting some random new people . . .'

'I do believe that recently you were expressing some concerns about draughts beyond the intensity required to play the game.'

Duncan shook his head. 'Yeah, well. We've never met these people before. We're going to their house straight from the train station. It doesn't feel like the smartest thing to do. It gives us next to no time to figure out whether they are psychopaths and whether we should really not actually be going to their house.'

'What do you think the chances are of these people being psychopaths?'

'Fifteen per cent.'

I frowned. 'How have you calculated 15 per cent? That's quite high for the general population, isn't it?'

'If you think about what they have done to get to this situation—'

'One of them has done. Only one of them's been in contact with me.'

'—and the proportion of people that have been in contact with you that have been not particularly sound of mind, which has been 85 per cent.'

'Really?'

'Eighty-five per cent,' he repeated. 'Is that about right?'

'I'm not sure I can really say that.'

'What percentage would you say?'

I told him I hadn't thought about it.

He told me to pick a number.

'I guess I would say . . . 65 per cent have been . . .' My mind went blank. 'I'd say about 40 per cent have been dodgy.'

'Mm.'

'And then 25 per cent have been *probably* dodgy, and then the rest probably all with good intentions are okay.'

'Okay, so that's a pretty high proportion for the general populace.'

'If my calculations are correct, that's 35 per cent normality.'

'And I'm saying 15 per cent normality.'

'You're saying 15 per cent psychopathy.'

'No, normally. Normal.'

'You think the chances of them being normal are 15 per cent?'

'No, no, no, I'm talking about the—'

'Tomorrow?'

'—the general populace.'

We were getting swept away. I changed tack. 'Okay. So if they are psychopaths—'

'Yeah.'

'—and you're in the car with me, and you realise on our way to the location of the draughts game that they're psychopaths, what's your plan?'

'We're probably not going to be able to legitimately get out of the car until they stop.'

'Mm-hm.'

'And so they probably don't have locks on the car doors

because they're going to presume that we're not going to know that they're psychopaths.'

'You do know psychopaths are legendarily very good at fitting in with the general population.'

'I know, I'm not necessarily talking about—'

'You mean weirdos that you don't want to spend time with rather than psychopaths.'

'I don't – I'm not too worried about weirdos. But whatever the right term for somebody who might murder you is.'

The word came to me easily: 'Predator.'

'There are plenty of weirdos,' said Duncan. 'Everybody is a bit weird. And that's not really a problem.'

I suggested we find a safe word, a code we could secretly wield to abort the mission. Duncan proffered the name of a Welsh trampoline park. I was confused. 'The one I want to visit?'

'Yeah,' he said, 'and we're like, "Okay they're crazy." Then we can be like, "Oh, we're thinking of going to Bounce Below. Have you heard of it?"'

'Wow.' By this point I'd completely given up on being an impartial interviewer. 'I'm just trying to imagine this scenario where you or I say "Bounce Below", then we magically manage to escape after Bounce Below is said. "Oh, remember that Bounce Below? RUN!"'

'Obviously not instantly,' Duncan protested, 'but—'

'Within five minutes of the station?'

'At a junction, or traffic lights.'

'Oh my gosh,' I said, distressed. 'Oh God, this sounds horrible. How awkward.'

'What?'

'You say Bounce Below in the first five minutes and then at the next set of traffic lights, I have to get out of the car?'

'If we think they're psychopaths, we need to get out. If we say "Bounce Below", it means one of us thinks this is a fucking disaster. And it doesn't matter that it's weird that we run away because we will never see them again.'

'Well, let's hope they tell us they're going to murder us in the first five minutes so we can follow the Bounce Below plan.'

'Do they live 10 minutes from the station?'

'Yes.'

That piece of information must have been too much for him. 'Do you want pasta or spaghetti?' he asked.

'Spaghetti, please,' I said. 'Even though that's also pasta.'

I brought the Dictaphone up to his mouth. 'Is there anything else you'd like to say? Maybe final words to people who are listening to this after your body has been retrieved from a drain in Basingstoke?'

'In hindsight,' he said, 'I'm pretty fucked off that this happened.'

# 13

# HALF-NODS

Strangely, on our way out of London, I was the tense one. With wine in my bag, and chocolates too, I sat on the train seat and juddered both legs. After several minutes Duncan asked if I was stressed.

Yes, I told him. Very stressed. I slumped back in my seat. 'Potential murder is one thing. What if he doesn't like me? I would really like this whole thing to work at some point.'

'Yeah.'

'I feel like I'm playing Russian Roulette.'

Duncan went back to the headlines on his phone.

I texted Lenny to say we were incoming. In a flash he replied that all was well; he would see us soon. Our train slowed down: problems on the line. At the same time, my phone lost signal. My stress levels ratcheted up another notch. I couldn't text Lenny to say we were now delayed.

Minutes later the carriage jolted. A new message from Lenny arrived: he would be wearing a purple shirt, he said, and holding his phone in his right hand.

We pulled in late. I hurried to the barriers, egging my

boyfriend on to move faster and stay by my side. Standing out from the crowd, Lenny appeared in his purple shirt as described. I did not give myself any time to register how I felt, what he looked like, if he met my expectations. Instead I switched to Socialite Mode, gave him a hug, quipped about trains, introduced Duncan, then finally inhaled.

'Thank goodness you're here,' said Lenny. 'Gordon's been doing circles in the car park.'

He led us to the forecourt. Duncan elbowed me as we went, reminding me to keep my phone's internet on so Nicholas and Clo could monitor our movements remotely. Together we bundled into the back of the car, where we said hello to Gordon. These men seemed normal.

Didn't they?

Lenny took his place and we were off – the two 'grown-ups' chatting engines and horse power in front of us, accelerating.

Now I had time for reflection, Lenny did resemble the picture I had in my head, minus the hiking gear. His accent was more northern than I expected, was all.

In extra-quick time thanks to Gordon's need for speed, we came into a cul-de-sac with a name that matched the address I had been given. I squeezed Duncan's hand and gave an approving nod. Lenny's blue sports car was parked out front. 'Look at this beauty,' he beamed. Indoors: a welcoming scene of board games, wine glasses, books and a well-laid, circular table.

Lenny and his friend were already in their element: Gordon pulling down military medals he'd collected; Lenny clapping his hands at the wine and chocolate, saying we could get 'sozzled' while he paced beside the table. I disappointed him by asking for water instead – I wanted to keep a clear head – while Duncan drained his first glass without delay.

The older men had met at work decades ago, we heard. They talked of hosting constant draughts nights – six evenings a week sometimes, with the seventh switching to chess. 'It's said they played draughts in the Trojan War,' said Lenny, urging us to look up the history. The more they went on, the harder it became not to share in their enthusiasm.

After ordering pizzas, we sat round the table, Lenny and Gordon introducing the basics of the game. The pieces called 'men', the flying kings, muffins, the crowned head, the four-handed variations. I tried my best to follow. At points I thought I had it. Then I didn't. 'It'll make more sense as we're playing,' Lenny assured me.

We partnered up – me to Lenny; Duncan to Gordon – and began to work together in our teams. I had no idea what I was doing.

Every time something went okay, Lenny said sweetly, 'Great work, partner.' Within minutes I regressed to grinning each time I won his approval. Alas, success at actual draughts was more elusive for me.

Wanting a break, I offered to make tea, then became immediately annoyed at myself for spontaneously taking on that role as the only woman present. 'I'll show you where things are,' said Lenny, escorting me to the kitchen. Together we retrieved the cups. The kettle wheezed. 'Oh, it's *so* nice to meet you,' he said. 'I can't stop smiling!'

I smiled back. 'It's really nice to meet you too,' I said, feeling that this was true – while also feeling wary of being too encouraging, too fast.

(Was Lenny fatherly? What were his vibes?)

Pizzas arrived. The grown-ups insisted on paying, but I snuck some cash into Gordon's hand, anxious to contribute on the sly.

Hours passed. I lagged behind in game after game, losing 'men' in droves. 'You're doing *very* well,' Lenny insisted after yet another duff move saw me penalised once more. I sagged onto my elbows. 'It really doesn't matter,' he said.

On the plus side, the fear of murder had shrunk; was no bigger now than a fleck of a dot of tomato sauce on a small wooden counter. The wine had made friends of everyone. Lenny told Duncan about the difficulties he had relating to his son. The men talked about the terrors of physically ageing. Everyone swapped favourite book titles.

At one point, Lenny answered a call from his mum, and kept her company as we played. *He's a nice man*, I thought. *One of the good ones.*

Still, I could feel myself wilting from losing and the avalanche of new social activity. It was clear that Lenny and Gordon could play all night, but the deadline for the very latest train I'd planned to catch was chugging towards us. With 40 minutes to go, I suggested I call a cab.

'We never pass on an excuse to drive!' said Lenny, insisting they were sober. Him, I wasn't so sure about. Gordon, though, hadn't touched his glass for a while. He took the keys.

\*

Our return to the station was like a race, me gripping the roof of the car to stay vertical. Arriving at the other end far sooner than any sat nav could have estimated, Duncan and I stepped out of the car and onto the pavement. Lenny leaned out of the passenger window. 'How do we do this then?' he asked.

'How's about a hug?'

He opened the door and stood up. 'That's something only the lady can suggest.' As we hugged, he continued, 'It's so nice to meet you. You're such a lovely girl. I've got a huge smile on my face.'

I echoed that it was nice to meet him, as my mind homed in on 'girl'.

His arms came back to his sides. 'Can I call you some-times?' He turned to my boyfriend. 'Is that okay? I don't want to intrude on anything.'

I answered for myself that it was fine.

And then we were off.

'I enjoyed that,' said Duncan while we walked. 'The con-versation was easy.'

I agreed. It had been easy. And also, at the same time . . .

'Lenny seemed very, *very* happy to see us. Is it wrong that I find that difficult?'

Duncan followed me onto the escalator. 'He probably thought that you'd be a psychopath and was relieved to find you weren't.'

'I could still be a psychopath for all he knows.'

'Think about it: Gordon was his safe guy.'

'You're my safe guy,' I said.

I wanted to pull Duncan in for a kiss, but the man was

allergic to public displays of affection. Instead I gave his ear a peck and lovingly pinched his arse.

'Hey!'

On the train minutes later, as Duncan napped and lolled with an open mouth, my phone pinged. It was Lenny.

*Thank you. Thank you, Georgie. If you two are up for it, I'd really like to meet again. I'm thrilled to bits you were brave enough to visit. And I'm thrilled to bits you were up for spending time with me. Top news on all fronts!*

There was promise there, I thought. A decent start. I composed a reply, wishing him and Gordon a good weekend. Sent. Sorted. My eyelids closed.

The phone pinged again. Duncan shifted. 'What's happening?'

'It's Lenny.'

'What's he saying?'

'He says: "LOL. I'm going to dream about you guys tonight . . ."' I paused. 'Is that strange?'

'Yeah.'

'He must be drunk still.'

'Lenny's going to dream of me? Paedo.'

'Firstly, you're not a child. Neither am I, *still*. Secondly, he's dreaming of us, not just you.'

'Double paedo,' said Duncan.

I took a couple of days to rest and recover. Assured Nicholas and Clo that no one had died. Swam lengths at our local pool. Inched through a new edit of the shark book.

When I next looked at my inbox, I found another gushing message from Lenny. It suggested I *must be a witch* for making him smile every time he thought of me. That same day a couple more text messages came through. Lenny was proposing we make draughts night a monthly event.

I felt like I ought to be pleased. Instead I was concerned. Thirty-plus years of being a daughter told me his delight was unsustainable.

The next morning, I received another email from Lenny, despite not having yet responded to its predecessor. When I clicked on it, I saw that he had copied in his son.

My eyes widened. I had no idea if he had even mentioned my existence to his son before; now this was happening? He wrote:

*I've cc'd this to Wyn (hiya Wyn!) because he could do with more exposure to words and writers and I reckon there's plenty of good material to read in these messages! Georgie is a pal, Wyn.*

*How's the city? How's your mother?? If she's heard of me, say hiya from me. What does she think of your project, I wonder?! Lol.*

Pausing on Lenny's messages, hoping inspiration would strike me later, I immersed myself in other parts of the inbox. I felt increasingly perturbed about some of the men who had written – not to mention the state of adult relationships more generally. There seemed to be some major gaps in communication.

Such as this, in one man's first email:

*Keen on the sound of your ad. Above your age range
(73!), separated, one adult son. Made my living in sales
for years, then started a company of my own. Now
based in Peterborough.*

*Very drawn to the notion of an intimate relationship
with an adopted daughter about your age. I
masturbate with this in mind every now and again.
Hoping you are slender, shaven, submissive and
appreciative of bisexual lifestyles.*

*RSVP Love T xx*

Being neither shaven nor generally submissive, I was
fairly sure we were not destined for great things. Yet the
bounce-back message – about my long-term relationship,
about my wishes, about my clear quest for something
platonic – did not deter this penfriend.

The second email:

*Georgina, Thank you for responding. Since you have a
partner my interest in your advert is most likely
immaterial. I am drawn to the notion of being a
benevolent but stern father to a daughter. Making you
act and dress like a late teen and introducing you to an
array of regimes and sexual disciplines. Any rebellious
behaviour would lead to swift corporal punishment.*

*Should that sound OK I'm pleased to answer any
questions and move forward. T.*

No, 'T'. Let us not move forward.

I supposed there could be respondents out there who

had never experienced purely friendly connections with younger women; who, partly thanks to the internet's wily algorithms, presumed the word 'daughter' I'd used in the ad was code for getting their cock out. (Or putting it in.)

What was becoming unignorable was that the space I had made with my dadvert could be claimed and distorted in ways I didn't want.

And yet, weirdly, I was almost grateful for men like 'T'. There was plainly no mistaking his intentions. The 'T's I could see a mile off, then take evasive action: thanks and no thanks.

Whereas the messages that skipped near desire and away from it – like Harold's noise, perhaps; like Lenny's dream – those were the tricky ones.

Was I wrong to think that a reference to home owner-ship was a covert way to suggest somewhere we might meet in private?

Was *every* allusion to being single a warning?

Was *any* kiss at the end of a message a red flag?

'Right, guys. This is crucially important.' Three writer friends and I sat in the loud, dark corner of a South London pub, united by the sticky square of a table. We hadn't met in person for several months. 'Are you ready?'

'Yes,' at least one of them said.

'Okay. So.' I cleared my throat. 'Is there any circum-stance under which someone who's not your close friend or family member can say they'll dream of you, and it not be creepy?'

My friends looked at each other.

'Er . . .'

'No.'

'Unlikely.'

I put down my glass. 'Didn't think so.'

Zakia asked where the question had come from.

I told them everything. They listened. They nodded. They had ideas.

Matt leaned in to speak over the bar noise. 'You need referrals. The kind of people answering your ads are necessarily going to be the kinds of people who have lots of problems. Normal people aren't going to respond.'

'You could argue that a normal person wouldn't have put an ad out like this in the first place,' I replied.

Zakia asked what I was looking for.

'Possibly a hybrid of Michael Palin and Ian Hislop.'

'We could do that,' said Leander without a pause. Leander was an actor as well as a writer, and said he knew 'someone who *knows* someone who knows Ian Hislop'.

'See?' Matt sat back. 'Referrals! *That's what I mean.*'

Zakia tapped my hand. 'What else are you looking for?'

'Someone who's platonic and reliable and is there and can share things and has interesting stories.'

'How about a dad who's the same age as you?' said Matt. 'That's basically what you're looking for, right? Someone platonic and fun you can hang out with.'

I referred him to a man who had contacted me days earlier. *I'm a bit below the age range you specify*, he had written, *at 46 myself.* The man was uncle to an 11-year-old boy, and said:

*I believe I've wanted children my whole life.*

*You referenced that this isn't a sexual thing for you and that's something that hit me too. In my efforts to find someone to be that person in my life I've wondered if I could be a special person for them. I've spent time in the arena of kink and fetish because of knowing about the Daddy/Little Girl element there. My explorations showed me that wasn't where I would find what I wanted . . .*

*I am curious about what motivates people, which has led me into the hobbies of landscapes, serial killing and, to a degree, what some call conspiracies . . .*


'I want someone who's a) not a serial killer,' I said, 'and b) old enough not to want sex anymore.'

'Have you seen the STI stats in nursing homes recently?' countered Matt. 'They're all at it.'

'Fine. Someone who's old, who's decided that sex is behind them, and who's comfortable with that.'

There were some tentative half-nods of agreement.

Matt would not settle. 'Why don't you go around asking good dads you know whether they have any decent friends who might want to be your father?'

'Won't the dads think it's a ruse and that I'm actually asking *them* to be my father? That's what I'd think.'

'I wonder how things would be going if you were look-ing for mothers instead,' pondered Zakia.

'Oh God,' I said. 'So different.'

Everyone nodded in unison.

\*

Yet mothers could be difficult too. The next time I called mine, her phone recognised my number, as it always did. Nevertheless, she answered with an 'Oh!' after a few rings. It was as if hearing my voice on the line was a total surprise to her. 'The prodigal daughter returns,' she said.

'What's that supposed to mean?'

'To what do I owe this honour?'

'Are you trying to say I don't call you? I do call you.'

'Is that so?'

Before I could gather myself, she moved on. I decided not to tell her about Lenny, Submissive-Shaven Guy, or any others. Instead I prompted my mother for the latest notes about her life. The responses I received were surface level. Flatly delivered updates about Pilates, neighbours, street parking.

I asked if she wanted to stay for a weekend. 'Duncan and I have places to take you. I think we might have found the ultimate almond croissant – it's only up the road.'

Mum made a non-committal sound. Muttered that the train tickets would be too expensive.

'Shall we come down to you then instead?'

'Can do,' she said, without enthusiasm. 'It's up to you, isn't it? It's your life.'

'I guess.'

I went quiet.

So did she.

After the call I looked up the exact origin of 'prodigal'. Verified that it referred to a parable from the Bible, in which a son demands money from his father, squanders it, returns to his gracious parent as a sinner, and is generously forgiven in a way he barely deserves. According to the dictionary, a prodigal son was 'a man or boy who has left his family in order to do something that the family disapprove of and has now returned home feeling sorry for what he has done'.

So Mum felt I had reasons to repent.

I hung my head and shook it, wanting to shake off the clash I could sense coming.

———

My mother and I sat in the front of her car on our way back from the supermarket. I was 25; Granny Codd was alive; we had just visited her at the care home. Behind the wheel, Mum acted more angrily than usual at the way other people were driving: not using their indicators, going too slowly, going too fast. I sat on my hands, looking out of the window, hoping I could dissolve the web in my brain. It had been an eventful week.

Mum interrupted my thoughts. 'I've got something to tell you when we get back,' she said, grimly. 'It's important.'

I asked what it was.

'Not now. It'll have to wait until we get home.'

'Why mention it now if you're not going to tell me?'

Mum did not elaborate.

I considered staying silent too. Couldn't do it. 'Tell me.'

'No.'

'What if I already know what it is?'

'I don't think you do,' she snapped.

'What if I do?'

Silence.

'Tell me!'

'I said "no". You'll have to wait.'

We reached the junction beside my old primary school.

'It's about my father, isn't it.'

My mother braked hard. 'What about your father?'

The air disappeared from the car.

———

# 14

# MOTHER

Clear-Headed Clive in the mountains sent a new email. He told me about his youngest child, a woman in her early twenties, with whom he seemed to have the strongest relationship. She lived in Scandinavia and they regularly spoke on the phone.

He sounded so enthused about her life, collecting and sharing the details as if his daughter was a national treasure.

*She took a tumble the other day and hurt her leg; out celebrating a promotion! X-ray showed no breakage, luckily, though it looks very sore and is holding her back from her usual outdoors activities, poor thing.*

I paused.

I needed more high-quality fathers like Clive. Reminders of why I had started this project, and what I might stand to gain if it worked out.

Around the world were various Father of the Year Award organisations, a phenomenon with iterations in multiple countries.

In the category of inspiring everyday dads I found Ben Taylor, 2018 winner in the US. Taylor was nominated by his son, who wrote:

> My dad has a long commute to his regular job and then works at night fighting fires ... What's more amazing about my dad is that he still finds time to coach my teams, to do the laundry for mom on weekends, and to teach all three of his kids to work hard, be respectful, and have good manners. (I'm told I have really good manners for a 12-year-old!)

There was an award for Brent Johnson, too, a 2019 prize recipient, who learned guitar and established a not-for-profit to distribute music for families with 'multi-disabled children' – his response to the challenges faced by his music-loving son, a boy with cerebral palsy, blindness and seizures.

I wasn't as touched by that year's other winning stories, including one of a CEO who'd so bravely ... raised his stock price 600 per cent. Or the bizarre 2015 decision to award ex-president George W. Bush.

*George W. Bush: Father of the Year.*

A few hundred thousand Iraqi civilians might take issue with that one.

In his acceptance speech, Bush did say being a father had helped him quit drinking long-term and get sober, which I found surprising in a less scornful way. And there were more surprises out there. Such as the fact that, between 2009 and 2019, the number of families headed by lone-parent males grew by 22 per cent in Britain. This meant that 14 per cent of all single-parent families – some 400,000 in total – were headed by fathers alone.

These days, 7 per cent of full-time stay-at-home parents are fathers. Not an equal amount to their maternal counterparts by any measure, yet still more than I'd expected.

As my tangential thought processes played out online, an obvious realisation kept repeating: just as not all men who father are 'fatherly', being a female who has a child does not guarantee 'motherly' qualities.

Of course.

Of *course*.

I knew that.

There could well be someone out there, a parallel version of me, who was just as unsure about the virtues and purpose of mums as I was about dads. Unsure – or even forcefully opposed.

A UK government survey on historic child sexual abuse, for instance, saw mothers identified as an abuser for 1 per cent of men and 1.6 per cent of women. While this was a lower statistic than that identified for fathers (the abusers of 4.3 per cent of male survivors and 5.8 per cent of female survivors), it nevertheless meant that as many as 1 in 100 men, and 8 in 500 women had experienced their mothers in this extreme, distressing and traumatic way. Statistically, at the secondary school I attended, between 17 and 18 of my peers could have been in this group.

Other types of abuse – such as neglect, discrimination and manipulation – are harder both to measure and survey.

As author Peg Streep has said, when interviewed about

her non-fiction book *Mean Mothers*, the 'cookie-cutter of the good mother doesn't take into account that the woman who gave birth has her own personality, has her own way of looking at things, has her own reactivity'.

I thought about Carl's mother – my paternal grandmother. That first and only phone call we had about Carl.

It would take a while for me to learn that she had not shared the whole truth with me back then; to see that this woman had her own way of looking at things. Her own reactivity.

The main issue for Carl now was throat cancer, she said.

But he was in remission, she said.

Poor Caroline died from cot death, she said.

Not the whole truth.

For the first time in several years, I looked up the notice about Carl's dead child; this girl who had been his daughter in a way I never had.

*Loving you always, Angel,* it said. *Mummy & Daddy xxx*

According to the internet, cot death was 'a sudden, unexpected and unexplained death of an apparently healthy baby'.

No. Not the whole truth.

Not wanting Lenny's son to feel ignored, I eventually answered them both. Saying hello, asking after Wyn's week, I felt like a weird old relation being coaxed from the family cupboard.

*I'm glad you're around,* Lenny answered a few hours later, now keeping his son out of the loop. *You represent a very pleasant opportunity to write without fear or favour.*

And suddenly it struck me that this, too, was part of the problem.

I was 'representing' things. To Lenny and to others.

Connecting to the real, hard underneath was too risky, perhaps – for us all.

I was looking for extra guidance when I found the Fatherhood Institute, a not-for-profit describing itself as 'the UK's fatherhood think-and-do tank'. The institute conducted research, ran campaigns and lobbied to help 'dismantle barriers to UK fathers' care of infants and children'.

Dismantling barriers to fathers' care. That's what I needed.

Dr Jeremy Davies, the institute's head of impact and communications, spoke to me via a call from Morocco, where he and his partner were fixing up a property. I wanted to connect with him over British dads: what made them tick, or tock; what gave them reason to bolt or come close. In response, he focused in on the obstructions – infrastructural obstacles; the systemic things that 'add an automatic pressure on mothers to do it all' and so keep dads out of the picture.

Quickly Jeremy reintroduced the topic Neil and I had spoken about at the wedding: maternity services – the starting block for being a UK parent. Like Neil, Jeremy echoed that the way these services operate is 'entirely woman-focused. They do nowhere near enough to engage with the fathers who most of the time are in the room – and if they're not, they would be if they were *invited* in – to view their journey into fatherhood as important from a state point of view: an important journey that should be acknowledged in very basic, low-cost ways.'

(His words would come back to me later as I read an article stating that, in all the 88 pages written for healthcare professionals on birth, the NHS guidance failed to mention the words 'father' or 'partner'. Not once.)

'The reason that matters,' said Jeremy, 'going back to the anthropological narrative, is that the pregnancy, and the first few months of a baby's life, are the period where fundamentally he *is* a second parent. There's no getting away from that. He can't carry the pregnancy, he can't give birth, he can't breastfeed, but that doesn't mean there's nothing going on with him. We know that once the baby arrives, unless he's literally 300 miles away, the hormones are going to kick in. That will go against everything he has been told and learnt: that this is all women's stuff.

'That sets up an internal conflict, which fortunately, the evidence tells us, the vast majority of fathers cope with really well: they work it all out, they roll their sleeves up, and get on with it as best they can. But we also know – because straight away they have no choice but to be positioned as a secondary parent, and the parenting-leave system absolutely spells that out; as far as the state's concerned, you're nowhere – secondary parents can very easily slip into "I don't matter. She's better at it than I am. It's her job. It's her natural state. I'm not interested," whatever, whatever.'

'Huh.'

'And it's not that I'm saying everyone in a family must, by the time the baby is 9 months old, be working two and a half days a week and looking after the baby the rest of the time. It's not about that. It's about giving families the power to make better decisions about who's going to do what and when, rather than what we do right now, which I would call social engineering: we force mothers to be the leading parents, and we force fathers to be forever the secondary.'

Perhaps I was forcing the dads to remain secondary. Perhaps I could be doing more to include them.

Peter, my quest instigator, sent me a quote on Facebook, allegedly first spoken by Anthony Hopkins. I imagined it coming through Hannibal Lecter's face-cage, which made for an interesting thought experiment. Now I tried hearing it in Peter's voice:

*None of us are getting out of here alive, so please stop treating yourself like an afterthought. Eat the delicious food. Walk in the sunshine. Jump in the ocean. Say the truth that you're carrying in your heart like hidden treasure. Be silly. Be kind. Be weird. There's no time for anything else.*

I imagined meeting Peter at his seaside home near Swansea. Bringing him in on all this strangeness, while I still had a chance.

I would do it, I told myself. I properly would.

It seemed right to include Mum more too. Duncan and I travelled down to the coast as planned. Took my mother to her nearest chocolate shop for drinks and treats and bowls of chocolate ice cream with chocolate sauce. She was cheerful then, more talkative, the barbs of our last phone call melting away. As we basted our insides with calories I reflected on how, as a mother, she gave me lots of what I wanted. I still had my childhood bedroom, even; Schwarzenegger photograph and everything.

Plus, unlike Harold, she seemed to appreciate my sense of humour – most of the time. For example, earlier that day, over a shared pot of Earl Grey, I had called an old school nemesis a cunt. My mother hadn't batted an eyelid. In fact, she had laughed and agreed with me. Surely a rare quality from a parent.

Coming up on my tide of gratitude, I proclaimed, 'This cunting sundae is cunting lush.'

Mum looked at Duncan and back to me. '*How* did you develop such a revolting vocabulary? You're getting worse.'

'Uncle Jeff showed me the ropes,' I said, defensive.

'Even Jeff doesn't swear like that.'

'He does! He taught me how to swear, and how sledding down a staircase in a sleeping bag is an unpopular move, especially when you crash through the lower banisters. And Uncle Jon taught me how to eat up to six puddings a sitting.'

I scraped the last of the sundae sauce from the glass.

'Meanwhile, you and Granny showed me how to become addicted to chocolate. And it's *cunting lush*.'

'I apologise for my daughter,' Mum said to Duncan.

After chocolate, we met with her friend Nick – the one who liked sea swims and cakes – for a lumbering walk and more sugary items. As Mum and Duncan chatted in front, I asked Nick about being a father. I knew he was a good one; a dad who listened, took an interest, showed concern; who was *there* for his son. Since I kept hearing that fatherhood changed people, I wanted to know if it had changed him.

'I don't know if it's changed me,' he replied. 'Not really. Apart from making me totally broke at a period of life when I'd much rather be drinking Pimm's in my retirement penthouse by the sea.' Nick went wistfully quiet, then: 'I'd say becoming a father changed my attitudes. There is an interesting thing that happens. When your partner is pregnant and in labour, heading to hospital, there is no question you would save her life over the child's if you had to pick between them. But as soon as that baby's out, straight away, it's the opposite. You would pick to save your baby.'

Our footsteps gave good rhythm for a few metres. In the quiet, my mind scanned for a certain statistic and found it: that one in seven women experience postnatal depression; and one in ten men, at least, experience it too. Just the other day I had written down a few choice quotes from these men, including: 'I would tell my wife that this was the end of our life . . . All I could envision was the cycle of hell that was going to be our lives.'

Then I mentally retrieved another statistic: that 10 per cent of non-resident fathers never have *any* contact with their children.

'I don't think every dad would pick their baby,' I said to Nick.

'Probably not,' he replied. 'But that's how I felt.' He ducked to avoid a branch and held it away from me.

'Some men might even feel like throwing their babies in bins,' I added.

Nick scratched his chin. 'I suppose that's always possible.'

Lenny's compliments escalated. Taking time to tell me how much, again, he enjoyed our correspondence, he wrote: *I think you're strong enough to say 'Whoa. Stop Lenny' if I say something out of order. I've always wanted a girl who could do that. What more could a bloke ask for?*

Always wanted a girl who could do that . . . Even *in* context it sounded like a nod to a girlfriend, partner, romance.

The temptation to build a duvet igloo and dwell in it for a week or more was mounting. Instead I made myself stay where I was and write back. Trying still not to judge. Trying not to come to a wrong conclusion.

*When you wrote in your last email that you 'always wanted a girl who could do that', what did you mean? That seemed like it could be quite an important sentence.*

Lenny responded later that evening.

*'A girl who could do that.' Apologies. Thought I'd clarified. All my life I've wanted a girl with the force of personality and intellect to not be strong armed by me. To hold her ground and say 'You're wrong! Here's why.' I*

*once lived with a girl. After some time she concluded
her future did not lie with me. I was tremendously (!)
hurt. After asking her why, she gave one reason that we
were always clashing. But to me we had almost never
clashed. I believed we had debates, we had union
evolving from my points and her counterpoints. We had
discourse. And to her mind we were clashing. So this is
the kind of girl I'm not after. I prize the reciprocity of
discussion. I prize opposing viewpoints. I prize those
whose intellect and insights enable them to stand up
for their position but to adapt this when discourse
unearths new facts or spotlights hitherto unnamed
flaws. How the heck else can any of us grow unless our
views and prejudices and persuasions are called into
question??? So this is the kind of girl I've been after all
my life. A girl who can question my biases, convictions
and understanding. Never found one though . . .*

The romantic comparisons. The dot, dot, dot.
And so many *girls*.

I couldn't leave it. I tried once more with Lenny a few
days later. Tried to get us both down to the real, hard
underneath.

*Back to the 'girl' line for a minute – the word 'girl' can
carry such a lot in it. I wondered if you'd meant that
you'd always wanted a 'daughter', but then, with what
you've written in your latest email, it sounds like
that's not quite it; maybe more like you've always*

*wanted a female presence who could do that. Is
that right?*

In his own reply came the couched answer I had suspected:

*As for 'girls', I meant girlfriend, wife, significant other.
Not once have I ever imagined having a daughter. Not
in your case, not in any case. I could see you were
someone with a sharp mind, clear self-awareness,
unique personality and clear imagination. Those four
attributes were the reasons that prompted me to
make contact. Finding those four attributes in a single
person is unusual. But they are the attributes that,
nowadays, I value, appreciate and approve of. I'm a
bloke who likes girls. But I've still never found one with
the personality to handle me. If only I had. That's what I
intended at the very beginning of all this . . .*

    *OK. It's tea time.*

# 15
# FATHER'S DAY

*So when are you coming to Mumbles?*

Peter of the cruise ship was asking more about the visit I had tentatively agreed to. He was now requesting actual dates, even saying I could stay for a night – *your bedroom awaits*. He asked, too, what I was up to.

*Unsuccessfully courting strangers to be my new dad, thanks to you*, I did not write, while steadfastly ignoring the bedroom reference.

Retaining his role as original prankster, Peter also spent more time amassing jokes, doctored photographs and clips, and sending these to me. There were images of goofball terrorists making dumb mistakes. Videos of a vixen and cubs in his garden, for whom he was reportedly leaving out dog food. A picture of a sheep in suspenders, captioned 'Valentine's Day in Wales'.

Occasionally he also now mentioned his cancer.

I contemplated the idea of seeing him next at his funeral. I thought more about it being too late to pass on the news of what he had set in motion. That would not feel good, I thought.

Moments later I thought about losing someone close to me. Again.

That would feel horrendous.

Peter sent a picture of an elephant holding a lion cub in its trunk. It was so obviously Photoshopped, and also somehow dadly. I said, 'Aw.'

In the next moment I suggested a concrete date for meeting up.

As soon as my message sent I started to fidget. Rearranged all my stationery and the positioning of my pigs. As the afternoon unfolded, a hyper-protective offshoot of my imagination created a scenario in which Peter didn't have cancer after all; that the libido he mourned was in fact fully functioning. Somehow he knew that death – cancer death especially – was my Achilles heel.

When Duncan returned home he listened to my troubles. Before dinner. During dinner. After dinner. I explained that I didn't want the regret of not sharing my project with Peter in case he *was* ill, and genuine. Only, what if he wasn't, and the Facebook chats and jokes were designed to lull me into a false sense of security? We'd never spent time alone on the cruise, just the two of us. Mum had been only paces away at most. Besides, remember Ted Bundy? *Anyone* could be demonic.

In the flurry I threw out a newly unearthed statistic. 'More than *90 per cent* of rape and sexual assault victims know their attacker,' I quoted, aghast.

At bedtime, Duncan concluded I must not, under any circumstances, go to Peter's house because of 'stranger danger'. I could still go to Mumbles, however, if I stuck to public spaces.

I took Duncan's arm and looked into his eyes. 'What if I turn up and he has lunch planned at his place? I can't say, "No, I'm not going to your house."'

'It's pretty risky.'

Thinking aloud, I wondered if secreting a knife on my person was the answer.

In the silence that followed, I realised: I was planning a situation in which I felt there was a chance of not only needing a weapon, but of needing to stab a six-foot-something man with it in defence.

I took Duncan's arm again. Asked if he would come with me.

'With you where?'

'Mumbles for a day.'

Rubbing his eyes, he dragged up his phone for a swift online search.

'There is a waterpark near there,' he reported. 'With slides and a wave machine.' He asked when I was planning to go.

'Hang on.' I got up, sped to fetch the calendar, and sped back with it. 'I suggested *this* day but you're away then. How about—' I dowsed above the page with my index finger '—*that day*.'

Duncan said that could work.

I reached for a pen to make it official, only to notice the small, printed scrawl that named it as Father's Day.

I told Duncan. He said, 'Fine.'

'But won't you want to do something with your dad then instead?'

'Nah. Father's Day isn't really a thing.'

'Oh.' I wriggled back under the duvet. 'So I could be seeing Peter on Father's Day. Is that weird? Do you think I should—'

My boyfriend's leg twitched. Asleep.

I texted Peter, offering the new date. I didn't mention its relevance; didn't want him to feel he was being put on the spot.

*Looking forward*, he quickly replied. *Have rearranged all my other engagements my secretary very efficient. Love to Mother.* Instinctively I grinned, before Serious Planning Face took over.

From across the street, I heard my neighbour pacing. Quietly frantic.

Duncan would accompany me on the train, we decided the next day. He would say hello to Peter and take the details of his number plate, then leave us to have some time solo while I kept him posted on my location via text. At the end of the day, my boyfriend would wait at the station for my return.

There was a lot that could go wrong, yet I could think of nothing foolproof – except not going at all.

I bought train tickets and the countdown began. Peter said he had booked us lunch for two. Perhaps I would not need a knife.

Shower time became a daily rehearsal: how to tell this man what he had prompted. How to perfect the tone.

As I practised, I received another joke message from Peter. It was the picture of a smiling baby, accompanied by a caption: *EVERY TIME I CRY THEY STICK A TIT IN MY MOUTH. I LOVE MY LIFE.*

'Jesus Christ.'

I told him my eyes were rolling.

At the same time I made a mental note: best adjust expectations for our meeting.

In the run-up to Mumbles, Clear-Headed Clive suggested we switch our email correspondence to the telephone. I felt the now-familiar stab of panic that came with unpeeling a fresh layer of anonymity. I also felt relief: I was keen to go deeper and make new progress, as well as to break from interpreting words through a screen.

It turned out I had planted the seed for this telephone call by accident. I had signed off one of my messages with *Speak soon!* and the phrase was taken more literally than intended.

*Was surprised how you ended your email, about speaking,* Clive replied. *I did think, at first, it was a normal ending – one of my brothers always signs off in this way – however, you exclaimed, so guess you were thinking it?*

Let's give this a go, I decided.

*Fuck it.*

For caution's sake, I used the same tactic I'd tried with Grant's workplace, dialling Clive's number in a way that kept mine hidden. As the tone filled my ears my shoulders clenched. I made myself stretch out against a wall.

'Is that you, Georgina?'

'It is!'

'Well, here we go then!'

Clive's voice exuded warmth; I could hear the smile in his words and smiled back at the softness of his Irish accent. Yet it took me a while to unclench. 'I find people a bit much,' he said, not long into the call, having described the tranquil area in which he lived. 'I do like my solitude.'

I reacted by asking if I should leave him alone.

'No, not you. Don't be silly!'

I became insta-child and giggled.

For a while we talked about politics. I sensed him scoping out my views – as I was scoping out his. We discussed his retirement. 'I thought I'd do lots of gardening,' he laughed, 'but it's a fucking pain! I'm looking for something else now. I want to do something right. Something worthwhile.'

The notion hung between us.

'It's funny,' he continued. 'When you first become a parent, you're not really very good at it. Well, some things yes and some things no. It takes practice and experience. Then it's almost a bit too late and they don't need you any-more. I don't think I've ever been as good a dad as I am now. You get better at this.'

'Maybe that's why grandparents are so great,' I said. '*Some* grandparents,' I corrected. 'If you're lucky.'

'That's right. If you're lucky.' His voice kept smiling. 'Hm. Georgina . . . Georgina . . . Can I call you anything shorter? Georgina is a bit formal. What about George? Georgie? Georgy with a "y"?'

I shifted on my seat.

'Does anyone ever call you that?'

'Sometimes . . .'

'Like, "Hey there, Georgy girl," ' he sang. 'I'm of that era,
see. Georgy. Can we go with that?'

I forced my shoulders back again. 'All right.'

'And you can call me Cly. Much friendlier. Or whatever
you want, really.'

'Okay. That sounds like a plan.' I tested it. 'Bye, Cly.
Hi, Cly.'

'And we'll talk again?'

'Yes, please.'

'Okay then, m'lovely,' he said in his lovely accent. 'We'll
do that.'

An hour later I was still smiling.

The subject of grandparents re-emerged later that week.
Duncan's mum was making comments; not-so-subtly pressing us to give her a set of grandchildren. It was something she
did from time to time, saying things like, 'I've got all your
baby books on standby, Duncan,' and, 'We're decorating the
room upstairs . . . so the grandchildren can play in it.'

The four of us were out for dinner again. Though we sat
opposite each other, Duncan's dad didn't speak to me at all.
Until his wife talked about how, 'When you have kids,
Georgie—'

'If,' I said.

Duncan's father's face turned my way.

'It's my womb,' I clarified.

He folded his arms. 'There I was thinking it was a joint
decision.'

'It is a joint decision,' I said. 'Between me and Duncan.

At the same time, it's my womb. I decide what goes in there.'

The father stared at the boyfriend. Changed his expression into a *good-luck* kind of look.

'Is anyone having dessert?' sang his wife, passing out the menus.

The afternoon before Father's Day I texted Peter to check he would definitely still turn up at the station.

*Yes most definitely was going to get in touch*, he replied. *Catch up on the gossip and life very excited. Have a safe journey I'll be there a carnation in my epaulette so you recognise me.*

I talked out loud as I prepared my backpack. Reminded myself he might not know it was Father's Day. Looked at the kitchen knives. Left them in the drawer where they belonged.

Overnight I felt extremely sick.

In the morning Duncan and I navigated multiple transport connections and delays, until both of us were sweating from the sprints between our stops. Our second mainline train was quiet and half an hour behind schedule. It meant we missed the bus we needed.

My jaw would not unclench.

Duncan stayed silent, not wanting to interact with my stress. I could hardly blame him: I didn't want to either.

I messaged Peter.

*Typical British Rail bloody never improves*, he replied. *Not to worry your No 1 guide and lovely lunch companion awaits. I'm out and about, sun is shining, carnation pinned.*

Another bus pulled up. We boarded and miraculously

were back on track: our final planned train left with us on it. I took multiple trips to the bathroom. Anxiety gripped my stomach at the thought that Peter would be different to how I remembered him; that our dynamic would be different; that he could be gravely unwell.

It was then that I noticed the state of my shoes. Once they had been pristine, black and smart. Now they were a faded grey, with a new hole above the big toe. I could not believe I had missed the hole. My stomach throbbed.

Duncan was preparing to play on water slides all day. That was his plan. I returned to where he sat and seized on the opportunity for distraction. 'You know you'll be a solo adult male in a place filled up with children in bathing suits?' I asked.

'Mm.'

'If anyone else did that you'd probably call them a paedo.'

It wasn't clear Duncan had heard. He was scrolling his phone with intent, skimming adverts for new bikes.

'Fingers crossed you don't get beaten up,' I said. Then, 'I'm jealous. *I* want to go to the waterpark. I want to go with you.'

'Mm.'

As the industrial smoke of Port Talbot's steel factories billowed into view, I asked my boyfriend for details of the day's safe word.

He kept scrolling.

'Hello? *Hello?*'

Duncan's eyes flickered from his phone. 'Sorry?'

'The warning signal. In case I get in trouble.'

'How about, "Did you enjoy the swimming?"'

'*What?*'

'What?'

'There's a pretty high chance I'll ask that accidentally!' Flexing my big toe against its hole, I said, 'How about "Scotch egg"? I don't think I've ever said that without meaning to.'

'If you want.'

'And to register you've heard and understood, you'll reply with a line that includes the word "coleslaw". Like: "Hey, Duncan, don't forget to buy a Scotch egg for your dad while you're in town." And you go: "Did he say he wanted coleslaw too?" And I say, "Yep, absolutely." Then you ring off and call the police straight away and tell them all you know.'

'Mm-hm.'

'Did you get that?' I elbowed him. 'Hell*ooo?*'

'I'm listening.'

'What's the safe phrase now?'

'Coleslaw.'

'Friend! This could be life or death.'

'Mm.'

I tried to grab his phone. He yanked it away.

'*I heard you.*'

'Prove it.'

We went through the protocol two more times. Sitting back in my seat I had a few seconds of rest before another thought lurched me forward. 'What if I try to call you and you're down a waterslide?'

He shrugged.

'Oh God,' I said to the windowpane. 'I am fucked.'

\*

The train slowed. We were pulling in at the station. The end of the line. I stood up and marched on the spot beside the train door. When we braked I almost fell, then stood up straight and wished I had actually fallen, in a way that cracked my head into several pieces. It would be better to be unconscious right now.

*No, it wouldn't.*

*Yes, it would.*

*No, it wouldn't.*

The doors came open. I was excited again.

Right down at the furthest end of the platform I saw him: tall and cheerful, with his neat grey hair, his glasses and a small flower in his lapel. Peter waved. I waved back. When we reached him he gave me a hug. 'Hello, lovely girl!' he said in his sing-songing south-Welsh accent. He stepped back. 'Duncan,' he added, shaking hands.

'Pleased to meet you.'

'Ah, the pleasure is all mine, boy.'

My boyfriend sniggered.

'Right!' said Peter. 'Your chariot awaits. Step this way.'

When we reached his car he opened the passenger door. 'Madame.' I ducked in. Once inside, he offered to drive us anywhere we wanted. I explained Duncan's plan: to get to the pool and slide around all day.

Peter peered at him in the rear-view mirror. 'The water-park? On a Sunday?'

'Yep.'

'It'll be chaos in that place. Like a circle of hell.'

'I don't mind.'

'Dear God.' Peter spoke under his breath. 'In that case,

I'll take you there.' He started the engine, glanced at me and smiled, as if he had momentarily forgotten I was beside him. 'Very good to see you, George,' he said. 'Why not for longer though, eh? It's a long way for a few hours. The pillows in your room are all fluffed.'

*Unconscious*, I thought. *In his house.*

'Because . . .' I scrabbled for an answer before producing one that didn't fit his question. 'I have something funny to tell you and I didn't want to wait,' I snorted, attempting to coax us away from weird-funny to ha-ha-ha-ha-funny. Peter, driving, made a noise of intrigue.

As we motored through town I sat on my hands, squishing them into the foam beneath me. We were in the main streets of Swansea already; time for Duncan to leave. I waved at him through the window, doing my best not to show my rising panic. 'Meet you at six-ish?'

My boyfriend waved, then went off to his watery wonderland.

Peter restarted the engine. Within minutes we joined the coastal road to Mumbles, him indicating local landmarks as we went: the old fire station, the hospital, the worst road in town. As he did, I felt the weight in my throat grow heavier. What was I doing? What did I want?

How much could this hurt?

In a gap between the tour commentary, I forced a gentle laugh. 'So . . . I've been up to something a little bit interesting lately.'

We changed lanes. 'Oh, yes?'

I asked if he remembered Invergordon.

'Yes.'

'And the practical joke you played?'

Peter tittered. 'Oh, yes.'

'Well . . .'

'Are you going to adopt me?' he asked.

A loud laugh escaped me. A real one. 'I could do.'

He chuckled.

'What I wanted to tell you is related to that actually. See, I've been doing a project since then, and, well, you inspired something.' I took a breath. 'Since the start of the year I've been putting out these adverts, or "dadverts"' – I snorted again – 'advertising to see if anyone might be willing to be my father figure? I've had quite a few people respond actually, and . . .'

I studied Peter's facial expression. All the humour and ease had drained out of it.

'That's the Olympic swimming pool,' he said.

'Oh.'

There was a pause.

'Okay,' I said.

My ears rang. I had to keep going. 'The advert said something like: "I'm friendly and fatherless, and looking for someone who might be willing to take on the role of father figure. I don't know if it'll work, it's a bit of an experiment," that sort of thing.'

'That makes me feel very uncomfortable,' Peter said.

I swallowed. 'Does it?'

'Yes, that makes me very uncomfortable. Very uncomfortable, George,' he repeated. 'It sounds like a sex bit.'

'It's not a sex bit.'

'I know how I'd read that.' He slowed the car and wafted a hand to his right. 'Bonnie Tyler's house.'

I craned to see.

'It's very strange,' he said.

'Bonnie Tyler's house?'

'No, your . . . What you've been doing.'

'Why does it make you uncomfortable, do you think?'

'I feel . . .' Peter sighed, 'vulnerable for you.'

My skin flushed. 'I can look after myself. And lots have fallen by the wayside. The ones that are a bit creepy and sex-driven. I've kept a distance. There were quite a few of those.'

'I'm not surprised, George.' He shook his head. 'Oh dear. Oh dear.'

My arms and legs were folded, my hands wedged into hard nooks. I made myself unfold them. Made myself say more. 'Some of them have been really funny, actually. I could read you a good selection later if you like.'

He pulled a face.

'Or maybe I won't . . .'

Peter drummed his fingers on the steering wheel. 'That road's the way to where the Zeta-Joneses live. Nice family. Local family.' He looked over at me. 'You're looking very well, girl. Still got good teeth.'

'Thanks?' My fingers were curling up again. I flattened them under my thighs. Told him he looked well. Asked how he was feeling.

'Can't complain, really. Still getting pain, trouble sleeping, all that. I did have a bone scan recently and they said there's no spread there. Happy days.' We took a turning for one of the beaches. The car began a steep descent. 'Everyone in Mumbles knows you're coming today.'

My voice squeaked. 'Do they?'

'We were in the pub last week and everyone started looking you up on their phones. I told them you were tall, pretty and leggy.'

'Oh God.'

'My mates were saying, "Very nice. I'd do her."'

'Wow.'

He chuckled again.

'That's gross.'

'They are barbarians round here.' His voice perked up. 'Anyway, I've got us a table for two at the most popular restaurant in town. Absolutely rammed, it is. Father's Day celebrations. Very smart.'

My pulse quickened. 'Oh, yeah? I think I saw some bits about that on my way down.'

He switched off the engine. 'We're having the Father's Day menu, if that's okay. Just right for my daughter, I thought.'

The two of us looked at each other. Both of us smirked.

Peter had taken me to a picturesque bay. As we left the car he announced it was where his ashes would be scattered. We followed a small path past the beach huts. The service was all bought and paid for, he said, and he had picked just one tearjerker song. 'Not a dry eye in the house, I'm thinking. Hit 'em where it hurts.'

'Nice one.'

'Who knows? You might be there.' He gestured towards a section of rocks by the water. 'That's my spot.'

We watched the water swirl and crash. Swirl and crash.

I sighed. 'I'll come to your funeral if you want,' I said.

He patted me on the shoulder. 'That'd be nice.'

Walking back towards the car, I came clean about the state of my shoes, pulling off the worst offender to illustrate the issue.

'No problem at all. I'll just tell them you're my hippy daughter.' He chuckled again.

I put the shoe back on. Stumbled along the shoreline. Asked if Peter ever went sea swimming. 'I don't do anything, George,' he said. 'I just go for lunches with pretty girls.' He winked.

For a moment I scowled to myself, imagining being the latest in a long line of possible daughters. The idea was disconcerting.

Then I thought about what I'd been doing: dad after dad after dad.

It took a while to find a lunchtime parking spot. During the manoeuvres I updated Duncan, knowing as I did that it was pointless: he would be slipping down slides in waves of bubbles, his phone stowed in the pocket of his jeans, inside a locker.

Peter tried another street for spaces, pointing out houses he'd attended during his decades in the fire service, describing the various infernos he had extinguished. Breaking through doors, throwing pets out of windows and into the arms of his colleagues. '*That* one,' he jabbed at a building on a parallel street, 'was a horror. We couldn't park any-where near it. Just couldn't reach the flames.'

The bistro was on the waterfront, and fuller than I thought possible. We found a place to perch at the bar, waiting for our table to become free. As per the cruise, Peter seemed to have words for everyone. While he greeted them all I had the sense that I was on display; various people stopped to introduce themselves. I shrank under the spot-light, while Peter grew.

A Moldovan waitress brought his beer and my water. She was one of Peter's favourite people in town, he announced, waxing on about what good girls we both were. She and I shared a look.

Another man interrupted us, a disturbing twinkle in his eye. A booth nearby had become free, he confided. 'You two can go sit on the loveseat.'

I hid behind my hands. 'Please. Make it stop.' When I peered through my fingers two sets of male eyes were still watching. 'You're both appalling,' I said.

Finally, we were called to our table, lunchtime begin-ning at almost half past four. I stared about me as we went. So this was what Father's Day looked like from the inside. Every table was occupied, a father or father figure at each one.

A smiling young woman delivered our menus. Peter instinctively surveyed her chest, before double-taking back to me with one of his pantomime-like facial expressions. *Dead and gone to heaven*, it said. Unaware of the perform-ance, the waitress wished us both a Happy Father's Day.

'Thank you, my dear,' said Peter. 'This is my daughter.'

She nodded, inviting us to order our drinks; none the wiser. So we were in it again.

'Have whatever you like, George. Don't hold back.'

'Thank you, Pops.' I looked up. 'A *jug* of tap water, please.'

What followed was a roving conversation, and an eye-opening one too – not least every time a waitress walked past our table.

Every time.

Between the disturbance of waitresses, I found out more about Peter than I'd previously known – information he'd formerly only hinted at. For instance: 'Sometimes mothers approach me and just want me to be involved in their children's lives.'

'Eh?'

'I met one woman on this cruise who had a little girl, and this girl was a bit besotted by me, I think. Always saying hello and running to see me. A bit weird, you know – the mother was hardly there – but I didn't mind too much. The girl was quite sweet. Anyway, the mother was all for it continuing after the cruise. She said: "Little Lily won't stop talking about you. She wants to stay with you." Used to have her sending messages and trying to get a date in the calendar.'

I laid down my fork. 'Have you *seen* the Michael Jackson child abuse documentary? Not that I'm saying you're Michael Jackson necessarily—'

He spluttered.

'—but when kids go to stay at solo men's houses it often doesn't end well.'

'I know, George. I know. It was very uncomfortable. All my friends told me: "If something happens to her, anything, you'll be in a world of trouble." I just – I would have said no anyway. It wasn't right.'

'Bleurgh.' I picked up my fork. 'Just to be clear, you approached me. This is all your fault.' I chewed through a squeaking wad of halloumi. 'Do you ever feel like you want a partner?' I asked. 'Don't answer if you don't want to.'

'I would like company sometimes. It's a bit sad, isn't it?'

'I don't know.'

'Lots of my friends get very jealous. They say: "You've done it right, Pete. Going all over the world, travelling wherever, no wife or kids to drag you down." I'm not so sure. Sometimes you want what you don't have, don't you? The grass is always greener and all that.'

'Maybe.'

'It's impossible to know, George. There's been a few times in relationships when I've been very happy and it's felt right. For a long time, I'm talking. Years. But every time they've wanted kids in the end, and that's it. Sometimes I get older women, independent-type women, sending invites to visit them or signals to start a relationship. But . . .' He shook his head. 'I'm just not into it. God knows what that's about.' He turned his attention back to his roast dinner. 'I don't have any family left in the UK now.' He gave me a nod. 'Apart from my daughter.'

I laughed. 'Thanks, Pops.'

'A pleasure.' He carved off a piece of roast lamb and held the silence.

'You never wanted kids?' I ventured.

More silence. Then: 'I had a gorgeous girlfriend years ago. Absolutely *stunning*.' He closed his eyes. 'Bit of a slapper, mind—'

'Pops!'

'Well, we were together for a while. She had this big family in Swansea, real rough they were, the brothers, the father – they hated me because I was from Mumbles; thought that made me a snob – but I liked her, you know. She had these *gorgeous* green eyes and *thick, black* hair. My God. And the boobs—'

'Inappropriate.'

'Perfection. Still, I knew something wasn't right. Money was going missing from my house; from my drawers. She denied taking it, of course. Very vocal, feisty – one day she punched one of the guys at the station; knocked him right to the floor. But that's what her family were like; ex-prison some of them. Anyway, I started hearing stories, rumours: people were telling me about seeing her in the clubs. She was very flirtatious, you know, always going out. The type to turn heads everywhere she went. But when you're with someone like that, it's difficult to – you don't *really* want to see what's going on. I liked her. She had a nice side to her. And I'm not possessive, George, that's not me, so I didn't ask much about it.

'Anyway, one day she announces to me, "Peter, I have some news. I'm pregnant and it's yours."' His eyes went up to the ceiling. 'I tell you, that very second I felt this' – he pulled out the words – '*chemical imbalance* in my brain. Like a nervous breakdown. Total depression. Total despair. Now, if it'd been a normal relationship, no issues, no complications, then I probably would have . . . I would've thought "Why not? Right. Time to settle down." But I couldn't do it. I just couldn't.

'It was terrible. I was a mess. Such huge emotions. So I told her, "You're going to have to get rid of it." Then all her family came round the fire station every single day for a week, threatening to kill me. "Let us at the bastard!" They started standing outside my house, shouting and swearing in the street. I hid in the office, hid in my house. It was horrendous. I didn't even know if the baby was mine and they're coming at me for the money.'

'It could have been yours.'

'I didn't want it, George. It never – it wouldn't have worked.'

By now, Peter had lost his comedic demeanour.

'My mental and physical health took a real beating,' he said. 'But I was hooked and it took me a long time to shake free. I still bear the scars today.'

Ultimately he insisted she have an abortion, just as Carl had wanted from Mum.

Unlike my mother, Peter's girlfriend had it.

'If my doctor told me the cancer had spread to the bones and I had six months left to live, I would take it all in and be fine,' he said. 'No problems. But if you said to me now you were pregnant, I'd have a nervous breakdown.'

'So would I.'

Peter laughed. 'You'd be wondering what I'd put in your coffee,' he said, coming back to himself.

'Remind me never to drink coffee around you.'

'Good girl, George.'

'I'm a woman.'

'Right you are.'

We sat back. My mind felt foggy.

Our late lunch meant it was almost time to meet Duncan. After Peter paid for our meal we started to leave, though not before he had sought out his Moldovan friend again. 'There we are.' He looked between us. 'My daughters.'

I frowned. 'You too?' I asked.

She shook her head. 'I don't know with this Peter,' she said.

'Don't you want a sugar daddy?' he asked her.

'WHAT?'

'Joking, George. I'm joking.'

'But are you?'

'Come on, let's go.'

My frown intensified. I didn't know with this Peter either.

In the car, heading off, I sensed we were going the wrong way, travelling in the opposite direction to the station. 'Did we take this road earlier?' I asked, already sure we hadn't.

Peter confirmed my suspicions. We were making a detour to his flat, he said.

My eyes darted to my watch. 'Duncan'll be waiting.'

'Tell him 10 more minutes. There's something I want to show you.'

I tried again. 'We only have tickets specifically for that train.'

'You've got plenty of time.'

I composed a brief text to my boyfriend and sent it on quickly, concerned.

'Won't be long,' said Peter.

Watching the suburbs pass by I focused on breathing. This was not supposed to be happening. This was not part of the plan. I wanted to trust the man. Yet I wasn't at all sure I could.

We arrived at a block of flats. Surreptitiously, shielding my phone with my bag, I started texting Duncan the address.

'In we go,' said Peter, coming round to the passenger side.

'One moment.'

The message sent. I grabbed my backpack and clutched it to my front. Followed Peter up the communal staircase. 'Shh,' he instructed, one flight in. 'My friends might be outside. Don't want to upset them.'

*Friends? Upset?* My internal risk detector went off: *Peter wants you to make less noise. If his neighbours don't know you're here, they won't notice if you never leave.*

I stomped a little harder on the steps.

Peter halted by the first-floor window. He beckoned at me, breath misting the glass. 'No sign,' he said.

I looked down to see the remains of where a large cream cake had been thrown to the grass. My insides unknotted a little.

'Do fox digestive systems like baked goods?'

'They have a hard life – why not?'

We climbed up the next flight of stairs. 'Here we are.' There was a cutesy Dalmatian doormat outside his front door. I commented on it, surprised. 'I'm in touch with my feminine side,' Peter quipped.

The door opened. I followed him into a hallway and open-plan lounge with a view of the town's grey stone

229

castle. The place was impeccably tidy. He strode to the kitchen counter and picked up a small box. 'Here we are. All yours.'

'For me?'

'Thought you might like it, George.'

It was a cosmetic face gel in fancy packaging. Apparently, he had been sold it at an airport by a woman giving out testers – '£120 down from £220, she said. I thought it seemed quite nice, you know. But what do I need it for?'

I tried to protest and hand it back. Peter wouldn't let me.

'But it's so expensive.'

'It's only money, George.'

'Really?'

'Really.'

I thanked him and unscrewed the golden lid. Took a sniff.

He asked me what it smelled like.

'I'm not sure.' I inhaled again. 'Wealth, I think.'

'I'll give you the tour.'

I checked my watch. Began to pull out my phone.

'Won't take long,' he insisted, spotting me. 'My abode is quite compact. But since you're here.'

I slipped the phone back.

'This is your bedroom,' he announced, showing me what looked like the spare. He lifted up the bedsheets. 'Clean and fresh today. I thought you might be staying longer. Never mind. Next time.'

'I thought you might be joking about that.'

'I never joke, George.'

He led me to his bedroom. 'The master suite.'

As soon as I stepped inside my body turned to ice. There, in the corner, was a giant axe, balanced within Peter's reach on a wooden platform.

A giant axe coated entirely in *metal*.

Peter reached for it.

*This is it.*

Picked it up.

My legs locked into position.

*Time to die.*

He swung back to me.

'My retirement present,' he cooed. 'The boys clubbed around and had her chromed. Isn't she a beauty?'

My voice broke. 'Impressive.'

'Get a load of that weight.' He held it out.

The heft of it pulled at my arm socket. 'Bloody hell,' I gasped. 'I expect that could do some damage.'

'If you want damage, take a look at this one.'

From atop his chest of drawers he picked up a boomerang. Long, dark and studded with rough carvings.

'A lost soul gave me this in the 1970s,' he said. 'I was working in a kitchen in Western Australia. He comes to the back door begging for food. I share what we've got and he gives me this to say thank you. Poor bugger. Proper hunting weapon, this.'

I touched the nearest edge. Sharp as a blade.

'Very effective,' Peter agreed.

Minutes later we emerged from the flat, descended the staircase, reached the car and started driving back towards the station. My mind grew murkier still.

Duncan was waiting inside the entrance, a broad smile

on his face. He had not only whizzed his way through the flumes, but infiltrated a game of laser tag between two warring families.

Peter gave me a *cwtch* – a hug – and called me 'cariad'. *Darling*. Duncan and he shook hands.

'Come again soon, my girl.'

We boarded the train, still waving.

The murk in my head solidified, then turned to mush.

# 16

# DAUGHTER

*if m saying hey . . . . . . . u maybe saying whatz this . . . . if
i ask for some talking . . . .u maybe say why?! . . . . if m
asking u for drinks . . . . . u maybe say wt nonsense . . . .
if i say i love ur profile . . . . . .u maybe saying m flirting
wt u . . . . . if i asking for frnship . . . . . . .u maybe say m
pushing . . . . . . so can u plz offer me hw to begin wid a
new exchange . . . . . . . . in fact connecting sounds great
new connecting, i saw a great movie where a line says '1
time ur living is when u r connected with some1' . . . ????
Before u reply m starting wid an ask . . . . . . . .& . . . i
seek frds ! wont disappoint surely!! Let's begin
connecting . . . stick n stones cud break ur bones, but i
wud never hurt u wid my words. gentleman's promise.*

*Quik info on me i am 6 feet tall, fair enough, have a v
athletic body, great sense of humour, and a decent
warm heart . . . .. A DREAM Sagittarian BY NATURE.*

I closed my laptop. Clear-Headed Cly aside, the stragglers still writing in to me were either too obscure or too

intense. Too aloof or too committed to being my father far too quickly.

(Didn't I want commitment?)

The consensus everywhere I turned was that I needed to cast the net wider. That I was being constrained by Britishness. One friend was heading out to Bangladesh for her studies. I gave her some dadverts to put up in her accommodation. Another friend touring South America offered to help. I emailed her words destined for Peru, Ecuador, Colombia.

I started to wonder how life would be if I had access to father figures from every culture; someone who could pass down all meaning and ritual, showing all the differing ways that dads could be dads. Then I wondered what would happen if everyone had that kind of access.

To achieve it, a daughter would need to translate her advert into every language, adapting it to suit every space it found. She would need to make audible versions. Tactile versions. Versions designed to be spoken and heard.

There were 7,100 languages in the world, the internet informed me. A 2011 study described 'over 3,814 distinct cultures having been described by anthropologists', a figure that was 'certainly a major underestimate'.

I wanted to be the daughter who could unlock that.

Peter messaged for updates about me and *Mother*; me and Duncan; our journey home. He invited me for a second visit. A longer one. I couldn't work out his intentions. Whether I should be concerned about the axe. Or the eye that coveted waitresses. I was trying to fathom how British society had shaped him. And how he might not live past the year.

A memory rudely forced itself into my mind. It was of a coffin.

I was staring at it from the front row of a chapel, holding a ball of damp tissue, wondering what reality lay inside.

I couldn't do that again.

My brain scanned busily for urgent diversions back in the now, at my desk. It was seeking hits of dopamine. Action; reward. Action; reward.

*Actor Dads*, blurped a thought. Those guys were trained for interactions and awkwardness; to manage uncertainty in expert ways; to give crowds what they wanted – even crowds of one.

Within the hour I contacted *The Stage*, a newspaper made for people in the theatre and performing arts. The magazine had a readership of 30,000, I was told, 43 per cent of whom were over 50. Such delicious statistics; my dopamine spiked. 'Yes, please,' I said, pulling out my credit card. Lights, camera, dadvert.

When Duncan came home there was more good news. He told me he had spoken to a colleague about my project. The colleague had then offered to help me corner the gay zone. 'He thinks he could help you find a dad through Grindr,' said my boyfriend.

'Invite him for dinner,' I clapped. 'ASAP.'

Several conversations in, Cly took on an almost spiritual, guru-like capacity. He had passed through addictions to drink and tobacco and come out far-sighted, renewed. He also talked increasingly about the news headlines – a bit excessively sometimes, I thought, tuning out again. ('That's dads for you, though,' said a friend.)

Cly spoke to my natural side. I enjoyed that he knew about plants. Birds. Climate. Carbon emissions. Plus he knew I had talked to other dads. And he didn't get funny about it.

We often came back to Buddhism. We often came back to death. 'I think the body dies,' he said. 'But not the energy.'

'I think that too.'

'It just moves away.'

'Yes!'

'Like a flame passed between two candles.'

'Oh, that's nice.'

'I mean, we think that mayflies have short lives,' said Cly. 'But what must the mountains be thinking when they look at us?'

'Mm.'

'Time doesn't exist anyway.'

Sometimes I called Cly 'Sensei'. I was 'Grasshopper'.

To me, his random comments felt ripe for his own book of philosophy.

He said: 'You know those 8-year-olds who wake up and know what they want to do with their life? I'm very jealous of them. I wish I knew what I was doing.'

He said: 'We want to cling to things, and make things special, and make things different.'

He said: 'People who watch *Love Island* are just not going to have the same concept of happiness as me.'

'We complicate things, we humanise them,' he added.

I lapped it up. Yes, yes, yes.

'Should I have kids?' I asked more than once. 'Is it worth it?'

'I loved having kids,' he answered, which surprised me. (Given that he had co-created six, it shouldn't have.) 'I love them when they're small especially. They make you feel so good. They bring out the best in yourself. You just . . . You want to be better.'

I thought about Carl and Caroline, his angel child.

'I'm concerned,' I told Cly. 'If people have kids to feel better themselves . . . it doesn't work, does it? Having a baby doesn't fix problems – they just make the problems more obvious. And plentiful. And then you're not just having your problems yourself, you're affecting a new person with them. Then getting disappointed because the baby hasn't fixed your problems. And then you're locked in. For a lifetime!'

Cly laughed. I wasn't joking.

Our chat went on. He said: 'My youngest kid sent me a card the other morning. I thought of you.'

He said: 'I always attract the nutters.'

In that moment, suddenly, I glowed. Cly was a nutter. I was a nutter. Everyone was a nutter.

Only after the call came a fading. The fear about what might be different face to face.

Some friends expressed doubts about using a gay hook-up site for my purposes. They included one of my cousins, who reminded me of the time I insisted we pay an after-dinner visit to Chatroulette. I'd been convinced we would make friends all over the world. Instead, as soon as we started, we were sucked into a carousel of live explicit videos; penises emerging in various states of arousal. When I tried to initiate conversations regardless, the owners of the penises switched us off.

Perhaps Grindr was a non-starter. Except Duncan's colleague, a gay consultant named Dale, was sure he could find a way to make my offering palatable. Besides, I still longed to bypass the dubious offers and sexual risks from men who wanted women.

A gay dad could be exactly what I needed . . . his queerness making him even more open, perhaps, to the notion that families built outside 'traditional' structures could be equally as effective and enriching as the norm.

Not that all 'traditional' stalwarts of those structures would ever accept this, of course. Reading a paper by British sociologist Jeff Hearn, for instance, I learned of research in the seventies and eighties which found that lesbian mothers experienced unfair discrimination and prejudice in family courts. They were 'assumed to be unfit and unsafe parents and that children would experience harm in their care'. In response, Hearn flagged landmark work from the early nineties by researcher Charlotte Patterson, whose in-depth assessment of all available studies established that 'there is no evidence that the development of children with lesbian or gay parents is compromised in any significant respect'. Moreover, as Hearn wrote in 2001, 'Empirical research has indicated that there is no difference in developmental progress of children in lesbian, gay and heterosexual households . . .' In fact, a separate sociological study published the same year found that gay men who co-parent with either women or men actually tend to be *more* engaged in childcare than is 'typical' for fathers as a whole.

Elsewhere, scientists have proved that neural flexibility in the brain enables gay couples to fulfil both cognitive (male-associated) and emotional (female-associated) parenting roles. Indeed, those scientists found that *all* parents, whatever their gender or sex, contained such neurological potential: 'When mothers are around, fathers' amygdala can rest and mothers do the worrying. When mothers are not around, fathers' brains need to assume this function.'

After noting the results of one study of gay men, which found that 76.4 per cent of them desired to become fathers, as well as the information that, before 2002, same-sex couples in the UK had not been allowed to be foster parents, let alone full and equal legal parents – a grim case of cultural norms impeding love and loving connections – I felt more convinced than ever: those older gay dads and I must partner up.

The queer world had been coming up with clear, creative familial opportunities for decades or more (no doubt far longer than records could show). Read tales about the kiki 'ballroom scene' in New York, for example, and anyone could see it: how some queer Black and Latinx young people found sanctuary in houses headed by elders who self-titled as 'mothers' and 'fathers'; how they formed non-genetically linked family units that offered support and belonging.

Inventive, essential ways to build a family in stifling times.

Dale came straight from the office, still wearing his suit. 'Think of me as your fairy godmother of Grindr,' he said. 'Everyone who I know who uses Grindr has made friends off Grindr. That's not its primary purpose. It's aimed at hooking up in the here and now. But actually, I have several friends I've met through the app.'

On the off-chance, I asked if any of those men were now Dale's father.

'No,' he said. 'But I do have a friend who I've not had any sort of sexual relationship with, who *is* a father, and has two children who are pretty much adults now. There's quite a lot of men out there who are in that kind of boat.'

I couldn't tell if it was Dale's belief in his own powers, or the effect of some rapid slurps of wine from the glass Duncan handed me, but I felt emboldened. The feeling lasted until Dale spoke again. 'Just to prepare you,' he said, 'there will be plenty of men on there who will be sexually into you. There will be plenty of men who are also into the age gap. So, to prepare you: you are not going to have a completely harassment-free time.'

I groaned. 'I thought we had entered the safety zone.'

Dale was appalled. 'I would never call Grindr a safe space!'

In the course of the evening we set up my profile. Dale familiarised me with the territory as we went and activated my account. When I gave it the name *Never Had a Dad*, he warned me that I might be opening up a sexual hornet's nest.

As if that hadn't happened already.

We agreed we'd leave things blank for 20 minutes, eat

some food and see if and how anyone nearby made contact. Within seconds there was a rustling sound on my phone. 'That's the noise it makes when you get a message,' said Dale.

Of course I had to check. Of course it only said *hi*. Of course I was then sucked in, clicking on the profile of the person who said *hi*, then window-shopping everyone else who appeared.

The numbers of people nearby were immense. Most were young, too young for me. I scanned profiles for grey or white hair and kind faces. Saw a wistful-looking man with a beanie hat. Beards that looked drawn on with felt-tip pen. Someone shared his fervent passion for sponge baths. As I browsed, Dale talked me through the tribes: twink, sober, rugged, pos, otter, leather, jock, geek, discrete—

'Daddy!'

'Daddy,' Dale affirmed.

And what did 'daddy' mean to him?

'Daddy is: you're looking for somebody for this dad–son kind of arrangement. You want an older man in your life. That doesn't have to be you cuddle up and you pretend that you're actually son and dad, but certainly that you're into an older man, or you are an older man, looking for somebody a bit younger. Although I think also if you're just an older guy, it's a way of saying, "Look, I'm an older guy."'

'So a tribe is either who you are or what you want from it.'

'Exactly.'

I guess I knew which tribe I would be aiming for.

We peeled ourselves off the app to drink more and eat.

Restless in my chair, I barely tasted anything, so keen was I to get going. Before the break, I had seen that the nearest man in my target age bracket was only a street away.

But first: a conundrum. What profile name could replace my original choice? It would have to be short and catch the right people's attention. Plus Dale insisted multiple times that I needed to be direct.

I went for 'Daughter'.

For the summary underneath it I wrote: *Female, not here for sex, trying to find a platonic father figure. I want to know what it would be like to have an actual dad (mine was not around).* Dale agreed it was chatty without being neurotic, revealing without being insinuating, open without being risky.

Before he left me to it completely, he advised I would need to be proactive; that I could not just sit and wait for things to happen. 'This is not going to be a one-night thing.'

Patience. I would need patience.

I reached for a new glass of wine.

# 17

# SEX BIT

As soon as I switched it on the next morning, my phone buzzed. Grindr was alive. It had things to show me. There'd been a delivery, I told Duncan, as he emerged from the shower. Two messages from one man. 'This could be it,' I said.

'Strong start,' he confirmed.

I entered the app to read it aloud. *Where are you?* said the first text. Then: *I'd love to go down on you hun, kiss kiss.*

I fake-puked. Dropped the phone.

My boyfriend sat down to clip his nails. 'Oh well.'

Irate, I picked up the phone again. 'Is this meant to be a joke? Is the guy messing with me? How much clearer could "not here for sex" be?'

I toyed with the idea of putting that into some kind of reply, then decided against it. This issue was getting too big for me to fix. Instead, while crescents of fingernail flew through the air, I huffed into my best duvet igloo construction.

'So you don't want your dad to go down on you?' asked Duncan.

'No. Do you want your dad to go down on *you*?'

'*No*.'

'Just checking.'

'You've got to be clear about these things,' he said.

I bust out of my igloo. 'So you think I need to change my Grindr profile to add some brackets: like, open bracket, "I don't want you to go down on me," close bracket?'

'No.' Duncan backtracked. 'I don't think that's necessary. I think it's clear from your profile.'

'It's clearly not clear.' My voice was loud.

'Your adverts were clear.'

'They're clear to me and clearly to other people they're an open invitation. Do you think this is just a project about how men don't understand that "no means no"? Or how men just don't –' I stalled. '*Some* men just don't listen to what women are actually asking for.'

I stared at my boyfriend.

'Really,' he said.

My gaze drifted up.

*Hello*

   *Saw your note in P Eye – I'd love a chance.*

   *I'm fabulous – may I plz?*

   *I'm in e UK*

   *Completely sincere + serious – &c!*

   *Ta ta 4 now.*

   *Roger x*

   *PS could do with some book assistance – can u*

*read / write complex(ish) words?*

'What is this?' I yelled. 'Go away!'

I left the house. Went walking in the deserted city district. Connecting to the internet to double-check my direction, I heard the rustling Grindr sound, and geared up for another come-on. Braced myself. *Wow that's an interesting profile!* it said.

I lit up. *Ha ha – yes, it's probably not the norm*, I typed. *But it seemed to be worth trying! Let me know if you know anyone who might be interested in the idea. Funnily enough, I've not been getting many messages . . .*

A tumbleweed silence followed. I finished my walk in a cloud.

The following day, the same man returned: *Why on Grindr for this?*

My hopes reignited. *Good question*, I typed, writing, editing, rewriting as I went. *There are lots of men in the right age bracket, I imagine there might be a few on here who haven't been able to have kids (but wanted to know what having a kid might be like), and I'm \*hoping\* to have fewer sex requests on here than I've had from advertising in magazines. We shall see.*

After hitting send I took a close look at his profile. The man was in the daddy tribe, the leather tribe and preferred being on top. He was looking for dates, friends and hook-ups, and described himself as 'open-minded, mature'.

Meanwhile, Peter sent a video. *Just fed your brothers and sisters.*

The troupe of fox cubs squeaked on his lawn.

I signed back in to Grindr, and saw the man I'd been writing to vanish. He had blocked me.

My guts started to ache.

When the next new Grindr message arrived I left it unread for a while, aware that this probably wasn't the kind of patience Dale said I'd need.

*How is Mother?* texted Peter.

I curled up around a cushion with a cocoa by my side. Took my time approaching Grindr again. The new messenger's profile said he was 40 – way too young.

His message read: *Tell me more.*

I snapped. '*You* tell me more.'

Dale had told me I needed to be proactive; that I couldn't sit and wait for people to come to me. Right then I wanted the opposite: to wait here until I was found. And so I sulked.

Duncan's ex-housemate Claire – the friend who kindly offered to be my mentor – agreed to come to the flat for an afternoon. Over tea we debated Matt's idea of obtaining referrals: good men recommended by other good men.

The conversation brought a forgotten vision back to mind: a brief, long-ago idea I'd had to arrange a speed-dating event; one where the female participants angled for fathers instead of partners. I told Claire about it now, adding, 'If we could get a group of women of a similar age, so that the focus is not all on one woman, and have everyone take turns around the room, then we can all compare notes at the end about who was the best dad.'

My mentor was keen.

We discussed which questions someone could ask in two

minutes to gauge decent dadliness. 'Something to do with their emotional availability,' said Claire. 'Like, "When's the last time you cried?" And it's about how they answer that question, how well they talk about their emotions, how well they listen to you about your emotions, and how secure you feel in telling them about your emotions.'

Immediately I felt like Claire could have done this project much better than I had.

Then she took things up an extra notch: she suggested we fuse the speed dating with Grindr.

I recapped: 'So recruit some contacts with Grindr, then invite them all to the same place, and then I meet them anonymously among a group of women?'

'That would be good for safety.'

'Everyone could be called Georgie!'

'Yeah.'

'Georgie One, Georgie Two, Georgie Three, so that they're not quite sure which Georgie they're talking to!'

'*Yeah!*'

We knew women to ask; we knew several venues; we just needed the dads.

The Great Grindr Hunt was back on.

Claire suggested I message five men a day for the rest of the week and see where that got me. Wedged by her side, I composed a standard message with a new excuse to get my foot in the door: that I was researching fathers, hence making contact. I opened the app.

'What about him?'

Claire singled out a profile. An average-looking guy with no alarming red flags on display, named 'M'.

*Hi M,*

*Random message, I know, but do you have a daughter? If not, have you ever wondered what it might be like to have a daughter? I'm not hitting on you, just really keen to hear answers from different people as I'm doing a project about fatherhood. I never had a dad myself.*

*Thank you!*

While adrenaline levels were high, I sent four more.

We paused to eat toast. As I was trying to follow the conversation with Claire, I caught the rustling sound of a notification.

I yipped. M had replied.

*A project on fatherhood,* he wrote. *Lol. I see.*

*I really am!* I protested, typing as fast as I could. *I know it sounds crazy.*

His profile vanished.

'He blocked me.'

Claire laughed. Suddenly I was laughing too.

Another guy we messaged, whose real name may or may not have been Fred, replied to me next. He was keen to talk, he said, just not on Grindr. He suggested I download a separate messaging app to connect properly.

If Claire hadn't been with me, I might have stopped there. Instead, the app freshly downloaded, we took a look. There were all sorts of groups that people could join if they wanted. I searched the word 'father' to see what appeared, almost immediately spotting a group called #fatherless.

'Bingo.'

Except the group was full. As was a father–son incest group.

Claire and I jointly shuddered.

Next, I searched the word 'daughter'. Nothing came up.

It took me a while to locate Fred. I reread his instructions, tried to stay calm, and spoke the conversation aloud as it unfolded.

| | |
|---|---|
| Me: | *Hi Fred!* |
| Fred: | *Hi* |
| Me: | *What do you think of the project and my questions? I know it's strange to do this on Grindr!* |
| Fred: | *It cool baby* |

Claire giggled.

| | |
|---|---|
| Fred: | *I'm looking for a truthful and not complicated sugar baby to share minds and have deep talks and to get naughty with sometimes. I have too many sugar baby that run off with my cash . . . Cash is not my issue . . . But I just need somebody who is honest* |

I considered ending the chat. Except, no, I should square up to this. Maybe there was more to it.

| | |
|---|---|
| Me: | *Oh that's interesting! Are they male sugar babies or female sugar babies? I* |

*am not looking for a sugar daddy, which I say clearly in my profile. I am only interested in hearing other people's thoughts about being a father. What do you think about being a father (sugar or not)? Did you have a father in your life growing up?*

We watched as he typed.

Fred: *You'll receive your allowance once weekly of $3000 thru PayPal and after that we would make plans for hang-outs to have some fun times, sex, spend time with you . . . And other things like this . . . are you OK by this?? So to tell you more of me . . . My character is extrovert and I have a great sense of humor. I am a generous and affectionate person. I love deeply, maybe I love too deeply when I am loving someone*

'Argh!'

'Ask if you can have it in pounds . . . Oh my God, you're not going to—'

Me: *Can I have it in pounds?*

Claire and I guffawed across the sofa.

Me: *Only joking!*

> *This isn't why I'm contacting you. I really just wanted to know your thoughts about fatherhood. I wish you all the best in your search for sugar babies*

Fred:     *OK.*
*Baby but I want you to cross your heart that you will not run away with my money after receiving your first allowance I love you baby if you stay with me I'll spoil you with money baby that's a promise from daddy OK*

'I'm not sure he's quite listening to me?'

I ended the chat.

In the lull, Claire asked after Peter. She was interested in how we met and wanted to hear what he was like in person.

Powered by a new giddiness, I offered to give him a call. Five times I tried to connect to his phone. None of those times could he hear us. When the line eventually worked I apologised. So did he. 'I'm not the best one to do these things,' he said. 'I'm a bit of a dinosaur.'

'I think I must be a dinosaur too, because I couldn't get it to work at all.'

'You're the educated one.'

Instinctively I batted away the compliment, discarding my master's degree in a single line. 'I'm not educated, Pops.'

He disagreed. 'I read your profile. I went on Google, remember?'

'You googled me?'

'Yes!'

He reeled off some facts from my website until he couldn't remember any more. 'It was a long time ago, when I googled you. Because I thought you were too good to be true . . .'

I tensed up.

'Quite an interesting little lifestyle you've led.'

'I do my best.'

'Indeed you do. Yeah, you've done very well for yourself. Good girl.'

I smiled, then glowered, then smiled; *God*.

I introduced him to Claire. After the niceties were done, he asked what we'd been up to.

'We've been having a day of . . .' My voice trailed off.

Claire rescued me. 'Brainstorming.'

'Brainstorming,' I echoed. 'Toast.'

Peter repeated, 'Toast.'

'Yep.'

Claire took the phone. 'Do you remember when you first met Georgie?'

I sat back as he paused to retrieve the memory. 'I think I just walked into the eating quarters one day, and I saw Georgie and Mother sitting there. I'm not too sure what I said but I went up and asked them, I think, "Is there any room at the table?"'

'And then you hit it off?'

'Then we hit it off, yes. The three of us got on well together.'

'What happened on the day when you went to the café?'

'Gosh . . .' Peter hesitated. 'This was . . . off the ship?'

With my fingertips, I started to smooth the padding of

the sofa. Claire prompted him. 'It was during the cruise – you went for a day trip, you stopped somewhere . . .'

I scrawled down 'Invergordon'.

'In Invergordon,' she added.

'Oh, Inver*gordon*, my God, yes,' said Peter. 'I've erased that from my memories. It's full of inbreds.'

I shook my head.

He started talking about the street and the houses. The town's mural of a fire truck.

Claire brought him back. 'While you were in the café did you meet anyone else?'

There was an uncertain intake of breath. '*Did we meet anybody else?* There were people off the ship, I believe, in the café; there were the local people, and—'

'Georgie's told me that you were sitting at a table, and then someone else wanted to join you.'

He went quiet, murmuring about the time that had passed. 'I can't remember off-hand.'

'Do you remember pretending to be Georgie's dad?'

Another pause. I felt rejection looming.

'I can remember something, and I said, "Oh, I'm her father and this is Mother." I'm just trying to think . . . why I said that.'

'That's what I wanted to ask,' said Claire.

'Was some guy *staring* at her or something? Whatever Georgie said is most probably true.' He went quiet again. 'It wasn't a foreign chappie, was it?'

'Just the one woman who came,' Claire recounted, 'and then you said something like, "Yes, do join us, me and my wife and my daughter."'

'Yeah, I do *remember* it. I can't think of the woman, though.'

'The woman's not important, really.'

'I've got one woman in mind but that might have been another holiday. She was on the ship, but she had whiskers—'

'Say you *were* in a café with Georgie and her mum, and you *were* pretending to be her dad, what kind of things would you say, or how would you act?'

'How would I act' – a laugh began to shimmer in his voice – 'if I was her *father*? Oh, gosh. Erm . . . That would be a new experience, wouldn't it?'

I looked at the pigs on my desk and kept a smile going. For Claire.

'I'd most probably feel a bit . . . Yeah, I do feel a bit protective towards her. And, um . . . never had any children or been married or anything, but I'd always liked – I've always fancied a daughter. If I'd had a child, I would have liked a daughter. With Georgie? Yes, I feel a bit protective towards her. I'm very fond of the girl; she's lovely and I would try and – Fatherly things? Yeah, days out maybe. Yeah, go for days out and I would show her around the area as I have done, just try to show her the best of Mumbles and Wales and stuff, yes. But I knew I would be protective of her in a way, yes.'

'Oh, that's nice.'

'Yeah . . .' Peter sounded unsure. 'I haven't had a lot of experience with children to be honest. But yes, I like Georgie. She's nice. Easy company, easy-going.'

He faltered. Claire and I waited.

'She's intelligent,' he said, 'she asks questions. Yeah. She's nice. I like her,' he concluded.

Now I wanted to be the padding in the sofa.

I held my breath.

Claire said, 'Have you ever thought that before with other women—'

*Yes*, I imagined him saying, *she's the only one deluded enough to* –

'No, no—' Peter was adamant.

'—or girls?' Claire finished.

'No, I haven't.'

'So Georgie stood out?'

He laughed. 'Georgie stood out. I don't know why. Because she said to me once, recently I think it was, "Do you fancy me, sexually?" And I sort of looked at her and I said, "No, never." And this is when I think the subject was being *broached*. And I said, "No, never thought about you like that. But I would look upon you more as a daughter." You know?'

The words puzzled me. I had no recollection of asking Peter if he fancied me sexually.

'I've never looked upon you as like an object or, erm, anything of that nature.'

My mentor regarded me with a raised eyebrow. 'Very good,' she said.

Claire and I parted ways not long after that. I wondered what had just happened and why. If Peter had memory issues. If he was worried about seeming predatory.

If he was ashamed.

A few days later, despite our best efforts – with Claire duplicating my Grindr account, sending identical messages from South London – our side mission failed. By the end of the week the app had offered only a collection of disap-pearing ghosts, a bunch of one-liners (*I have a daughter so don't need a second one . . . You sound as if you're writing a dissertation or thesis . . . Vote Labour*) and an extraordinary photo of two penises nuzzling each other.

Duncan and I returned to the house of his parents. His father remained closed off in his office. His mother insisted her husband needed to boost his company's web content, and seemed certain that I was by far the best person to help him.

I looked at my boyfriend. He looked at his phone.

Prising myself off their widest chair, I knocked on the office door.

'Yes?' said its gruff inhabitant.

'I hear you want some rebranding assistance.'

'Do I?'

'Apparently.'

'Another time.'

'It's a date then.'

'Is it. Bye.'

That was that.

When his wife and I were alone in the lounge, sitting at either end of their extra-long sofa, she asked me for another project update. 'Is it helping to fill a hole?' she wanted to know.

'I'm not sure it's filling the hole exactly. Just making it feel smaller by enlarging what's around it.'

She nodded; patted her knees. 'What's in the inbox today then?'

I thought about my lack of replies from *The Stage*. 'It's getting quiet.'

'Go on, let's have a look.'

I slumped, retrieved my laptop and returned, pulling up one of the messages I had not replied to.

My boyfriend's mother sidled closer. 'Well?' She began to read over my shoulder. 'Ooh, look, he's given you his full name. Is that normal?'

'Yes, quite a few of—'

'"I caught sight of your very sorry ad in *Classic Boat*" – ha ha!' She changed her angle to read better. '"I'd be interested to learn more about you. I'm in the age bracket you've specified, I have three sons but have never had a daughter!"' She broke off to look at me. 'Promising!'

'Except—'

'"Perhaps we could help each other for missing out on a large part of life?" she continued. 'Oh, that's sad. "Sailing is my passion and I'm planning a world expedition in two to three years' time, might you be interested?" Gosh, that's a bit . . . isn't it? "I imagine you've had many replies, but respond if you're interested. By the way I live on the east coast, divorced years ago, zero baggage and a solid lifestyle. Brendan."' She clapped her hands together. 'So what next?'

'Nothing.'

'Why?' She frowned.

I clicked to view his reply to my bounce-back. 'For one thing, he doesn't ask me a single question in either of his emails, or answer any that I've asked him. Which suggests he's a man who wants to project his fantasies onto someone, rather than actually wanting to get to know them. It also suggests that he doesn't necessarily pay much attention.'

'Riiight.'

'For another, more crucially, this man is double big.'

She narrowed her eyes.

I directed her to his email address: a mash-up of capital Xs with a reference to being enormous.

'Do you think he's . . . ?'

'Alluding to what he thinks about his penis. Yes.'

'He could be talking about his boat.'

For a nanosecond *I* was unsure. I shook myself out of it. 'If you were a man going to write to a younger woman, and you wanted to make a completely platonic impression, wanted absolutely nothing sexual from her at all, would you use that as your email address?'

'Not everyone knows the importance of first impressions.'

'I think he's trying to convey a very particular first impression. A double-big one.' I shut the laptop.

'What about the chief exec, Champagne Man? Is he still writing?'

'Sometimes.'

'Are you writing back?'

'Sometimes.'

'And you still haven't met him?'

'No.'

She wanted to know why.

What I didn't tell her: *When I meet a 'dad' we both become real to each other and it's terrifying.*

And: *I'm starting to doubt that anyone out there can give me what I want.*

Instead I told her about the patterns: that men who mentioned wealth tended to have a different agenda; that men who described relationships with younger women were usually no-gos; that men at the lower end of the age range were most likely to get flirty; that men with sons and no daughters seemed to be horniest, whereas men who'd never had children were sometimes the hardest to read. Champagne Man Kit, the chief executive, had referenced extramarital relationships, was still in his fifties, had never had kids and was eager to share his elite job status.

'He did write well, though. Might be worth a shot?' Duncan's mother got to her feet. 'This is all a bit of a minefield, isn't it?'

'Yep.'

'Gosh.' She walked away, entertained. 'Rather you than me.'

I revisited the exchange between me and Kit. Since his first email I had repeatedly underlined that I was looking for an extra parent, not an extra partner. He still asked if I wanted to meet and named a date a few weeks away.

My instincts told me the exercise was pointless. My instincts told me he wasn't the right kind of person.

Except the people I'd *wanted* to meet so far hadn't been right for me either.

Kit suggested coffee in town the next time he was in London. He had also told his wife about our contact: *She hasn't read any of these emails yet but she's aware we're in touch. She probably will read them at some point if things continue to progress well, though.* There was merit in the friendly, pressure-free way he proposed a meeting, I supposed. Plus I liked the font he used: rounded letters that seemed neat and friendly.

(As if the sense of a person could be understood in terms of font choices.)

(And who knew? I had no idea.)

I thought it would be helpful for us to start at a museum or gallery as I had with Harold; a venue where we could walk side by side and focus on something external; a helpful aid to distract us should things turn awkward or feel too much. Kit told me he didn't mind where we met, so I made a shortlist of places I hadn't tried. The Charterhouse Museum. The Anaesthesia Heritage Centre. The City of London Police Museum.

Kit plumped for the Police Museum – *mainly because I know exactly where it is* – and I took a closer look at what was there: a collection of truncheons, uniforms, 'criminal tools' and two bombs planted by militant Suffragettes, all situated in a complex built over London's oldest crypt.

Call me intrigued.

Prepping at home, I picked out the same outfit I had now worn multiple times. Only this time, for some reason, I deliberated over whether or not I should be applying mascara.

I brought out my make-up bag, stashed it back, brought it out again; caught in another exasperating loop. Eventually I confronted myself: 'Is it because he's a chief exec? Why should Chief Exec Dads get mascara?' I stashed the make-up bag properly, concealing it in a drawer under boxes of jewellery, earrings, perfume: a cache of items bought for me by Duncan and his mother.

The dilemma reminded me of a phenomenon I'd seen online for the first time recently: daddy–daughter dating. These were the videos, covered in sparkling graphics of hearts and roses, of fathers taking their daughters on 'first dates'. Showing their 4-, 5-, plus-year-old girls how they 'ought' to be treated by men. Inviting them out for dinner, giving them flowers, telling them they looked beautiful with their made-up eyes and fancy dresses, sometimes slow dancing together on the patio.

My nose wrinkled. 'Why not snog her and show her how she ought to be kissed, you first-date thieves?' I said.

Slamming the drawer shut, I stretched my arms, trying to dislodge my discontent.

The standard nervous sensations came up quickly as I walked to where Kit and I were scheduled to meet: the sense that anyone could be him, and that everyone was watching. Once more I fought to hold back my expectations.

We were due to meet at three o'clock. I arrived outside the museum 10 minutes early, feeling too conspicuous in the pink scarf I said I'd be wearing.

And there I waited.

Wholly on edge.

A young woman came towards me in a wheelchair and glanced about. I watched her from the corner of my eye. She didn't move on.

After a few moments, I started thinking she had set me up – had pretended to be a businessman named Kit – and was now inwardly revelling at my ignorance.

*Why are people so mean?* I asked myself.

I checked the space around me for hidden cameras. In my bag was the latest copy of *Private Eye*. I pulled it out and mimed reading, waiting for her to approach me and reveal what she had been doing. It would be good if I could make myself laugh at that moment.

*I'm sorry for pretending to be a businessman dad*, she might say.

I might reply that I was *Sorry for pretending to be . . .*

*Pretending to be . . .* what exactly?

A daughter worth having?

I sighed. Maybe the wheelchair woman could be my father. Why the hell not?

A large man wearing a creased suit slowly ambled into view. He was holding a briefcase. 'Kit?' I tried.

The man half smiled, saying nothing while coming closer. He looked like the epitome of reluctance. More than that: total discomfort.

Soon he was right beside me, and still not speaking at all. Perhaps he thought *he* was being set up. Or perhaps he wasn't Kit.

The man looked up at the building behind us, contemplating the rooftop.

I took a leap. 'Have you been here before?'

'What is it, a council building or something?'

'I think it's been a lot of things.'

Silence. My every cell was flailing.

'If you want, we could just have coffees?'

'That sounds much better,' he said.

He must be Kit then. And Kit must not be a man for a random museum after all. Sagging slightly, I walked beside him, away from the truncheons and feminist explosives.

The first shoots of a conversation emerged. He had an interview to join the board of a business tomorrow, he told me. I pounced on the subject and began to ask more, until I realised I didn't have a plan for where we were walking. To something independent, I reckoned. With interesting cakes.

Kit gestured at a branch of PAUL, a chain café that appeared on almost every main street of London. 'That'll do,' he said.

Once through the doors, he asked if he could buy me a cake and coffee.

'Let me buy it for you,' I said. 'You're the one who's travelled furthest.'

'No, I'll buy it.' Again, no room for debate.

After he placed the order, we sat near a window and picked up the chat. I wrestled with a pistachio croissant, wincing as pieces of nut flew across the table, envying the genteel restraint of his raspberry macaron.

Almost as soon as the small talk began, I forgot what had been said, so intent was I on preserving some level of dignity. 'Am I how you expected?' I dared to ask, when the last of the pesky croissant had been dispatched.

The long hesitation told me all I needed to know: Kit was disappointed. I recalled his earliest messages: those *younger women*, plural, with whom he'd had a continuum of relationships. Sparkling ladies all of them, I imagined. Well spoken and up for champagne. 'You speak like the person who wrote the emails,' he offered.

(I wondered if he'd prefer to be meeting Mascara-Wearing Georgie.)

'Your ad clearly set off something for me,' Kit added.

All I heard was his use of the past tense. At which point I gave up. This connection was nothing special. There were no shining golden threads between us.

Fine. Whatever.

The adult inside me decided we might as well have a decent conversation. For some reason that adult wanted to talk food, and to recommend the experience of eating a deep-fried Creme Egg. In return, Kit told me about a time he ate deep-fried jam sandwiches. Somehow, this led us on to tales of jury service: I was once called for a long trial at the Old Bailey and had to duck out because I was between jobs; no employer would sub me. Kit had once helped convict a man who had sexually assaulted his young child.

There was more to be said, we both knew it. Yet neither of us was capable.

We had barely been 40 minutes in the café when Kit made his excuses to leave. He had places to go. On the pavement I judged the mood and decided to try out a hug regardless. As I pulled away he seemed shell-shocked. I became convinced my face was frightening.

'We could head to the Tube together?' I nodded, indicating where I was going to walk.

'Ah. I'm going in the opposite direction.'

'Ah. Fair enough. Bye, then.'

'Goodbye.'

'It was nice to meet you,' I called, as the suit retreated.

# 18

# ELEPHANT

There was a key quote in my notebook I kept coming back to. It said: 'Fathers are particularly important for helping girls learn to interact with males.'

Did I not know how to interact with males?

I received a new message from Peter. My phone said there was some kind of image involved but wouldn't show me a preview. It must either be something majestic and Welsh, or something dirty and prankish. Maybe both. I told myself not to look for a while. Leave it. Rest. Make time.

My mind conjured up the coffin again.

This time it was Peter's coffin.

I grimaced and slumped on my desk, downloading the image he'd sent.

The picture was of a woman in her teens or twenties, with long fake lashes, a brilliant smile and large breasts with nipples prominent through her T-shirt. The nipples were long and augmented. In her hand was a fast-food drinking cup.

*Disgraceful*, read the caption. *KFC are still using plastic straws!*

Of course I couldn't stop staring at her nipples. Of course that was the point.

Points.

Two points.

'Wurgh.'

Had any dadvert respondent thought it might be wise to send me this joke, I almost certainly would have stopped corresponding. Peter, though.

Peter.

I was sure I had seen something else to the man; another side that was genuine and paternal. Yet how was I supposed to interact with this?

Cly and I had another phone call; I did not mention the KFC image, nor did he know the ins and outs about Peter. Even then, without prompting, he told me, 'There are no professional parents.'

I laughed at first and wrote his statement down. Later, I argued with it. 'There should be professional parents. My God, why leave this to amateurs?' As I mulled I suddenly thought of the care system. Was that not professional parenting in action – at least in theory?

The next day, a pig by my side, I contacted an organisation called Become, the national charity for children in care and care leavers. They put me in touch with Becca, a trained social worker whose job it was to offer advice and support.

On our call, Becca explained that those adults who *were* professionally trained weren't necessarily cutting it for children either. The care system was failing in its parental duties on multiple levels, letting down masses of vulnerable kids. 'Care-experienced young people will very likely have experienced trauma,' she explained, 'and that's why they'll be going into care in the first place. But actually, going into care itself is a traumatic event. What you need to support growth and healing from trauma is stability, routine, reliability, but care-experienced young people are often changing homes multiple times, moving between different foster carers, or different relations, or different residential homes. That means changing schools, changing social networks, changing professionals. All that stuff, all that instability, is a huge issue.'

Interestingly, there was such a thing as a 'corporate parent'. Becca brought up the term in relation to children who have been in the care of a local authority for more than 24 hours; commonly referred to as 'looked-after children' (although many young people in care feel the label is a misnomer: they don't feel they *are* being looked after, so prefer to say 'care-experienced'). As one council defined it: 'Put simply, the term "Corporate Parent" means the collective responsibility of the council, elected members, employees and partner agencies, for providing the best possible care and safeguarding . . .' Those responsibilities apply until the young person turns 25 and involve working closely with social and fostering services.

'That's what the local authority is referred to as,' said Becca. 'Horrible, isn't it?'

I agreed the phrase sounded dismal. '"Corporate parent": like, strokes you with the tip of their umbrella at night?'

Becca went on. 'There's been an independent review of social care that came out recently. Part of it is about making the care system more loving. But how do you ask professionals to quantify "love"? That's really philosophically difficult.

'There are some fantastic social workers and other professionals out there who really care. But it's quite difficult to ask someone – to say you must show the exact same amount of love. However, if it's the local authority taking the child into care then they should show that love, because that's what they're saying: they're going to be your family.'

What a family that could be. A family who, when its offspring came of age, would put them in a holding queue if they phoned to ask for support. Brag about its achievements in council-branded leaflets. Start expecting monthly payments in the form of local taxes.

Except, wasn't that also what most parents did: expect some kind of return on their investment?

The theory left me wondering if there had ever been any such thing as a selfless parent; someone who took on the challenge without wanting care, time, love or recognition to come to them in return – whether while that child remained a child, or after they'd flown the nest.

After my call with Becca, I thought more about people who choose to adopt – on the face of it, one of the more selfless choices an adult can ever make.

Beside me was a book I'd taken out of the library on fathers and adoption. The book was supposed to be a guide for dads as adopters, rather than for any children being adopted.

Still.

The book's author, Paul May – an adoptive dad himself – confirmed the inherently selfless nature of the process by design: that it is 'first, foremost and *only* a service for children'. Yet, while recognising the trials and tribulations involved, May also acknowledged the potential overall benefits to adopters, writing, 'Adoptive fathers never lose the sense that they are somehow special: that they have been given a special opportunity in life, and a special relationship to which they owe a lifetime's commitment.'

(Perhaps a person could enjoy that sense while also being selfless?)

On the phone, I spoke with a close friend of mine who had become a parent to an 11-month-old when he was taken from his biological mother – a woman my friend was related to and who suffered from drug addiction. The man thought to be the child's father had issues too, and did not step forward to claim any parenting rights. (As my friend explained, 'He is not named on the birth certificate and refused a DNA test. Interesting that British fathers have the option to deny their parenthood where mothers do not . . .') My friend and her husband were now undergoing the formal process of adoption.

I asked if she saw her act of parenting her son as a selfless one. She replied that, 'Within parenting, every day, there are acts that you only do for your child that don't benefit you personally. There are a lot of selfless acts.'

Did she not, on some level, do these acts to get love from her child, though, I prodded?

I could hear my friend smile at the question. 'But if you didn't get any love back from your children,' she said, 'you wouldn't be such a good parent. Children need to love their parents, and they need to *feel* love, and that's when they turn into human beings and not monsters. They need to be able to give love back, because giving love back gets them more love in return. It's like a virtuous circle of love.'

'Interesting . . .'

'I guess it's the act of caring for someone,' she continued. 'Caring is a very powerful thing, isn't it? A baby is completely dependent on you and the baby really *needs* you to love it, because if you didn't love your babies, it would be a nightmare. Because it's really a massive pain; they're constantly waking up crying, and pooing all over the place and stuff.' She laughed. 'The *act* of caring – the older I get, I think just doing things makes it so.' In other words, the act of caring makes you care.

'So . . .' I pondered. 'Parents need to love their babies so it doesn't become so arduous that they just give up parenting. And then a natural response is that the child then learns how to give it back, and therefore to build meaningful connections later in life?'

My friend agreed. That sounded about right.

In his book, Paul May describes how roughly one in five British adoptions breaks down as families complete the protracted, sometimes years-long process it entails; a process that presents 'a daily opportunity for the prospective adopter to withdraw'. In a minority of cases, this breakdown occurs after every step of the process has been achieved, and the child has entered the family. (A 2017 BBC article on the subject reported that this happens in between 3.2 per cent and 9 per cent of adoptions, citing reasons including severe, untreated trauma causing child behavioural issues, a lack of access to specialist therapy services for adoptive families, and a general deficiency in support from the ultimate corporate parenting bodies of the government and local councils.)

On the call with my friend I shared some of these findings. Asked about the process of attachment she and her son had experienced. Asked, too, when she first realised that she loved him. Her thoughts went back to the day they met. 'It's sort of about how much you're *allowed* to love someone,' she said. 'He was my cousin's baby . . . I did know her, but not at all well, and I could imagine myself in her situation to a greater extent than I could imagine myself in his situation. It's pretty awful to be driving away with a child when someone is sobbing in the background because their baby's being taken away. It doesn't matter whether that's the best thing for the baby; it's still terrible, it's still awful.

'I remember being in therapy and . . .' My friend hesitated. 'It's hard to describe, but it seemed wrong to want him because it was somehow going against his mother. I remember my therapist saying that it would be really important for him that he *was* wanted, that someone wanted him. And I remember that sort of made it okay. I'm allowed to want him and that's okay. But it's difficult to pinpoint, isn't it? Because love somehow creeps up on you.

'Loving him doesn't really feel like a choice.'

I spent the rest of that day reading May's book, on the hunt for information I could (not-at-all-selflessly) use to help me now; to boost my chances of being someone who could love and be loved by a father figure in the way I thought I wanted.

Becoming an adopter has to be approached gradually, May advises: 'It's like eating an elephant – an elephant with some very unpalatable parts at that, but one that can be consumed if the portions are small enough, and there's enough time to recover between courses.'

As far as my own adoptive process was going, parts of the elephant seemed to be stuck in my throat.

It wasn't just Peter's KFC picture – to which I eventually fudged the reply: *Glad to see you're taking an interest in environmental matters.* No, naively I had thought my mission would be fun. Expansive. Healing. Clarifying. Instead I felt as if things were narrowing down to a bleak, murky dot.

There was nothing new from Grindr. One respondent to *The Stage* said: *I fully intend to respond in a fulsome way . . . I'll be back in touch.*

And wasn't.

I kept the door closed with Car-Boot Harold. Ended the chats with Draughts-Player Lenny and his silent son. I also said goodbye to Jerry, future incumbent Mayor of Blackpool. Intriguing and poetic though he had been, our dialogue was so one-sided – I shared so little of myself – that when, after months, he wrote, *I hope you feel half as much about me as 'Dad' as I feel about you being my 'daughter'*, I was transfixed. It was a marvel to see how he filled the space I had left open; what daughter he had created in his mind. And I knew with certainty I could never be her.

To my astonishment, Champagne Man Kit had suggested we meet again – yet I felt so averse to repeating that arduous experience I said no. At the same time, I was increasingly late sending responses to Clear-Headed Cly for our next phone call, and constantly deferred meeting in person.

All the while, intrusive thoughts of Carl were threatening to throw me off course; the thought of there being a father who, once upon a time, might have chosen to fill the gap. Who chose to reproduce again instead of returning to me; co-creating a second child whose loss was apparently insurmountable.

Wanting to be out of my head and solely in my body, wanting a break from all the strain and unease, I booked a massage for me and Duncan both. This would not be a one-to-one massage, but a three-to-one. Not a vigorous rubbing and raking, but a gentle laying of hands.

My boyfriend went first and emerged from his session ethereal. 'I think I'll sleep well tonight,' was his review. I didn't doubt it.

When it came to my turn in the room, the trio placed their hands on me, touching head, sacrum, feet. 'There's tension everywhere,' I told them.

'Yes,' the leader confirmed.

Heat emanated from his fingertips. The room fell mute.

After five minutes or so, a woman lightly cleared her throat, then whispered, 'I feel your heart needs holding. May I?'

I nodded. Lightly, she placed her hands on my chest. In moments my face was scrunching. Tears poured out and rolled down into my earlobes, dampening the soft hands of the man who was cupping my head.

\*

The day after the massage I went to Mabry's. She was having a difficult time at work; her clients were being nasty and lashing out. As the two of us shared our troubles over dinner – picking at homemade cheesecake; flattening into the cushions – she asked me about Peter.

'There are so many reasons why he's not a wise choice,' I said. 'Some of the stuff he says comes across as super-sexist, we're politically on different planets, he makes highly inappropriate comments about the female anatomy—'

'You're smiling, though. I can see you like him.'

'What does that say about me?'

'Does it have to say anything?'

I pouted. 'He does make me laugh sometimes,' I said. 'I think he's kind. He's attentive.'

'That's great.'

'Yes, but . . .' I explained that I wasn't sure I understood him; wasn't sure I could really relax around the man, or if that would ever change. 'Plus maybe I just *shouldn't*. I want him to act like my dad sometimes, but why?'

Mabry reminded me that there were no rules. 'You're two adults, male and female, with very little shared history behind you. Clearly there's *something* there.'

Perhaps it was in the way we'd met.

Perhaps because he'd started it.

Perhaps it was something else.

'And how's your mum?' asked Mabry.

My head drooped.

I had started a new side project: booking trains for Mum to come to London and stay with me and Duncan. It had been tricky to find dates that worked – I was putting a lot in the calendar without entirely thinking it through – and abruptly her responses stopped.

I left it two days before checking in, writing to openly wonder if she was okay.

She replied at last: *The answer is no.*

Then:

*I'm struggling to get over this feeling that I've become another thing to tick off your 'to do' list. Must be frustrating to have a question mark in your diary when I'm sure you could fill it with something more fun and interesting than me! At the moment I'm not feeling social. I don't know when or if that will change, so if you want certainty, organise something else for those dates. Sorry. Xx*

I bit my lip. Wrote back: *I can definitely see why you feel like that.*

And: *It's nothing personal.*

And: *I don't have much extended time for anyone.*
*The fact is that everything is a tick list at the moment.*
*Things are getting overwhelming.*

My mother's silent period only lengthened.

It was late summer. In part to deal with the overwhelm, in part because of Fuck It, I signed up for involvement in a medical trial. For 10-plus days I would be sequestered in a hospital ward, quarantined from the outside world and dosed with droplets of avian flu.

Outside, the London sun was hotter than ever, scorching

all records. Inside, I wrote emails in cool sterility, recalling snippets on the joys of dads to recharge myself and stay motivated.

Like the friend whose father threatened to lob a brick through the window of his son's non-paying employer – and thus satisfyingly elicited instant payment.

Like the new freelance client who applauded my plans and insisted, without hesitation, that '*everyone* deserves a father'.

Like the rest of my conversation with Jeremy from the Fatherhood Institute.

'What's been your experience of fathers in your own life?' I had asked him.

His voice surged. 'This could keep you going for a couple of hours,' he said.

I encouraged him on.

What followed was Jeremy's story of becoming a father himself, and how he came to join the institute. 'I did a PhD when my son was little, which was all about gay dads – because I'm a gay dad. I suppose being a gay dad now is quite standard; it wasn't then. I wanted to find out more about what gay men were doing with fatherhood and whether it was different from the standard way, whatever that is. It ended up turning into a job.'

I could hear him thinking back. 'My experience of fatherhood was . . .' There was a long pause. 'I mean, I loved it, I just loved it. And still do. It's a magical thing.'

I asked him if he felt 'changed'. If he had felt new hormones in his body.

'Absolutely,' he replied. 'I remember when they handed

him to me. I remember being in a room with him on my own – this was probably within half an hour of his birth. And he was just *there*: I was holding him; he was looking straight in my eyes. It was unbelievable. It's unbelievable.'

For a moment I tried to picture Duncan having this sort of reaction.

Then I tried to picture Carl the first time he held Caroline, my half-sister. The baby he chose to commit to.

My mind was a blank. Yet I wanted to see those reactions. I wanted to see those dads.

Jeremy continued. 'My son is an interesting case study in fatherhood, because he has three fathers – or father figures. He's got his mum and his stepdad. He's got me and my partner, who's been around since he was small. And each of us is quite different. We all play different roles. I think this is partly about who we are as people. My partner and our son have a lovely relationship; they laugh a lot. I've always been very close to our son too, both physically and emotionally. But while I wouldn't want to overplay it, I do think there's a difference in status that results from the biological relationship.'

Jeremy took time to think about his next words. 'As a biological father,' he said, 'there is a big societal expectation, and a kind of legal and cultural context to your fathering. Consciously or subconsciously – or a mixture of those two – I've felt that. That sort of shaped my "doing" of fatherhood. In the context of my son's life, I guess I inhabited that sort of biological father role, whereas the other two men inhabited step-father roles. There was a sort of in-built relativity, if that makes sense.

'What I don't want that to come off as is that I was the

most important, because both of them were there from when he was really young, so it's not like either of them has done anything less than be highly involved and highly important to him. And what the evidence shows is that fathers through time have been very flexible and have the ability to "step up". There have always been step-fathers as well as biological fathers and some of those step-fathers look very much like biological fathers – or our idea of biological fathers.

'My son has had four parents basically: four parents in two households. That's all he ever knew.'

I thrilled at the possibilities. I marvelled.

I *wanted*.

On a couple of days, the researchers took biopsies of my lungs. They flushed my airways out with water, collecting what came back out for analysis. It gave me all the excuse I needed to double up on orders for cake. The virus wasn't gaining hold. What did take hold was the thought that, *Ha! I'm coping! I don't need Mum after all.*

After the procedures, I wrote to Cly and Peter. Peter replied without hesitation, checking in; checking the state of the nurses.

The silence from Mum got louder.

Talking to my ward buddies, both of whom were now swampy with flu, I asked after their parents. I heard tales of one dad who constantly called his adult daughter pet names. 'The names make me cringe,' she said from her bed, against the opposite wall. 'They also make me happy.'

'My father taught me how to invent things,' shared my

other ward-mate. He was a father himself now too, and grafting through his own patents.

I wondered what Carl might have taught me, had he stuck around – and how much of it would have been positive.

Chattily, Cly wrote back to me, sharing his own news from the outside world: his afternoon with the hedge trimmer; the holly tree he was tackling; philosophers he rated; the power of looking, and observing what exactly is doing the looking.

*Hope you are OK*, he added. *Have been a little concerned about you. You know, isolating yourself in an experimental laboratory. Is everything alright, with you and the world?*

In our conversation, Sophie Lewis told me she believed fathers could 'mother' too, defining 'mothering' as labour, 'fathering' as a moment.

'When you say "fathering" you're talking about the instant of authorship,' she explained, 'the patenting of an embryo. Like a Property Act, really. That's what it means to "father" someone. It doesn't mean to "be a father figure", it means to knock someone up. So my policy currently is that if a parent cares ongoingly, that's mothering.' She looked away. 'But I suppose I couldn't, um . . . I couldn't deny that there's, like . . . not necessarily been enough . . . curiosity for me?'

I wanted to ask Sophie what she was getting at. Before I did, she got there herself. 'About what? This question you're asking. What are dads for? Because I've thought so much about what mums do. And how the whole institution of motherhood is patriarchal too, right? I talk about a sort of dialectic of mother*ing* against mother*hood*. But, yeah. Basically . . .' There was a long pause. 'I think I've been a bit like "hashtag no dad", you know what I mean?' She flashed a grin. 'I mean, I think the idea of "*dad*" is . . .' The grin was fading. 'Maybe you'll persuade me otherwise, but that's not a function I see as doing more good than harm.'

It seemed I did want to persuade her – or, rather, to meet somewhere in the middle. In the next moment I said to Sophie: 'The more research I've done, the more I get into it, the more it seems clear to me that for some family units, "fathering" and "mothering" are kind of unhelpful terms.'

While agreeing that fathers could 'mother' too, and that 'mothering' was labour, I reckoned the verb ought to be 'parenting' – since it seemed the only things a father can't do are carry the baby and breastfeed; since if men and women were encouraged to think about fathers as primary parents too, it could benefit everyone.

'But then again—' I looked at the floor. 'Families themselves can still be so exclusive.'

I was thinking about Carl again. Thinking about Carl's mother.

'*So* exclusive.'

After I had been released from the experiment, my scheduled phone call with Cly came around. He answered slightly out of breath. He'd been throwing apples, practising his 'fast bowl' in the garden.

We talked about mindfulness and seeking help. We talked about estrangement. A son had recently cut off contact, though apparently from the whole family and not just his father. Cly had written back in response: *If you want me, any time, I can do whatever you want.*

I wrote that down.


Again, I tried messaging Mum. Offered what I sensed she wanted from me. Duncan and I could come down from London again. A long weekend.

Tentatively she replied, saying she might like to go to a restaurant.

I spent our train ride looking for different places she might enjoy, vetting them with Duncan. We arrived with a shortlist. Greeted the dog. Mum and I shared a rigid hug. And every restaurant suggestion I made was dismissed.

I lasted about five goes until I was straining. 'Where do you want to go?' I asked again. 'What do you want? Please just say.'

My mum folded her arms. 'It's so patently obvious you don't want to spend time with me.'

I exploded. '*Seriously?*'

The two of us glared at each other. Without saying a word, my boyfriend took his backpack to the living room, sealing himself inside.

'I work really hard for this relationship,' I shouted. 'And it's never good enough!'

'Oh, you do, do you?'

'Yes!'

'That's not how it feels to me.'

My anger rocketed upwards. 'I spent over an hour looking at restaurants you might like and you've shat on them all.'

She volleyed back, 'You might as well give up then, since I'm apparently so difficult.'

'Fuck's sake!'

'Stop it! You're upsetting the dog.'

'I know!' I yelled. 'I'm sorry! *I'm* upset!'

'*You're* upset. What about me?'

'This is about you! It's all about you!'

My mother stomped past me and up the stairs. I followed closely behind, demanding she not walk away.

'You're being aggressive,' she said. 'I don't have to talk to you. I don't want to.'

'I'm being upset! My voice has got loud!' My tears were flowing freely now. 'I'm agitated and when I get agitated my voice gets loud! I can't seem to stop it!'

'It's extremely rude and I'm not talking to you until you calm down.'

I felt the early pinch of hyperventilation. Insisted she stick to the subject. Holding on to the wall, I tried to wipe the messiness from my face. Pictures of Child Georgina looked out on the scene: holding a fire truck; posed in a studio; stunned. 'I'm fed up with feeling like I have to do everything,' I said.

Mum turned away, moving towards her bedroom.

'I feel like you want me to parent you,' I said. 'I don't want that. I want you to do your own thing. I don't want to feel responsible for your emotions or guilted into spending time with you. I have *so little time*.' As I spoke, the rush of anger rose again.

Then Mum's mouth crumpled.

Mine crumpled too.

'If you really have no time,' she said, 'how is it you found a day to spend with Peter in Swansea, who you barely know?'

'ARGH!'

Her lips pressed together in a tight, thin line.

'I want to be able to see friends and meet new people,' I said. 'I want balance. I want to live my life, and explore things, and learn.'

She shook her head.

I asked her what she was waiting for.

Mum's eyes narrowed. '*Waiting* for?'

'Surely there must be something. Something you want to change about me. About this. What are you waiting for?'

'I'm still here, because I hope one day I might be useful to you.'

I took a long breath before I answered. 'You can't be waiting all your life for me to come back and find you useful.'

Her lower lip wobbled.

'Seriously, Mum,' I said. 'That's *too much pressure*.'

When my mother replied, her voice was quiet and low. 'You're the best thing that's ever happened to me,' she said. 'I know it would have been easier for you if I'd found some-one else, but I feel safe when I'm at home with the dog. He's the only one who likes me.'

'I like you.'

'No, you don't.'

'*Stop telling me what you think I think. You don't know.*' I flapped my arms about. 'I like you!' I yelled. 'You're the one who doesn't like me.'

Mum shook her head again. 'I don't always like you, no. But I love you.'

The scene was too familiar; too much like that time in the car seven years before. Too much like the fallout that followed.

———

Me: 'It's about my father, isn't it.'

My mother, braking hard: 'What about your father?'

I held my breath. 'That he's dead,' I said. 'He died on Thursday.'

'How did you know?' she fired back.

'I contacted him.'

There was rage in her voice as she asked me when.

'My father has died,' I shouted, 'and your number-one reaction is to be furious – at me?'

———

This time, the air between us settled more quickly. This time there were no debates about who of us should attend the funeral. No persistent questioning of the details I'd been unearthing without her. No dismay that I'd been so interested in the notion of knowing Carl. All that shock transmuted into anger.

This time, within an hour, my mother and I tired of clashing and agreed to go for a walk. We left Duncan behind, still typing away on his laptop, absorbing himself in the security of the screen.

On our way to the beach, Mum said, 'I've failed you.'

'Please,' I responded. 'Don't say that.'

As we reached the car park above the cliffs, she added, 'Maybe I do expect too much of you.'

'Maybe,' I echoed quietly. 'I don't know.'

'It hasn't been easy for me,' she said. 'Is that how you feel too?'

'I feel like this is really fucking difficult. And I feel like nobody's perfect, least of all me.'

'That's how *I* feel.'

'Well, snap then.'

Later, as we said goodnight, my mother pulled me close. Tenderly she kissed me on the cheek and refused to let go. She sniffed my face and told me I smelt lovely.

Overcome with a flood of endorphins, I didn't want to move.

# 19

# STATUS QUO

My notebook said: 'Children need their fathers, but fathers need their children, too.'

*Fathers should be crossed out*, I thought. *Just 'parents'.*

In my inbox, a casual respondent wrote, *In all relationships there is a power dimension and in the case of parent–child I think it reverses, so in adult life the child has the power.*

I was not powerful. My stomach felt weird, my breasts sore again. I took a pregnancy test while Duncan was out. No blue line. No baby.

In the UK a number of organisations exist to support single-parent families, none of which I had ever heard of before. I would make contact now, I decided; ask for their help. But there were few I could get through to. After calling numbers, leaving messages, sending multiple emails, I received nothing.

Perhaps these organisations were being affected by funding cuts, staffing problems, a general lack of resources. Perhaps they were being impacted by the issue Robin Hadley had raised: that, for a cause to have money, it had to be popular. Championed by academics and celebrities.

Maybe being the child of a single parent wasn't popular enough.

It should have been. Nearly 2 million single parents with 3 million dependent kids formed part of the UK's sociological fabric, I discovered.

That was 5 million whole people. More than half the entire population of Greater London.

As I researched, I found a take on single parenthood I hadn't encountered before. It came from a 2018 study led by Sheffield University, and said: 'On average, those who have been in a single-parent family at some point report higher levels of life satisfaction than those children who have never lived in a single parent family.'

Powerful, positive stories. That's what I wanted.

Stories of single mothers. Stories of single fathers.

Stories of people doing their best as people.

Following the recommendation of an old uni friend, I disappeared for a while with a queer US parenting podcast called *If These Ovaries Could Talk*. Not everyone featured on the show was going solo. In fact, most of them weren't. But powerful and positive? Yes and yes.

Skimming through, I found the story of Ash. While Ash had been born female, in adulthood they defined themselves as non-binary, as well as bisexual and solo-polyamorous. That last term meant they not only made space to have multiple lovers, but consciously aimed to 'decentralise' any romance in their life. Or, to put it another way, they did not view romantic relationships as their priority.

When giving their podcast interview, Ash was in London and pregnant, having had sex with a friend for the sole purpose of making a baby. The process which led to them choosing that friend had been both thorough and lengthy, with steps including joint therapy and a legal agreement. Romance had no part in the equation. As Ash put it, 'They're such different things. Like, being romantically and sexually compatible with someone, and having compatible parenting values – they're *so* different; what are the chances those things are going to align?'

I could not help thinking of Mum's pairing with Carl. Sexually compatible they may have been. Parentally compatible? Clearly not.

Ash told the hosts the plan was for friends to help them raise the baby; that they felt more supported and less isolated than many people in nuclear family arrangements seemed to be when expecting. They also said they wanted to avoid gendered labels like 'Mum' or 'Dad', feeling that these terms were unlikely to properly signify the specificity of their relationship.

The way Ash spoke sounded revolutionary and highly rational, reminding me of Sophie Lewis's arguments to rehaul parenting structures; to find more inclusive means of relating in familial ways. Several months after the interview first aired, I was eager to learn how such rational intentions were playing out in reality.

After contacting the podcast hosts, I was kindly put in touch with Ash, who agreed to chat with me about their child-rearing approach. We scheduled a call, fitting it around their baby's shifting sleep habits, and briefly I explained the path that had led to me seeking them out.

'Obviously my child doesn't have a dad,' Ash said,

speaking from a restful room on the other side of the city. 'There are lots of people in J's life. And I'd much rather have no dad and lots of other adults than have a *bad* dad. Or, you know, a parent or two parents in a bad relationship. But I definitely do have some kind of immediate defensiveness or guilt about the fact that I'm not giving J a dad. To hear that you've gone on a huge quest to find someone to fill that role is really interesting to me.'

I asked Ash if they had a dad in childhood, and – contrary to my expectations – learned that their father had been much more present than most. 'Dad was kind of the primary caregiver for our entire childhood,' they explained. 'He was the one who was at home cooking and picking us up from school and things like that. I have a very good experience of a dad. I think I have a less good experience of relationships. My parents divorced when I was 16.'

'Ah.' Yet more of Ash's rationale fell into context.

From all I had read, rearing children seemed to loom as the crucible through which large volumes of couples combusted, at least in the UK. Of the 95,000 kids with divorcing parents in England and Wales in the latest published data – 95,000 children *in just one year* – 20 per cent were aged 0 to 4 when their parents legally separated; 44 per cent were aged 5 to 10; 36 per cent were aged 11 to 15.

That was a lot of children impacted by the ending of relationships, or relationships impacted by the beginning of a child.

And these were just the couples that reached divorce – not the families who ground on in anger and sadness, refusing to call it a day 'for the sake of the children'.

'I've had some really good relationships,' Ash told me. 'I'm currently in a really lovely relationship. But the fact that relationships are meant to last for decades, that just doesn't seem realistic. That's for me the main reason I'm not parenting in a relationship, because I don't think I can make a commitment that I will still be with that person for the rest of J's childhood.

'Very few people can make that commitment,' Ash continued. 'So that's the reason I'm doing it. Not because I think that if there was a dad, the dad would be bad.'

But was there anything about fathers, I asked, that Ash felt their child might be missing?

'I'm non-binary, so what does "dad" actually mean? Is it the masculine energy that they provide? I'm a builder and a carpenter, and I'm going to teach J how to build stuff. I've got a lot of that kind of thing that you'd imagine as the "dad role". My dad was a stay-at-home parent. He was playing much more the "mum role". So for me, I don't think that a dad really gives anything different to what I will be giving, or two mums, or two dads.

'I don't think gender actually has much to play in it. It's much more important who's the primary caregiver, who's taking on the role. But we don't live in a society where we have these varied types of families. I think that the concept of "dad" ends up having this kind of cultural baggage attached to it that J may well feel they're lacking. And it's: "I want that, because I can see everyone else is enjoying having it."'

I wanted to explore this with Ash: the idea that two-parent families look to the outside like enjoyment. After all, that was my feeling too, despite all the stats on divorce. Instead technology got in the way. My internet connection broke. My train of thought derailed. When we reconnected my mind came closer to home.

Was the present matching the expectations Ash had in pregnancy? I wondered aloud. *Should I get pregnant too?* I didn't say.

Ash said it had been even better than they'd imagined. 'I've loved every second of it. The kind of "single parent-hood" aspect of it has actually really surprised me in terms of this stage: there's not been a single moment where I want another person involved.'

'Huh.'

'It feels very uncomplicated because it's just one on one. There's only me meeting J's needs, so it's just really easy to know what's happening. I think if there was another person, it would be a lot of negotiating, like, "Okay, well, you did this, this time. Okay, so I'm going to do that." Obviously, at different stages in life, it will be very different. But for now, I've found it really straightforward and lovely. A very, very good experience.'

After talking with Ash I could not help but think of Duncan. There were some things on which we seemed strongly aligned in terms of parenting ideals: baby names, education, a move to the countryside, freedom to roam, discipline styles that were firm but fair, plus an agreement to shake things up at some point and spend a few years overseas. Yet we also had heated debates. Such as whether or not our non-existent baby would be vegetarian (like I had been since the foetal stage) or would eat meat (as Duncan had done since he started on solids). 'Making it veggie would be indoctrination,' was his argument.

'That's my point about eating meat, though. Why's mine indoctrination and yours not?'

He didn't see it.

'Fine. Compromise: you take it to an abattoir when it's old enough to know what's going on. If the child's happy to eat meat after that, it can start then.'

'My parents aren't going to like it,' he said.

'It's not their child. We're the parents.'

'They'd both want to give their grandchild meat.'

'And you wouldn't back me on that one?'

No reply.

We debated, too, about surnames. Duncan insisted our non-existent baby must have his name. Only his name.

I asked why.

'It's a great surname.'

'So's mine.'

He brayed with laughter.

I explained that being called Codd was character-building. 'Plus you develop a natural affinity with marine life. Plus it's just a good name.'

His nose stayed wrinkled.

Mine wrinkled too. 'So I have to carry an expanding blob of cells in my abdomen for nine months – half of which are yours – potentially blow out my groin to deliver it in a way that not infrequently requires surgery and some-times life-long urology appointments; lose sleep, lose money, perhaps lose my sanity; get bitten on the nipples day and night, suffer repeated boob infections, and you won't even let me give it my surname?'

'That's not fair. I can't carry the baby, can I?'

'Would you carry it for me? Would you choose that? Honestly? I wouldn't.'

No reply.

'How about we combine names then?'

'Too many syllables.'

'What?'

'It wouldn't work.'

'No?'

'No. No.'

I believed we could find a way through if we wanted.

(Would we want to?)

(Did I?)

In my alone time I read about 'couvade' – an umbrella term for rituals by fathers-to-be marking their transition to parenthood, one I had heard directly during my conversation with anthropologist Frank L'Engle Williams. Frank had told me how, through couvade practices, fathers in some cultures – including minority groups in India, Thailand, Russia and others – are ritually 'indoctrinated into the idea of fatherhood'. His book shares some fascinating examples: 'Among the Paraiyan [of South India and Sri Lanka], the husband was practically starved for seven days following the beginning of labor, only receiving some fruits and tubers.' For one inland tribe in the Southeast-Asian archipelago, couvade is 'likened to hatching an egg, whereby the socially recognised father must not leave bed for five days after the birth of his infant; he is treated as an invalid, and may not even bathe for two to five days, depending on the location.' Elsewhere, 'Among the Jivaro of Ecuador and Piojes of Putumayo, a father was required to sympathetically enact the birth outside the home; then, after the birth, he was in so weakened a condition that he was confined to bed to recover from the shock of assuming the social role of fatherhood.' Each experience marked a man's adjustment to this new phase of life.

In other circles, multiple medical studies, encompassing many communities worldwide, pointed to the existence of something called 'couvade syndrome', whereby expectant fathers experienced pregnancy symptoms such as nausea, toothache and vomiting while their partner's pregnancy reached full term. One statistic claimed that this may affect between 10 to 15 per cent of fathers-to-be across the world. (Another study found the proportion of first-time fathers who experienced couvade symptoms to be as high as 65 per cent.)

I asked a writer friend, whose son had not long been born, whether he had gone through anything like that himself. He told me his hair had fallen out – 'but that was probably going to happen anyway. A ritual would have been super helpful, though,' he added. 'We were in the hospital one night, *one night*, and then everything changed. Forever. That was it.'

It seemed to me that some men changed alongside their partners, while some men clearly didn't. And not all the changes were necessarily desirable. Some became sympathetic; some apathetic; some straddled the two.

It seemed such a gamble to enter parenthood with someone you loved.

If they transformed in unexpected ways.

If the things that were positive turned negative.

If, as a result, they grew resentful.

If you grew resentful.

If either one wanted to leave.

On Christmas Eve a dadvert request went out via Facebook to the London Gay Men's Chorus – this being Mentor Claire's latest idea, arranged through one of her friends. I wondered at the timing of it: whether we might catch someone yearning for new family over the festive season; mulling their past choices and future options.

In Mum's kitchen, I prepared food for the next day. She poured a glass of wine for herself and me, and put on the radio. As I worked, an interview began with a man named Nadim Ednan-Laperouse. A few years before, the programme explained, his 15-year-old daughter Natasha had died of an allergic reaction to a mislabelled baguette. Trapped on a plane, on a flight between London and Nice, Nadim watched the fatal reaction unfold, as EpiPen injections failed to reverse the catastrophe. When she died in his arms, he said, he saw five short figures appear beside her, along with a soft yellow light.

Mum and I stopped moving and listened more carefully. Nadim's story continued.

Weeks after her death, the grieving father had entered a darkened room in his house. The then-prime minister, Theresa May, was discussing his daughter's death at a national conference. Nadim recounted giving his thanks to God that Natasha was being remembered, when 'suddenly the whole room lit up. Went *whoosh*, like someone had put the light on. But not the normal light. It was a soft yellow light.'

The vision stunned him.

'I remember going, "Oh my *gosh*, what's that?" and as I did that the light went. And then it dawned on me very quickly afterwards that this was God saying, "I hear you, my child. I'm with you."'

I pushed away the chopping board. Sat down.

'It doesn't change the fact that Natasha's dead,' I heard. 'It doesn't bring her back. It's not for that, but it really made me feel that I have a father. Someone bigger than me. Someone – thankfully – stronger than me. Someone with no ego like me, you know? And it's such a relief to know that there's someone else there who takes care of it all, and you don't *need* to be like that. You know, *give it up*, basically, if you like. It's a road to nowhere.'

*Give it up.*

Mum poured more wine and asked me about Peter. How he was and what he was doing.

In response, I asked what she thought of him. *Really* thought.

'I never got the impression he was at all threatening,' she said.

'No?'

'I thought you got on really well.'

Her words surprised me.

'I think he's probably a man who enjoys female

297

company, but he is a little bit unsure of himself. I don't know. I find him quite difficult to fathom out. But then, when he told us about his illness, something sort of fell into place.'

The dog snuffled between her feet, detecting crumbs and morsels. She picked him up and nestled him into her lap. 'It made me think about what I would do,' she said. 'If I had a terminal illness, I don't think I'd be going off on cruises on my own. I'd probably be wanting to spend time with my nearest and dearest. But the fact is, he didn't really have anybody, did he? I know he's got a lot of friends, but what he's missed out on is having a lasting relationship with one person and children. He's probably realised that a bit too late.' Mum poured another glass for us both. 'Are you thinking of adopting Peter?'

I told her I didn't know.

'Well, if you're not thinking of adopting him, that means he's falling short of your ideal.'

'Does it?' I stalled.

'Remember *Georgie's Book of Men?*'

My memory jolted. I had forgotten that. Now I could picture it clearly: the repurposed school textbook filled with adorations of various men, in Biro.

The TV detective Jonathan Creek's hair and humour.

The long leather coat and low voice of Keanu Reeves in *The Matrix*.

The medic in *Band of Brothers* who put himself in harm's way for everyone else.

'Think about the ones you idolised,' said Mum. 'Arnold Schwarzenegger. That was weird. Why would you be attracted to an Austrian bodybuilder who couldn't really act? Was it because he was strong?'

'I liked him from *Terminator 2*,' I said.

'He didn't speak much in that film.'

'No. He just ran around and was slightly frightening.'

Mum raised an eyebrow. 'But he saved people, didn't he?'

'He did. He saved the child.'

Christmas Day. My extended family and I congregated in my aunt's living room, one of those increasingly dwindling occasions when the majority of us were present and freely talkative. I lay on the floor, sprawled by a wall, while a handful of cousins, their parents and Mum nestled on the sofas nursing teas. 'So how's it going?' one cousin asked. 'This project of yours. All these dads.'

I opened my mouth to reply and did not have the chance.

'I feel very uncomfortable about all this,' Mum declared. 'I feel very uncomfortable about it.' She addressed the group, not me. 'It suggests that you feel you missed out.'

I looked at her. 'Of course,' I began. 'Of course I feel—'

My aunt shook her head and faced Mum. 'You *couldn't* have been a father.' Her comment came out at speed, so fast that I sensed an old argument had awakened; one I had not witnessed before.

'Look,' I said. 'I had a great childhood. I didn't feel strongly then that I was missing out on anything. But . . . it's like . . . Like *everyone* has a father, and I just want to know what that feels—'

'*Everyone?*' a cousin interrupted. Her father had died when she was a child. Cancer. Of course he had.

'In my mind,' I clarified. 'That's what it feels like. Rationally, I know that's not the case.'

Sensing more discontent beneath the surface, I guided us on to the realm of crazy men, the more weird and worrying anecdotes. Soon my family was laughing again. Safe territory, maybe. Everyone back on board.

Except they weren't.

I went to the bathroom for sanctuary, locking myself in. It had struck me that Mum must have been pulled in to this debate time and again, prompted by people around her asking, 'Doesn't your child need a father figure?' and, 'Aren't you letting her down by not providing one?'

Perhaps she had been fending off these arguments for a lifetime. And I had landed them right back in her face.

I flushed the toilet.

*Arnie saved the child*, I thought suddenly. *He also saved the mother.*

My reading turned briefly fanatical again. Any book or website that had the word 'dad' in it was fair game.

This time I learned that in Sweden, in the early twentieth century, a law had been passed to support the idea that every Swedish child was formally entitled to two parents. Legislators believed it to be so important that kids have a father figure, they established a practice called 'possible paternity'. This meant that in cases of children born out of wedlock, in which no man officially stepped forward as Dad, other men who could conceivably be the father – who had slept with the mother around the time of conception – could be designated the child's official parent. After that they would carry the obligations of fatherhood, especially the financial.

As one sociologist put it, quoting a Swedish law committee of 1915: 'it was enough that the man had "completed what according to the order of nature could have caused the child" . . . Underlying this view was the belief that men had to take responsibility for their sexual actions.'

The law shifted again in the 1920s, when blood testing was introduced to determine paternity, and the search to find the biological father, rather than any father, took priority.

I wondered how a law like that, in the UK today, would affect men's behaviour now. What if Carl had been ordered to stay in my life – forced to see things through and face the consequences?

Before New Year I interviewed Mum. Put my Dictaphone between us and everything, shooing the dog away from sniffing the mic.

I said: 'I don't think that you did the wrong thing at all by not having a dad in my life as a kid.'

She contorted her lips. 'Mm,' she said.

'The opposite,' I said.

'Good.'

'Yeah.'

We went quiet.

'I think it would've been very difficult for me to have formed a relationship with a man who could become a father figure to you,' she said. 'Given that I was quite emotionally damaged and also kind of in survival mode. It was all about working hard and keeping things on an even keel. I'm sure I failed in many respects . . .'

'You can only do your best.'

My mother looked pained.

'I have no regrets,' I added.

Her face relaxed. 'Good.' She paused. 'Excellent.'

We went quiet again.

I pointed at the dog. 'He has no regrets.'

'He has. But then again, too few to mention.'

I sniggered. Asked if Mum would like to be the interviewer.

'I don't know,' she replied. 'Been there. Done that.'

Quiet.

'I think the secret of successful interviewing is knowing when to shut up and just let people talk,' said Mum. 'That's when you get the most revealing things.'

'Is that a veiled hint?'

'No, I'm just giving you that as a word of advice. If you have any killer questions, leave them right to the end just in case your interviewee takes umbrage and walks out.'

I searched my mind for the killer question here. My mind was empty.

I told her I would interview her again.


Who, really, was benefiting from the status quo? From the discrepancies in expectations; from most British mothers taking on childcare, and most British fathers returning to work; from maternity leave being up to 52 weeks in the UK, and paternity leave being just two weeks? That had been my killer question for Jeremy from the Fatherhood Institute.

And Jeremy wasn't sure; maybe capitalism, he suggested.

I came across the researcher Dr Mario Liong, who had

written a book called *Chinese Fatherhood, Gender and Family*. Seeing the title made me wonder what fathers were like in the People's Republic of China – the republic 'fathered' by Mao Zedong in 1949; a republic ostensibly on the opposite side of the spectrum from capitalism, where the striving was for collective progress, rather than the separate progress of individuals. (At least on paper.)

Deciding to write to Liong, I asked if he might talk with me.

I spoke to Cly about the subject during our next catch-up call.

'I'm the same age as the People's Republic of China,' he responded. 'Isn't that funny?'

That was funny, I concurred. Then something inside me came up and out. 'What do you think about this?' I said. 'That our current nuclear family structures are instruments of capitalism. They keep us in these tiny boxes where we're compelled to keep working for our little family and are stuck in work forever. Instead of doing something about it and living for ourselves, we give up and pile all our hopes onto the *next* generation, hoping that *they'll* reap the benefits, but then they just follow our lead and pass on their chances too.

'Meanwhile everything we and they do is actually really for the benefit of a handful of mega-wealthy individuals and *their* little families, and then we die kind of thing.' I itched my knuckles. 'I think this might be what's happening.'

'Well, Grasshopper,' he answered. 'There might be something in that.'

'Maybe,' I said. 'Maybe.'

# 20

# NOT SURE

While I waited to learn about China, I wanted to try again with Peter. To see if I could stop worrying about his motives, crude gags or the chance of him suddenly dying. To just see him, and see what happened.

'Becoming a father is not a single event,' as my note-keeping habit informed me.

I realised it would be only our second meeting post-cruise. I wondered how many more we might need. How many more we might have. I wondered if it was still too early to visit him solo – except I had no choice. Claire was working. Duncan was working, and anyway he had now completed the waterpark.

'What are the plans?' I asked Peter in a quick call a few days before, thinking that might help me feel more grounded.

'Mystery trip with Pete's Tours,' he replied. 'Could be a book in it.'

'Mystery?'

I did my best not to think of his axe, while packing an umbrella with extra-sharp prongs.

On the train, killing time, self-distracting, I found my

horoscope in a free morning paper. 'Do you have an ambiguous opinion of someone?' it asked. 'You could find that reaching out and connecting with this person is worthwhile. They may have a lot more to offer than you thought and a positive friendship could develop.'

I put it aside and drafted a message, sending it to Duncan and friends. *If Peter makes me text that I'm fine when I'm not, I will write XOX, which actually is my SOS code.*

Then I imagined Peter finding the message, thus uncovering my masterplan.

*Will now delete these words off my phone before I self-destruct,* I texted next.

I wiped off everything.

When the train came in to Swansea, he was late. I hid myself in the waiting room. Pulled out my Dictaphone, my silent witness. Minutes later Peter appeared at the waiting-room door. The smile. The wave. The jacket. The hug. He pointed at the umbrella I'd brought, then gestured at the volume of sunshine streaming through the windows. 'You look like Mary Poppins.'

'It was raining in London.'

'It never rains here.'

'I'm recording, by the way.'

'You're recording? As we speak?'

'Yeah, like a thing of our day.'

'Are we gonna be famous?'

'I don't know. Maybe.'

I followed him out of the station and into the car park.

'The itinerary,' he said.

'The mystery tour,' I said.

'The mystery tour, my gosh.' He stopped. Squinted at the Dictaphone.

'I won't be recording all day,' I said. 'I just thought it would be fun.'

Our tour involved another drive down the coast. On the way, I stopped the recorder, feeling less and less like I needed it. We started talking about his old job again. He told me about a fire he had attended in town. 'You know these gas cylinders,' he was saying, 'the small ones you make a cup of tea with? There was one of those in the attic and a house fire spread to it – the house was empty at the time – and this cylinder exploded. It was such a force you wouldn't even think it. The whole roof lifted off the house and moved, so when we got there the roof was, sort of, four foot off the main brickwork, and all 'cause of this little gas cylinder.'

I puffed the air out of my cheeks.

'When the owners came back they got a bit of a shock,' he laughed.

We arrived at the pub he had booked for lunch. Except for an older woman sitting at the window, the place was ours.

My recorder was tucked away now. The defensive prongs of my brolly were in the car. Slowly, very slowly, I was relaxing. Enough that I started to enquire about Peter's humour. By way of response, he told me about a friend.

'His nephew's in his twenties,' he said, 'and I was in the kitchen with him one day, chatting we were, laughing and joking. My friend was there. And I said to his nephew, "Have you got any naked pictures of your girlfriend?" "No," he said. I said, "Do you want to buy some?" And we were *roaring*. My friend stopped it straight away. He said, "Peter, please. I cannot have that in this house. It's very upsetting." And the nephew's looking at me. I think, "Oh God, here we go." And I had to apologise. He really gets upset, you know? He said, "Well, who's this girl coming from London?"'

I leaned forward. Peter didn't pause.

'"That's Georgie." He said, "What does she come down for? It sounds very strange to me – she comes down for five hours and leaves." I said, "Well that's just the way she does it." I said, "She's more than welcome to stay." "How old is she? What does her mother think?" I said, "Mother's fine about it. What's the problem?" "Oh, I think it's improper," he said. "You realise there are, you know, lines not to cross?" I said, "She's my friend, you know?" but he – no – doesn't. "Oh," I said, "I'm not gonna jump on her bones." "Please, please," he said, "I can't. I can't take it." Very liberal, yeah, oh God.'

I gulped a big mouthful of water. 'You know I'm liberal too, right?'

'We all make mistakes, George. You'll learn. Atta girl.'

Peter leaned back in his chair, surveying our surroundings. The empty bar hung with pint glasses. A seagull plodding outside. Within moments he caught the eye of the older woman in the window. Raised his voice. 'Just having lunch with my daughter,' he told her.

The woman cocked him a look. 'She's not your daughter.'

Peter seemed surprised.

I didn't hesitate. 'What does this look like from the outside?' I asked, both desperate to know and fearing the answer would feature that two-word phrase with the 's' and the 'd'.

The woman cradled her chin in her hand. 'Like friends,' she said.

'Good. Okay.'

Except: friends was not what I wanted.

On our way out I thanked Peter for the meal. Switched my recorder on to catch the noise of our footsteps, and the birdsong.

'Nothing but the best for you, George,' said Peter.

'Aw, thanks, pal.'

'I thought you said, "Thanks, Dad," then.'

'Thanks, Dad.'

'That's okay.'

Our footsteps marched. My chest tightened.

'I think I'd go with Pops,' I said.

'Pops, is it?'

'How does that sound?'

'Yes . . .' He paused. 'That sounds . . .' He paused. 'Er . . .'

Peter still wasn't sure.

In the recesses of my computer were a couple of photos I'd taken in my mid-twenties. They depicted the letter I had sent to Carl, captured for my future reference. For some reason, though, they only showed the last two sides of what had been enclosed.

When I came home from Wales, for the first time in years, I opened them. Seeing borders of varnished floor around the paper, I was instantly transported back to another flat. Another time.

I saw I had written each word out carefully, more neatly than I had ever seen my handwriting elsewhere.

'. . . not anyone else', began page two, completing a line or emotion I could not recall.

I made myself read on.

'All my life I have been interested in learning more about you', I had written.

My mother has told me bits and pieces, but I can't say I understand what you're like (especially given she must have bias as far as you're concerned).

A while ago, curiosity compelled me to search for information on the internet. Again I didn't find out much, but it was then that I discovered you had lost your daughter Caroline. I was truly sorry to hear it and cannot imagine what impact that had on your life.

I also don't know what bearing that has on you hearing from me now. This is obviously a very strange situation for both of us – there are lots of unknowns on either side.

I am 25 now and feel more and more as if I need to know who I am and where I came from. From time to time I do and say things that don't tally with how my mum behaves and I wonder if this is a side of me I share with you.

I have heard about your skills as a photographer and, like you, am quite creative. Also, weirdly enough, the only instrument I ever chose to take lessons for was the bass guitar. I'm afraid I eventually gave it up, but when I did Mum told me you were a talented player. Perhaps there are more things like this we have in common. At some point, when the time is right for both of us, perhaps we can meet face-to-face and find out.

As I've mentioned before, I don't know your background or how you will react to this letter, but I would be delighted if – one day – you could bring yourself to get in touch. My current address and phone number are at the top of this letter. When you're ready, I really hope to hear from you.

Take care.

My signature, '<u>Georgina</u>', was underlined.

There was something about the feeling of these words that pulled at me. The formal tone. The matter-of-factness.

There were also the memories I had of writing it: the careful weighing up of every option. The anticipatory dread. The feeling of sending myself out to a point of no return.

Just like I'd been putting out a dadvert.

Mario Liong, the Hong Kong Chinese author of the book about Chinese fatherhood, was happy to talk through the internet. The two of us shared more mutual ground than I had anticipated. After swapping our greetings, I learned that Mario's familial experiences, and general uncertainties around parenthood, had led him to start his own investigations. 'At that time, I wanted to be a father myself,' he said, from an apartment in Taiwan. 'I wanted to know what fathers would be thinking and doing.' He had been studying unemployment for his master's in Hong Kong – researching the aftermath of the Asian financial crisis of the late nineties – when he met a sixty-something male interviewee.

The interviewee was looking for jobs, said Mario, 'which was kind of unusual at that time, because he was supposed to retire. He revealed to me actually, he had a 25-year-old son and he was supporting him. His son was physically healthy. He was able to work, but he wasn't willing to work. He just stayed home playing video games – that kind of guy – and then his father still felt responsible to support his son.'

I shook my head.

Mario nodded. 'I was actually quite surprised. I started to have this kind of curiosity. Because I've read academic works of books about fathers in the West, like some of Europe, the UK, and I didn't seem to recall this kind of account: fathers feeling responsible economically for adult children. I was curious.'

Mario's primary focus became Chinese fathers in Hong Kong, through which he learned that this father's approach *was* unusual, while also being an extension of how Hong Kong Chinese men express fatherhood overall. Repeatedly, Mario's interviewees equated earning money with loving their children. 'In Chinese culture we don't really show love and care through a lot of physical touch,' he explained, 'sometimes not even emotional dialogue or conversation. So instead we do things for each other.'

That was probably just as well: at the time of our conversation, statutory parental leave was just five days for Hong Kong fathers, having not long increased from three. If working long hours in an office was *not* love, what were these people doing?

As for fathers in the socialist People's Republic of China (PRC) specifically – which, unlike capitalist Hong Kong, had developed without any direct Western influence – Mario believed there were similarities in terms of fatherly mindsets: work equalling love, for example. However, due to the PRC's now-defunct one-child policy (active between 1980 and 2016), there was more concern on the mainland around the progress of children academically, particularly around competition with peers for the best grades and jobs.

Another difference: 'In mainland China, the grandparents are heavily involved in taking care of the children,' whereas middle-class Chinese families in Hong Kong typically hire nannies from Southeast Asia. Although, Mario pondered aloud, academics from mainland China were different again; or, at least, the ones he had met. 'They are kind of reluctant for their own parents to get involved,' he said, 'because they feel that their values are very different. But they're exposed to more foreign influences, and they have more living experiences abroad.'

The world was working on fathers in myriad ways.

Mario said things were shifting for Chinese fathers in Hong Kong. New identities and forms of self-expression were being claimed by younger generations – by the fathers attending a local men's centre that Mario formerly worked with, for instance.

Later I spoke to another fatherhood specialist in Hong Kong, Winn Tam, whose own work confirmed this. Winn was the director of a not-for-profit called the DADs

Network, which had supported and promoted fatherhood since 2015. His email signature described him as a *DADvocate for Active Fathering.* (I approved of the pun.)

Winn's directorial origin story was about the father he grew up with. 'I don't have the impression about how my father influenced me,' he said. 'I only see the bad side, the dark side; that he didn't participate much, that he didn't help my mother, and he didn't give me too much in my life. Somehow, I would like to say I hate him also.'

Then his old school principal, a fellow DADvocate, gave Winn counsel. 'And he told me to be fair about dads. Because in the traditional Chinese culture, Father would be out while I was growing up, and he has his feelings also.

'After that, I chat with my father and I ask him what he feels about his life. He told me that he was quite sad about that, that he didn't have many memories about me and my brothers. So even though he has a very successful business, he thinks that his family life has failed.

'I have to pay much more effort in this organisation to help much more fathers get awareness as fast as possible, so they don't take the route like my father.'

In my conversation with Mario, men's centres were also a key topic for discussion. The one Mario worked at defined good fathers and good men as those who could both maintain economic stability *and* were 'able to show love, being involved in housework, in children's lives'. (Much like most mothers I knew.)

Out loud, I wondered what happened to Chinese men

who actively disengaged from their children, like Carl had done with me.

'They would be condemned,' reported Mario.

'By the community?'

'Yes, family members or friends.'

'Oh, wow.'

'I recall there was a high-school teacher and his wife left him. His friends actually challenged him if he was a responsible father. Even when he was living with his children, taking care of them, his friends pressured him to be an involved father, to be a good father.'

Mario's own father was also highly involved. When at age 7 or 8, in their small Hong Kong flat, his mother decreed he could no longer share the bed with her, he switched rooms to share with his father. 'My mom was pushing me away. She was a homemaker. And my father was the only bread-winner, but he was really involved. He would look at my homework and play with me, even though he was very tired after work.

'I had pains in my knees when I was a child, so sometimes in the middle of the night I was awake because of those pains. And my dad actually took care of me, even though he was very tired. Some months ago, I recalled these experiences, and I was very touched. When I grew up, gradually we were becoming more distant.'

Mario told me he wanted more closeness. Yet that distance was persisting. 'Now I'm in Taiwan, I don't live with my parents anymore. Sometimes I talk over the phone. And usually it is my mom talking. I know that my father is still there even though we don't speak. But yeah, he's listening. Yeah. That's our relationship.'

Mario's personal parenting journey also went differently to how he wanted. 'At the end, I didn't become a father.' He and his long-term partner broke up. His research also affected him. 'Probably I met too many divorced fathers who told me these sad stories and issues with their kids. I wasn't discouraged by them, but I thought it was a huge responsibility to be a father. I cannot take it lightly. Several fathers actually shared with me that fatherhood to them was really a very valuable experience, because they were able and confident of bringing up another life. But as a person who, I mean, who is not even able to take care of plants – no, I'm not confident of being a father.'

# 21
# FINE

Confidence.

I couldn't find it.

Everywhere I looked, it wasn't there.

Peter: giant question mark.

The inbox: mostly dust balls.

The gay choristers of the capital: not a peep.

As for the dadverts I'd sent overseas: *kichu'i nā*; *nada*; nothing.

This was not meant to be happening. I was meant to be forming bonds with new people everywhere. To be learning if it was true that, in the words of J. Neil Tift, a man representing the Native American Fatherhood and Families Association, 'Through almost every studied culture, fathers have assumed three primary roles: the protector, the provider, and the disciplinarian.'

At least Cly and I were still talking. I felt more optimistic about that one. Confident, though? I wasn't sure.

Tired sometimes. Yes.

Wishing we could talk less about politics.

He and I discussed future plans semi-regularly, over the

phone: how Duncan and I could ride a train for a few hours and reach him; how Cly could pick us up from the station; how he could show us around his area. We were welcome to stay as long as we wanted, in his old house with his old deerhounds. The warmth in his voice was inviting. I liked how often he laughed. The timbre of that laugh.

I started researching trains. Considering dates. Gently brought myself closer to pressing *Book Tickets*. Yet felt, somehow, that now was not the time.

Instead I baked a crumble. Spent £20 on jars of luxury jam. Went cacti shopping with Duncan, agonised over the options and picked the three cheapest choices available, bringing home a trio of tiny plants. Against my boyfriend's wishes, I named all three. Gonzalez, Günther, George.

'What's the point?' he moaned, as I began formally introducing them. 'It's fucking weird. They're plants.'

'They're plant babies, you dickhead. Be nice.'

'Dickhead. That's nice.'

'I think you owe the babies an apology.'

When the time was overdue again, I emailed Cly to suggest a call. The time came, the call connected; he sounded delighted. I could sense him listening attentively while I went into details on how much I'd been lacking pep. Apologised for not being as quick to communicate as I'd wanted. I told him how, in fact, I was failing to communicate in all sorts of ways. With Mum, with Duncan, with everyone. And that I had made a resolution to be better.

He replied to reassure me I was totally fine as I was. As he did, I noticed something different about the way he spoke. His voice was louder than usual. More effusive.

And it slurred.

Resisting the obvious assumption, I chose not to comment. Pushed it down.

Then, about 40 minutes later, in a gap between anecdotes about dry-stone walling, Cly confirmed what his tone was already conveying: he was no longer sober. Was drinking again. Smoking too. After many years of going without.

Verbally Cly shrugged it off, as if this should mean nothing. In the next breath he diverted to another topic of conversation: how, if I took daily cold showers, I might feel life become more manageable. The laugh I gave was artificial. Grim awareness of what was happening seeped into my brain.

Fathers and drinking did not mix. I thought Cly knew that. I thought we'd discussed that. That we were on the same page.

'Are you okay?' I asked. 'Is everything all right?'

He chuckled. 'Fine, darling, yes. I'm tired and that's how it is.'

'Are you sure?'

'Yes.' Cly would not go there.

For a while he expounded on philosophy. My head felt warped and weird, not taking it in.

*He's not the same.*

*This isn't the same.*

*But the alcohol . . .*

Going through the motions, aiming for all the right noises at the right times, I listened and agreed where it was needed. Until the space shifted again.

From nowhere Cly cried out, 'I love you to bits. Don't *ever* not call me if you feel negative!'

I seized up. Stammered. We'd now talked to each other over such a long period, sharing lengthy conversations over months, and it was the first time Cly had shared anything like this. I managed to say, 'That's kind.' Tried to talk about my cacti.

He stepped things up. 'Really, Georgy. I only speak to four people in my life and you're one of them. Why don't you call me more?'

'I—'

'I would so love it if you called me more. I lost a child, remember. I don't want to lose you too.'

Panic gripped my insides. I had forgotten about the death.

I told myself it was Drink talking.

Drink kept talking. 'I love you, Georgy,' said Cly mournfully. 'I love you! Come to stay with me! You must come!'

'We'll work something out. Give me time.'

'Ach,' said Cly, irritated. 'There's too much time.'

'Life's – it's complicated, isn't it?'

'It is if you choose to make it that way.'

I let go of the phone and closed my eyes.


Carl had been a drinker. Mum sometimes said that he liked his booze – and that he had lost his licence for drink-driving. But the situation must have grown worse after they broke up.

Must have grown much worse.

The next day Cly sent a message. He wrote how lovely

it had been to talk to me, reiterating that he had been *extremely tired.* The reason he drank alcohol, he dropped in, was because a friend had been soul-searching and needed help. He had therefore consumed a glass of wine at her house.

*I do so worry about you,* he wrote, *and am really hopeful that I can help, by being there for you and listening.*

I wondered if he recalled how he had spoken. If, after all our conversations about dysfunction, about life, about death, about dads, he could perceive how that landed.

I racked my brains. What had I told Cly about Carl and drink? About why I had no half-sibling?

I wallowed in emails. A friend from university sent me an article from the *New Yorker.* Apparently, it was all about 'Japan's Rent-a-Family Industry'. I put my head in my hands.

It had been over a year and my project was liquefying. Not into a heart-warming, homely bowl of soup, but a hot and nauseating slurry of unidentifiable components.

I didn't know who I was meant to be.

A daughter to who?

A writer for when?

A female in her thirties, reaching out to discover –

What?

What was there?

It was a few weeks until the shark book came out. Researching online again, I found what I needed. Placed an urgent request to see a new therapist.

The therapist allotted to me was male, and thankfully

too young for my project's boundaries. Slowly I made my way to his rooms, a 10-minute walk from the flat.

There we talked about having a purpose. I didn't want to *have to* have a purpose. Except the dad project had been my purpose and now it was dying.

I supposed having kids could be a purpose instead. Should having kids be my purpose? 'Is that why what I've been doing makes people angry?' I asked. 'Because I'm trying to make dads instead of children?'

I cried and cried.

In patience, the therapist waited. He asked why I was crying.

'Because I feel empty and pointless. No one seems to want to know me, especially online.' A tiny snot bubble grew out of my nostril and popped. 'I know that's not true. I know I have friends. There's just a part of me that really wants more.'

'What's the solid you under there?' asked the therapist. His killer question.

I mopped myself with a tissue. Told him I didn't know. 'There isn't one,' I concluded.

(Was I looking for the solid me? Was that what I had made fathers out to be?)

Once upon a time, I thought releasing a book would be what finally caught my father's attention.

I had imagined Carl passing a bookshop and seeing my name in the window.

Imagined *him* contacting *me*.

Tracing circles in the flat, petting pigs, staring at cacti, my mind came back to Jeremy from the Fatherhood Institute. He'd had a killer question for me too, hadn't he?

I brought out my recording of the interview and scanned the transcript. I was wrong. It hadn't been a killer question. It had been a killer statement. Several of them.

'For a child,' Jeremy told me, 'whether a father is present or not, the idea of a father is there, whether they want that idea or not: it just is there. Whatever the route to fatherhood, whatever the story of why he's not there, it's a very powerful thing for a child.

'Of course, you don't stop being a child by becoming an adult in that meaning of "child". You remain the child of your mother and father, or whoever your parents are, for your whole life. That's a position that you carry with you until your dying breath.'

I took in his words. I slumped.

'I don't know what the story was with your mum,' Jeremy continued, 'but I can imagine that she might have found all sorts of sources for support, or maybe she did it all on her own. Either way, she got through and she did the best she could. People from the outside would have thought well of her, I suppose, for doing so.

'It leaves a whole set of questions about him, your father. And it leaves questions about you, his child, for whom obviously – from this conversation and the fact that we're having it – it's clear that in some way he, or the absence of him, is still very much a part of your life.'

I'd not ever conceived it that way before. I supposed, aloud, that this must partly be down to the notion that mothers are all children need.

Jeremy laughed. 'Well, fathers are "optional"!' he said, alluding to the consensus. 'They're "disposable". And in all sorts of ways, literally speaking, that's true. You seem like a lovely person, like you're doing well in your career, so on and so on. Big tick for your mum. You're objectively, unless you're a serial killer—'

'Side project.'

'—you're a success story, and a demonstration that mums can do this on their own. And there are plenty of examples of mums doing it on their own. So, in that sense, fathers are optional. But. But. There is a big "but".'

Joy, a mother speaking to the BBC on parenthood: 'Just because we have the equipment doesn't mean to say we have the disposition . . . If I had my time again, I would never have children.'

The man across the road screamed through a new night. Duncan's phone was on the floor. I picked it up and called social services. 'Can someone help him, please?'

The operator asked his address.

'Ah, yes, he's known to us,' they said. 'His mother died last year.'

'Are you supposed to share that kind of stuff with strangers?'

'I'll make a note you rang. But best call the police.'

Duncan shifted.

Jo Nicholl, relationship coach and psychotherapist: 'Any absence is a wound.'

*

My therapy sessions were almost over before they had begun. Facing the man who was counselling me, I went off on one. 'I mean, do I have children or not? Should I? My boyfriend says he wants them with me *one day* and maybe I want that *one day* and maybe everyone wants them *one day*, when they're this nebulous thing that you can just imagine and don't actually have to clear up after or live with, but I don't have until *one day* apparently, because my womb will expire, and so will my boyfriend's sperm for that matter – that's if either of us is functioning right now at all anyway. And you can't put them back in, can you?'

The therapist: 'What do you mean, "in"?'

'You know.' I gestured to my crotch. 'Back up there. Once they're out, they're out. And then there's all the physical stuff. Like, my teeth could fall out and—'

'That's very rare.'

'*It happens.*'

'Unlikely, though.'

'I used to work in a clinic; I've seen women who were incontinent because of pregnancy – and not just urinarily, but *faecally*—'

He squirmed.

'—and I heard this woman on the radio recently talking about how she watched the skin on her stomach split open like a tectonic fault in an earthquake and—'

He held up his hand. 'I'm going to have to stop you there.'

I looked at him. I looked at the clock. We had 20 minutes left.

'I know we're supposed to have a last session next week but there's a chance I might not be here: my wife is having a baby.'

I slapped my hand to my mouth. 'I'm so sorry. Is it your first child?'

'Yep.'

'Are you scared?'

'Yep. And excited. Mostly excited.'

———

Years before dadverts. My first ever therapist. Our penultimate session.

I sat down. Dumped a large, stuffed bag by my feet.

'You'll like this,' I told him. 'Guess what?'

'What?'

'I'm on the way to meet Carl today.'

'Sorry?'

'My actual dad. My father. He's in hospital.'

My therapist leaned forward. Said: 'I think we need more sessions.'

———

# 22
# ESCAPE

Peter left messages on my voicemail. I'd invited him to my book launch and he wanted to hear all about it. Where it would be. Who would be going. His friends were keen to know more.

I clicked on the link to 'Japan's Rent-a-Family Industry', thanking the friend who'd sent it. The article's introduction revealed that, in Japan, 'People who are short on relatives can hire a husband, a mother, a grandson. The resulting relationships can be more real than you expect.'

As far as the internet told me, we didn't have family rental services in the UK.

Fine.

I composed a new message. Destination: the Family Romance agency, Japan.

*Good morning*, I wrote.

*Thank you for establishing this amazing service. I live in London, England, but I am looking for a temporary father because I never had a father of my own. I do not mind travelling a long way to experience this.*

*Please could you tell me how much it would cost to arrange time with a father in Tokyo? I would be hoping to come to the city for approximately one week to spend time with him. Do you have any father substitutes who speak English? I would be very grateful for your kind response.*

*(I am sorry for my lack of Japanese.)*
*With many thanks and warmest wishes,*
*Georgina*

Message sent.

Another note from Peter pinged its arrival.

The English-speaking world had few articles about Japanese dads. Most were about the 'Ikumen Project', a government campaign launched in 2010 to encourage greater paternal involvement in child-rearing. Its title combined the words for 'childcare' (*ikuji*) and 'hunk' (*ikemen*), and the project:

painted the father as a heroic figure, emphasising his masculinity and sexual allure; one of its posters depicted one man tearing off his suit and shirt, Superman-like, to reveal the project's logo on a t-shirt underneath, with the slogan 'Ikumen strength for society'. The implication was that these 'heroes' were not just protecting their family; by nurturing the next generation of workers, they were helping to save the country.

Mum called. Asked if I'd spoken to Peter.

'Why?'

'He's trying to get hold of you.'

'Is he okay?'

'Yes. He's just worried that you're not okay.'

'Well, I'm fine. Properly fine.'

'He and I spoke for about an hour. I said I'd make a banana cake and bring it down to Mumbles.'

'That's nice. I'm sorry. I'm busy. Can I call back?'

'In a significant minority of the world's cultures,' writes Professor Ross D. Parke,

> males and females divide the care of young children more evenly. Among the Trobrianders of Melanesia, for example, the father participates actively in the care, feeding, and transport of young children. Similarly in a number of other cultures, including the Taira of Okinawa, the Aka Pygmies of Africa, and the Ilocos of the Philippines, father and mother share more equally in infant and child care.

A *Guardian* article gave more info: 'Are the men of the African Aka tribe the best fathers in the world?' As well as describing the interchangeability of men and women in hunter-gatherer and childrearing roles in this culture, it explained that these men of Central Africa were even engaged in a form of breastfeeding: 'male nipples are there as a stand-in for when mum isn't around . . . a male nipple, deficient though it is in terms of sustenance, gives a more pleasant sucking sensation than, say, a dummy.'

Dads as pacifiers.

Mum had been thinking, she told me, in her next call. Thoughts about the breakdown of her own parents' marriage. How Grandad Codd had tormented Granny by curbing her budget for household supplies. How severely he reprimanded her for adding an extra pot of cream to their grocery account. How he refused to take her to hospital during the agony of kidney stones. Berated her, sometimes hitting her, in front of the children.

He had sex with a nun, he told Granny in spite, then divorced her to marry Barbara from the tennis club.

'Out of me, you and your grandmother, only one of us had a good experience with a father. That was Granny's dad – your great-grandfather – and he wasn't even her biological dad. Granny was conceived while he was at war and he still treated her as his own when he came back. He never let on.'

'*That's what I've been talking about*,' I said. 'Biology didn't work. There was a better way for Granny which did.'

(Where was the better way that would work for me?)

In Paraguay, men and women from the Aché community had formed an unusual parenting practice. Anthropologist Anna Machin has described how, as a result of constant warring and violence against their neighbours, the Aché exhibited:

a relatively rare form of fathering that results in children having more than one dad. Relatively common in South America but absent elsewhere, this method of parenting means that a child doesn't just have a single biological dad but has a number of 'social' fathers as well . . . The rate of mortality among Aché men is astonishingly high, and children who do not have a father are left unprotected and at a significant risk of being killed by invading tribes . . .

It is with this very real threat of death that the need for more than one father becomes clear.


I reflected on the dynamics between Granny Codd and my grandfather. How in Germany, after the Second World War, children of non-persecuted groups mostly had 'fathers who were active culprits or complicit' in Hitler's genocide. In the Allied countries, however, nearly all fathers became instant national heroes. While the men in persecuted groups, who were rounded up, tortured, killed, had other shapes jaggedly carved from their family units.

Grandad Codd was captured on German soil. In his prisoner-of-war camp he made giant barley cakes, wrote and painted. He was welcomed home by a street festooned with bunting. He was a 'hero'.

What if Carl had been alive to fight in the war? Would he have been a 'hero' too?

Would he have stuck around to be my dad?

And what if he had come of age in that lengthy period of human history, from the sixteenth to nineteenth century, when childbirth was even more gruesome for women than now; that period when almost a quarter of children lived in lone-father households?

What if he were Swedish in the 1910s?

Inspired by the Ikumen Project?

Peer-pressured by his community in Hong Kong?

Offered big chunks of paternity leave?

Getting help from the Fatherhood Institute?

Might Carl have then worked harder to be present?

And on that first night he babysat Caroline alone.

When he –

On the other side of the Atlantic, another curious mind had been examining the close links between history, culture and fathers. Jordan Thierry, a filmmaker from Oregon, set his sights on examining dad dynamics among African-Americans.

In *The Black Fatherhood Project*, Thierry interviewed fathers and leading researchers to gain an understanding of parenting in Black families prior to slavery, during slavery and in the decades since official abolition. In his film, one professor described slave traders' methods of breaking up family units, purposefully separating people from others they might know, and from those who spoke the same dialect. Another interviewee described how many oppressed men had cared for children as their own, even when those children were 'fathered' by men who were not present – or who indeed could not be present against their will.

Many men still felt a sense of profound, lasting shame for being unable to safely harbour their loved ones, the film reported – a feeling sustained as intergenerational trauma; sustained through decades of racism; sustained through the modern-day, disproportionate rise in incarcerations among the Black male population. Contained in the resulting culture were fathers who had been systemically hindered from protecting. Hindered from providing. Damaged by the discipline of others.

I spoke to director Jordan by video call – he was working

down in Mexico – and asked how his documentary came to exist. 'The original vision was just going to be a short film interviewing Black fathers,' he recalled. 'Then I realised that I had to not just try to counter the stereotype of the deadbeat Black dad, but actually acknowledge it, and address why that stereotype exists. Why there is this reality that *does* exist.'

He told me that he had started by looking at the 1980s crack epidemic and the war on drugs. 'That is such a huge part of Black American history,' Jordan said. 'It's like something that we all survived; that our families survived. Nobody was untouched by it. But there wasn't much conversation on how that impacted Black families. I was like, okay, that provides some context. But then what about before then? What about before *then*? And so on.'

What Jordan learned time and again by going back, was that families and fathers are never isolated units. That they are constructed, constricted and sometimes destroyed by their surroundings. By the year in which they are born. By their colour. By their peers.

By the people with power around them.

'Oftentimes we have these conversations about family in a vacuum,' said Jordan. 'We don't acknowledge those political and systemic forces that have shaped family structures. And that goes for the role that religion has played, and the role of culture, the role of economics and work. All those things shape what we see and feel and understand to be family and relationships. That's the part that I think is really important.

'That's not talked about enough.'

\*

The shark book was in its penultimate phase before it would be published. While I waited I was invited to experience another mechanism systemically shaping masculinity. It was how, on a grey weekday morning, I found myself at Her Majesty's Prison Grendon in Buckinghamshire, surrounded by a range of men serving time. (A prison where incidentally, two years later, Black and minority ethnic prisoners would officially flag 'concerns about discriminatory and ill-judged behaviour from staff'.)

Impulse told me I had to go, for an open day arranged by the Friends of Grendon – of which a freelance contact was one. When I looked up the prison online, the first article to appear was a news piece titled 'Hi, I'm Adam, I killed my daughter'.

The impulse grew stronger.

Peter didn't like the sound of it. As soon as he heard of my plan, he left a message. 'Careful, George,' he said. 'Watch your back with the inmates.'

'It's a therapeutic prison,' I told him when I called back. 'They're not inmates, they're residents.'

'Dear God.'

Within the brightly lit waiting room was a small collection of books and toys for children coming to visit. Meeting their uncles, cousins, older brothers, family friends.

Meeting dads.

'No formal auditing of men's parental status is in place within prison,' I discovered in my preparations. 'Surveys, however, have revealed some figures: in 2003 it was revealed that 25% of young men [in young offender institutions] are fathers or expectant fathers and it was estimated in 2003 that 32% of [the] male prison population have dependant children under the age of 18.' Overall, an estimated 312,000 children in England and Wales were believed to be affected by parental imprisonment every year; almost 2.4 per cent of the total under-18 population. While 65 per cent of sons of prisoners ended up in the criminal justice system themselves.

This rippling, cyclical situation had me thinking not only of Jordan Thierry's spotlight on Black American oppression and incarcerations, but also of Jeremy Davies, the voice of the Fatherhood Institute. 'There's this sort of great big black hole that never gets talked about,' he had said. 'Which is: what do fathers lose by being expected, still, to take on a greater provider role than mothers?

'If this gets talked about at all, it gets talked about as a problem of men selfishly paying themselves more, almost escaping the "drudgery" of childcare. Well, okay, that's one way of describing it. But another way would be of men missing out on the most important relationship, or one of the most important relationships, that any human being can have, i.e. the relationship with their children. Which is worse? I don't know. They're quite different lacks, but they're both very lacking, it seems to me.'

Here, in Grendon, many men missed out.

A group of us were led through multiple sets of locked gates and scanners, and into the prison itself.

Inside, in a carpeted anteroom, it smelled like tea and biscuits. Two residents served up hot drinks from a cosy hatch. More residents filed in to speak with us, wearing casual clothes like sweaters and jeans, picking their chairs for a chat. They did therapy just about every day, they said. They ran their wings collectively, electing representatives, sometimes voting to eject residents who weren't fully embracing Grendon's therapeutic model – thus sending them out and away to other prisons. The set-up was hard and also helpful for making transformations.

I wondered which of the men before me were dads. I wanted to ask them about the black hole of being kept separate from their sons or daughters.

Except that some of the men here had done especially awful things to children and young people.

And for those men, I wanted to ask: what about *your* fathers?

We moved on to a larger room inside one of the wings; it was painted with a mural of books on shelves. Guests and residents sat together, and we introduced ourselves one after the other. Some gave their crimes along with their names, as part of the process of taking accountability. The guy beside me, who wore a pair of glasses with a logo that read 'Icy' embossed on the arms, briefly explained how he had been in a robbery that went fatally wrong. Like the others, he praised a technique widely used there called psychodrama, in which residents re-enacted their crimes within groups, each group member taking on different roles. A resident could be themselves, be the victim, be an accomplice, be a witness. Try to connect with all the feelings their actions had unleashed. Fully realise what they had done, and not repeat it.

By lunchtime, now in a small, school-like canteen, I had still not asked a single thing about fatherhood. Instead I spoke to another resident about his former life in London. This man was in for kidnap and forced imprisonment, and the two of us were getting on pretty well. I finished two large helpings of chocolate brownie and stopped myself eating a third. These men seemed like decent people, I thought. They didn't look like criminals. Perhaps a couple did. But the rest . . .

A female volunteer took me aside. Asked how things were going.

'Well!' I said. 'It's been really inspiring. I'm also scared to ask what I want to ask, but I think that's okay?'

She nodded. 'Let me tell you something,' she said. 'I've been coming here a few years now—'

'Cool.'

'—and some of these guys will tell you they're murderers. What they won't tell you is that they ate the eyes.'


Having the wrong kind of dad could cause irreparable damage. I knew this. I knew what might have been my lot.

Damaging, too, was having a dad who was absent behind bars.

In his film, Jordan Thierry had reported that on any given day a million Black children in the States have a parent incarcerated. He concluded: 'It is up to extended relatives, neighbours, teachers, police officers, and other people in the community, to step up as partners in the development of young people so that they can avoid addiction, gang violence and other ills that derail so many of our talented youths from the paths that they should be on.'

Which led me back to the 'corporate parent' idea. And then took me further still. Because it wasn't just local authorities who could play mum and dad.

Neighbours were a parent. Teachers were a parent. Doctors were a parent.

Drink could be a parent. Drugs were a parent. Violence was a parent.

Police, judges and wardens – they were parents.

Books, newspapers, websites – in their way, they were parents too.

Protectors, providers, disciplinarians.

And their child-rearing styles could be admirable; could be wretched.

Whoever manned Family Romance chose not to write back. I considered writing again and saw myself land in Japan, wearily hauling myself over to a capsule hotel before trying to be a daughter to someone who did not speak my language.

The voice of Cly popped into my head and urged me to think about the carbon I'd be burning for such a trip. I pursed my lips. An online tool said a return flight to Tokyo would melt 10.4 square metres of Arctic sea ice. It said 3.5 billion people emit fewer greenhouse gases than that in a year.

I suspected I knew how well that would go down with Cly – yet it had been weeks now since we'd properly engaged; since I'd last looked to him as Sensei.

I was a coward. I was in hiding.

Logging in to my inbox, I saw Cly had sent a new email. It came with a quote from a now-dead Indian guru – a quote he thought might ring true for me. On the first read I found it dense and opaque. I read it again and again to extract meaning. *Question*, it began:

*Do you not think that the desire to free oneself from conditioning might be a consequence of conditioning?*
    *Answer:*
    *Of course. Desire to free oneself from conditioning only furthers conditioning. But if one understands the whole process of desire – not to destroy desire but to understand desire – in the understanding of desire, the freedom from conditioning comes. If I set about deliberately to free myself from my conditioning, that desire creates its own conditioning. I may destroy this conditioning, but I am caught in another conditioning. But if there is an understanding of desire then that very understanding destroys conditioning. Unconditioning is a by-product; it is not important. But it is important to understand what creates conditioning.*

After several reads, I found the nub of the paragraph that made sense to me: *If I set about deliberately to free myself from my conditioning, that desire creates its own conditioning.*

My mind chose to interpret it thus: the harder we try to escape something, the more we find we've escaped into the same thing.

I knew I did not want a dad who needed drink to feel okay. Or needed a son or daughter for the same reason.

That guilt of missed phone calls and visits. The sense that I was not giving enough. It felt to me like Cly and I had leapt forward; jumped straight to the hardest aspects of having a parent.

This time I told Mum what was happening with Cly. At the same time I told her that I wanted to keep looking. This project could still work for me. Somehow. Some way. 'How does seeking out a bunch of strangers tell you anything about what a father is?' she said.

'It tells me more than I get from just living my life without doing it.'

'You're not going to find a dad for you out there, are you.'

The sentence was not worded as a question.

I made myself come out of hiding. Made myself stop being a coward. *Hi Cly*, I typed.

*How are you? I've been thinking about you recently and hoping all is well. I hope you can forgive me for the silence. I've been stuck in a rut.*

*I was quite worried to hear last time we spoke that you had been finding solace in alcohol again – not that I can blame you in the slightest. I really hope you are looking after yourself, and that there is good support near you too?*

*I have zero idea of when I'll be able to do another phone call, but you've been in my mind. I wanted to let you know I haven't forgotten you.*

I pressed send and logged out.

'I need professionals. No more amateurs.'

Mentor Claire arrived at the flat looking eager. Ready. It rubbed off.

'I want to *feel* like I have a real father,' I said. 'I want to completely *believe* it.'

Sitting beside her, online, I searched *hiring man for dad*. A page of options appeared, including an article stating that 'Mums can choose to pay up to $1,000 (£782) to rent a father who will fulfil the clichéd roles – cooking BBQs, playing sports and even talking to youngsters about "the birds and the bees".'

'Specifically only about the birds and the bees?' asked Claire.

On closer inspection we found it was a sugar-daddy service. Vetoed.

In New York, one guy was branding himself as 'Rent A Dad': available to help young people negotiate on house-buying, set up websites, build flat-pack furniture – even shop for wedding rings. I sent him a message, then switched tabs to make my calculations. Heathrow to JFK Airport per passenger: 6 square metres of Arctic sea ice turned to slush.

I refocused the search. Only England.

'Man and van,' I read out. 'That would scare the man in the van, wouldn't it? "I'm here to move something." "Thanks, Dad. Sit down. Let me get you a cup of tea . . ."'

Another idea: escort services offering sex-free options.

Only, most of the escorts looked utterly intimidating. I filtered them to create a shortlist: people who claimed to be good at conversation (I liked to talk); people who enjoyed walking (I liked to walk); people who could ice skate (I'd never learned); people who liked role-playing (ideal – boom!). One profile bested the others – a no-brainer. It showed a man in a velvet jacket, smiling at the camera.

My voice rose as I scrolled to learn more, reading aloud what I'd found.

He was £75 per hour.

Six feet tall.

'And he teaches self-esteem!'

'Oh my God, Dad!'

'That's a great dad skill.'

We scrutinised his pictures. 'He looks like James Bond,' said Claire.

'I want him with a suit.'

Except he was 48.

'I think you should contact him,' said Claire. 'Never mind the age.'

Immediately I emailed the agency.

I felt stronger again. No, *exhilarated*. I high-fived Claire on her way out.

After that I waited several days. And, of course, the agency did not write back.

How I envied Japan's solution. Envied the opportunity to hire someone, no strings, and request they perform the dad role in a way that I could choose.

Would I really have to travel to Japan?

The costs of the journey were epic.

Would I really need an escort?

Perhaps that would only lead to more sexual grey zones.

There was nothing like what Japan had in the UK.

Zilch.

Except . . .

I started to type.

*

Peter sent a card to the flat.

'To my wonderful daughter', said the front, in intricate silvery writing.

Inside, he signed it, 'Love Pops xxx'.

I couldn't believe it.

The next day, we planned a call. I held the edge of my desk as the phone connected. 'Hi, Pops,' I grinned when he picked up. 'It's Daughter here.'

He laughed.

I ploughed on. 'I loved the card.'

'Just a little jokey thing, George,' he said. 'Thought it might tickle you.'

A jokey thing.

'It did,' I said, sitting up.

'Nothing much,' he added.

A jokey nothing much.

I cleared my throat.

We talked about logistics for the book launch. There were people who wanted to meet him, I said. My friends wanted to vet him and his credentials.

He laughed again. 'Looking forward,' he said.

Before the call ended I asked about his cancer.

Peter replied in the same voice he used to comment on the weather – a forecast of sun with a hint of cloud. 'Oh, I'm in more pain, George.'

'Yeah?'

'There's not much more they can do.'

The harder we try to escape something, the more we find we've escaped into the same thing.

*

What did I want?

1. To state what behaviour was okay and what wasn't, and to have that respected.
2. To have a nice time.
3. To know what it would feel like to have a dad who was actually there.

'You've already got someone who'll role-play random dad stuff,' said Mabry on the phone. 'That's Pops, right?'

'Yes . . .'

'You've had the experience of faking it in front of strangers. In Invergordon, yes?'

'Yes . . .'

'So what is it that Pops *can't* give you? What is it you haven't been able to get from anyone else?'

What I hadn't been able to get from anyone else was Carl.

But no one could play Carl for me – that would be impossible.

And what I knew of Carl was not ideal.

And yet.

What did I want?

I returned to the brief I'd been drafting.

'Fuck it.'

I laid out my plan.

# 23

# DAD FOR HIRE

The book launch happened on a boat, which was moored to the side of the Thames. There was Mum. There were cousins and friends. There were writers and divers. There were people who knew about sharks. There was Duncan, chatty and hosting.

There was not Duncan's mother. (She was on a skiing trip. She sent money for snacks, and sent love.)

There was not Duncan's father. (He didn't feel well, he texted, not sending love.)

There was Peter. Neat grey hair and glasses, looking perky.

I gave a speech.

Peter looked on as I did, standing next to Mum, reunited for the first time since the cruise. He made her laugh with comments that I couldn't hear.

After the speech I ate loads of snacks and drank wine. Zipped around, reluctant to pause, only staying still at the table where people wanted me to sign books.

In glimpses I watched Peter talk to Mabry and Claire. Watched him talk to my ex-colleagues. Watched him chat with Mum. Watched him find my female cousins and introduce himself.

I saw them cover their eyes and shake their heads. I saw them laughing. Happily.

I sent my brief to John, an actor. I had obtained his details through Leander, my friend who wrote and acted too; the friend who kind of almost knew Ian Hislop. (A referral, if you will.)

My brief said that:

*I would love to find someone willing to play the role of a father, who is meeting his adult biological daughter (i.e. me) for the first time.*

*You wouldn't need to know any details about my actual biological father's life, or pretend to be him in any way. Ideally, you would ad lib/create whatever character you feel best fits the scenario of someone who couldn't be around for the birth and upbringing of their estranged daughter. As long as the character's not mean/dismissive/rejecting, that's all I ask! Leander thought you would be a great choice. (For the record, I will be playing myself.)*

*I would travel to meet you for the experiment (I'm guessing you're in London?) at a date/place that fits your schedule. I'm imagining that we'd meet at around lunchtime in a pub or café, then carry on to somewhere like a museum, bowling, etc. – I'm open to suggestions, too, if anything strikes you as appropriate. We would both stay in role the whole time, then say goodbye to*

*each other before dinner (so around midday until*
*5/6pm).*

*I would pay for your food/ticket entry/public*
*transport or fuel expenses for the meeting, and for*
*your time that afternoon. If you feel you would need*
*preparatory time, too, let me know what you're*
*imagining, and if you feel that would need extra*
*remuneration. Leander suggested that £200 a day for*
*an acting workshop-type arrangement was appropriate,*
*so I'm working off this figure. I hope it sounds right;*
*please shout if not! I don't have loads of money*
*(maybe one day) – but I do very much want to pay you*
*a rate that feels totally fair.*

*I'm envisaging the 'reunion' as a one-off.*

*Of course, if at this point of reading my message*
*you think, 'Holy crap, no thanks,' that's fine and*
*understandable. I'm hoping that won't be your*
*reaction, but: no pressure.*

*I hope to hear from you soon.*

*Warmest wishes,*

*Georgie*

The anticipatory fear I felt was now more than familiar;
it was par for the course. This time I knew how to handle
it. I breathed. I booked a massage.

Occasionally I had a call from Peter and missed it. I
texted him. Apologised. Let him know I would call back.

Then I picked up a new card that had come with a box
of treats from his favourite Mumbles café. 'Saw these and
thought of you. Enjoy. Love Pops xxx'

Duncan was on a trip to his parents' house for a family bonding session, his mother now back from skiing. I hadn't been invited. I planned a walk with Mum.

She told me Nick was around that weekend. Nick, her ex-colleague; my one-time ideal dad. 'I'll invite him along too,' she said.

'Good idea,' I said.

Nick could be the buffer.

On a hill in Dorset that weekend, during the standard walk between tea rooms, I prepared to voice a question.

Keeping my eyes on the distant outline of hills, I let both Mum and Nick know I needed advice.

'What is it?' said Mum.

'Fire away,' said Nick.

'If you were going to hire an actor to play the role of dad for an afternoon, what kind of thing would you do with him?' I asked.

Nick let out a laugh.

Mum didn't. 'You're not doing that, are you?'

'Yes.'

I explained the set-up in Japan.

'Sounds very strange and interesting,' said Nick.

'The zoo,' said Mum.

'The zoo?' I echoed.

'That's a fatherly place to go.'

'The zoo,' I repeated again, under my breath, trying to watch the idea play out in my head. Historically, I wasn't a fan of zoos, or keeping animals confined in small spaces. Neither was my mother. And yet she had suggested it.

I thought aloud: 'So lots of distractions, something to look at, instant conversation starters. And animal dads.'

'Animal dads?'

'Like chimps and apes who act as fathers to babies, even when they're not biologically linked.'

'Right.' Mum sounded unsure. She changed the conversation and engaged Nick in debating the merits of different tea shops in the area.

*The zoo*, I kept thinking. *There's something about the zoo.*


John replied. He was in a play and the cast had not been well. He would write at greater length as soon as he could. In the meantime, he wrote: *I am open to the idea.*

My stomach lurched.

I heard from John again while I was working for a freelance client some days later and made myself hold back until I was able to give his words my full attention.

Kept my eyes wide and steady when I clicked.

*Hi Georgie,*

*Apologies, half term for my kid followed hard upon illness. My head is now clear.*

*Intriguing business model they've set up in Japan.*

*As a creative myself I understand the value of treading down new paths in search of clues and inspiration. I'm a father to an 8-year-old so have some understanding of parenting. I am, on the whole, kind and empathetic.*

*I'm very happy to be a part of a process that enables you to find something.*

*How are you envisaging the context? Who made contact with who? Have they spoken over the phone prior to meeting?*

*I'm very free next week onwards. I can stay with you until 5.30. The venue should be your choice. I'm sure you instinctively know where you want to spend the day.*

*I'm wondering if it might be useful for us to chat on the phone to work out the parameters of the meeting? I'm clearly going to be very much 'me' when we meet. But it would be useful if you could list things you need that might not be me so I can have a good think about them and come up with alternatives.*

A noise came out of me that I couldn't identify.

That night my plotting continued. In the morning I passed it on.

*I'm most interested in creating a similar scenario to a meeting with my estranged father (had his personality been totally different, of course, and had he not been in a long-term relationship with my mum, since that's something you wouldn't be able to successfully ad lib without a lot of prep).*

*Backstory/parameters-wise:*

- *I made first contact after doing some detective work to find out your name and details.*

- *I did this by sending a letter introducing myself in an open and non-judgemental way, and raising the idea of meeting up to talk and get to know each other a little.*
- *I didn't pressure you for a response and you replied surprised/pleased to hear from me, and happy to meet.*
- *Before you received the letter from me, you were aware that I existed, but didn't know where I was and (for whatever reason) didn't look. If you can think up a reason why your character didn't look that would be helpful; it will probably be something we talk about for a bit.*
- *Going further back: unlike Carl you had a brief fling with my mum and barely knew her then, or remember her well. At that time she lived in Somerset. She was a journalist and copywriter. Her name was Denise and she was 6ft tall, with dark wavy hair and blue eyes, aged early 30s. You met during a night out, which she was at with her workmates, and you got talking to her at the bar when she was buying a drink. You probably don't know/remember much else about her. It was a long time ago.*
- *Denise found a way to get in touch with you while she was pregnant, letting you know I was yours, but made it clear she was happy to raise me without you as a co-parent, since the two of you didn't have a relationship. She let you know again when I was born (1987), and then lost contact with you somehow (again, a reason as to why 'you' think you lost contact*

*would be helpful – and did you try to regain it? Not try? Why?)*
- *When we meet, I will be interested to learn more about who you are and what you've been doing since 1987.*
- *We haven't spoken on the phone.*

*On that last point, I can see the value in having a pre-chat. At the same time, I'm hoping we can avoid talking by phone before the day. My instinct is that speaking beforehand could dampen the sense of spontaneity and unknown-ness in that moment of 'reunion', and might prevent me from being able to stay in character with you. It's important for me that we don't break character under any circumstances, even as we are saying goodbye.*
    *Does that make sense?*

When John wrote back the next afternoon, it seemed we were good to go; seemed that I might get to meet my father the right way. That I could finally play my part in depth.

Logging on to dadmails, I saw a new message. Not from Cly, but from somebody who hadn't written before. Respondent number 51. Conversation 158. Somebody who already knew my name. *Hi Georgina*, it started.

*I'm clearly a strong candidate.*
    *We could indulge our shared love of Dorset, chocolate, ice cream and country walks together.*

*I've known your mother for more than 30 years and*
*we're still speaking.*
*You were a bridesmaid at my wedding for pity's sake.*
*Shall I go on?*
*Please let me know the next stage in the process.*
*Happy to submit a more detailed CV.*
*It is, of course, your decision, I will continue to be*
*friendly if you choose another.*
*To be honest you've got me for free so I'd get a rich*
*dude involved too.*
*Nick x*
*P.S. my financial situation is dubious*


I got out of my chair and did a quick lap of the flat, then dropped to the floor and clutched the pigs to my stomach.

'Nick sounds great,' said Mabry, being the fastest friend to respond to my phone request.

'He is great. Too good to be true. When I was a kid, God, if he'd offered then . . .' The sentence was too big to finish.

'And what about your actor?'

The two pigs bounced in my lap. 'I need to do that too. I want the reunion. But my head is melting. I'm melting.'

She asked what the issue was.

'Pops will die. Nick's going to reject me. The actor is going to reject me.'

'Oh, Georgie, I don't think—'

'Yes! Even though he's an actor and *I'm paying him.*'

'No.'

'I know, I know. If I think about that rationally, it's unlikely. I know that's probably just the child part of me speaking. But it's speaking very loudly. And it's terrified.'

Mabry tried to reassure me. 'Even if you hadn't had all that stuff with Carl, it's possible you might feel this way.'

I wasn't sure.

'Seriously,' she insisted. '*Anyone* doing something like this would probably have worries that the stranger they're going to meet won't actually like them.'

'True?'

'True.'

The pigs bounced higher.

We switched to the next thing.

'I'm worried I'm booking a one-way ticket to Trauma-town,' I said. 'This acting gig could open up all sorts of issues. And if he's *mean*, if he's *mean* . . . Except he's my friend's friend, who is apparently lovely. And also he already has a child, so hopefully he has some of that natural paternal thing down?'

Mabry asked what I might want to say to him; if I had any idea how I might feel.

My response was that I simply couldn't predict it. 'Or can I?' I pressed deep into the hollows of my skull. 'Okay. One of the fears is that I won't be able to get into character or stay in character. Another fear is that I get really upset. Or angry, even. God, I might get angry. Like, "Why did you leave? No, *really*? If having a baby was *such* a hideous prospect, *why didn't you wear a fucking condom*? Why does that have to be on Mum?"'

'If you get angry, let it out.'

A pig dived for the floor. 'You think?'

'Yes! It's an experiment; this guy knows it's an experiment. You can't predict what's going to happen. Your actor has a basic idea of why you're doing this. And, actually, if you think about it, this could be the absolute ideal scenario for voicing that anger. It's a safe space. He's being paid; you're in a public place; you'll be able to come out of character if it gets too much; he can leave; you never need to see him again. There's no tie. There's no right or wrong. Whatever happens, you'll learn something.'

I hesitated. 'You're saying I could get angry?'

'You can definitely get angry.'

'I might get angry.'

'You have reasons to feel angry.'

'But what if I'm just terrible at acting? What if I'm *so* bad at acting that he can't focus, and—' I stopped myself. 'I've noticed I'm feeling like I have to organise all of this and make it perfect.'

'Yes.'

'I think I'm forgetting that this is going to be collaborative. And that I don't have to do everything. *He's* the actor. I'm literally paying him to share the load.'

Mabry paused.

I could hear her working out what to say next.

Slowly, carefully, she let it into the open. 'As someone who's known you for quite a long time . . . I'd say you often seem to feel you have to do all the heavy lifting with the men you're in relationships with. You make the effort, you plan, you feel you have to give and give. There's this attitude that *you* have to do everything, when these men could be doing a hell of a lot more for themselves. These are people who could be taking account of their actions.'

The second pig took a tumble.

'Does that sound fair?'

Staring past my feet, I nodded to no one. I knew who her words were directed at; was too afraid to go there. 'Mm.'

*But if I didn't have Duncan . . .*

The call fell silent.

'How's Pops?' asked Mabry, rousing me.

I exhaled. Told her he didn't seem to expect me to do all the heavy lifting. 'Just occasional responses to politically incorrect memes and videos.'

'That's good . . . Problematic, but good.'

'He's sent me some parcels of cake from Mumbles. And he's started suggesting some trips we could go on together.'

Pops and I had been standing apart from the others. The book launch had quietened down. Now only the cousins, Duncan and Mum remained.

'Can we go on an adventure?' I asked him, when no one could overhear.

'Absolutely, my girl,' he said. 'We can go anywhere you want.'

I smiled now to recall the exchange. 'We're making a plan for the summer,' I told Mabry.

'You need more men in your life like that,' she said.

There was one more person I wanted to talk to. Someone else's input I wanted to get. I had now known this person for seven years, since a call during which I learned news that I hadn't expected.

Cancer had got my father in the throat. Now alcoholism was rotting his liver away.

There wasn't much time.

'Would you like to meet him?' I heard through the phone.

'Yes,' I confirmed. Yes, I would.

# 24

# CARL

Michael and his wife lived a way north by train. Before my meeting with the actor I travelled to stay with them, as I had done multiple times now in the years since he first made contact – visiting both on my own and with long-term boyfriends. On this trip, I brought my Dictaphone.

Michael was on a mission to learn photography: buying multiple cameras and lenses; converting part of his home into a darkroom; trying to understand his subject better.

Trying to understand Carl.

We talked about how it was going, finalised plans for lunch and dinner, and discussed the idea of an interview. Over the months I'd been letting slip bits and pieces about my project. Michael was acting interested.

He cleared a private space for us in the spare room. On my way in I passed an other-worldly black-and-white photograph of a farrier; the old man seemed to be meta-morphosing into steam. Carl had captured the image. Had developed it.

Michael closed the door. We smiled at each other. Jointly awkward. I turned the Dictaphone on and let it run. Came around to the point. 'So I'm doing a project, interested in fathers.'

'Yes.'

'And I was thinking, well, seeing as I'm doing a project on fathers, I should probably think about my actual biological father.'

'Yes.'

'And you are the person who knows the most about him.'

Michael nodded. He was Carl's brother.

The man had learned of my call to their mother a few months after I'd made it; heard about my attempt to contact Carl. He thought I should know my father had been hospitalised and asked if she might help enable a visit should Carl agree, insisting I had a right to be involved. When his mother showed resistance, Michael wrote me a letter, requesting that I ring him when it reached me. Ever since, he had been my primary point of contact for the family.

As I settled into the tidy spare room, I asked how he would describe my biological father to a stranger.

'I'd say that he was a charismatic sort of person, who— People enjoyed his company, generally speaking, in a social sort of situation. People were easily charmed by his humour. But it was very much skin deep.

'He was, I think, an unhappy person. The humour was a bit of a mask . . . He was very guarded, extremely guarded. And a very contradictory character, and a very difficult person to pin down. Gentle at times, very gentle at times. Obviously, like everybody, he could be all different things.'

I kept quiet.

Michael said, 'I think he was very, very sensitive, and sort of tended to side with the underdog . . . Hated authority, I think. And, to me, he was very caring, in the sense that he never imposed anything on me. So he was a nice brother to have. But . . . I would say, on balance, he was unreliable . . .'

'Oh?'

'Carl didn't like telephone conversations very much . . . And he didn't have a phone in his home. They wouldn't have been able to afford the bills. He was a hopeless communicator – letter writer or anything like that . . . You wouldn't hear from him at all. He'd just disappear.'

Michael told me Carl rarely let anyone close. Neither before I was born, nor afterwards. This was news to me – and some relief. It could be why I never received a reply to the letter I sent him: the man did not reply to anyone's letters.

When I was ready, I brought myself back into the wider story, asking Michael to consider an alternative outcome to what had happened: one in which Carl was present in my life. I wanted to establish what he would have been like as a father. What exactly I'd missed.

'I don't think he was capable,' said Michael. 'I mean . . . he ran a mile, didn't he . . . I just think that, you know, all you can do is look at what actually did happen. And what did happen was, he just didn't engage at all.'

And what about Caroline? I wondered.

What about Caroline.

Carl's partner had been out celebrating her birthday with

friends. It was her first night away from Caroline since giving birth.

Over the years, after Carl's funeral, I had pieced what happened together through others who seemed to know it better; the few people Carl had confided in who also confided in me. They implied that the 'cot death' written on Caroline's death certificate did not tell the whole story.

Carl had phoned up friends that night to say he couldn't get Caroline to settle down; he seemed to be panicking about getting things wrong.

By the time his partner came home, I was told, Carl had fallen unconscious.

He had been drinking to handle the stress that night – drinking because he felt way out of his depth. A parent by name and not verb.

As Carl stirred, his partner spotted the baby trapped beneath him, compressed by the slump of his sleep. She screamed him awake.

The baby was still, but not sleeping.

She had not been able to breathe.

The eve of my meeting with John the actor approached. I was once again solo. Duncan had planned a trip to the ski slopes alone, inspired by his mother. He would be whizzing down mountains, sleeping soundly, free from the stress and the flat and the jams and the cacti.

One day soon, I knew I would have to address this issue of my partner's absence. Or, rather, his absent presence.

Why my heart had chosen him as family. And whether and when such choices could be unmade.

But not today.

My phone showed forecasts for heavy snow and icy rain – unseasonably harsh weather. That night there was no screaming from over the road. Instead fierce gusts and rain thrashed the bedroom windows. My mind thrashed with it. Hours before my alarm my eyes flicked open. Watched the too-bright streetlight through the curtains. Things were eerily quiet out there.

After some time I raised myself onto my elbows. Swung my legs out of bed. Vapours of breath curled into the air.

Preparing for this meeting felt different to the others. For starters, I picked a new outfit. I wanted to wear soft and warm things. Hugs in fabric.

With hours left before our meeting time, I paced the floors in the flat, trying to get myself into an appropriate kind of headspace. I wanted to act authentically; to really feel I was going to meet Carl.

'I'm going to see him,' I repeated. 'This is it; it's happening, it's happening.'

I was not expecting any success with this tactic. After all, it hadn't worked when I met Grant. Yet strangely, after a few minutes, something shifted. I was me in that room, and me years earlier, waiting for something I'd wanted for so long. Only this time, it was coming.

A dark chasm opened up between my lungs.

Parts of me began to vanish into it, while other parts oozed out.

It was a mess and I was believing it; I was feeling it. Crying.

It hurt.

Suddenly another force overtook me. The lung chasm closed over. As fast as they had arrived, my tears stopped flowing.

'Eh?'

Stretching my arms, stretching my neck, I tried to get back to the feeling that the day was all reality and no performance. That Carl was going to be there. Me and my father. The repetitions began: those same set phrases.

This time I met resistance.

I wiped my eyes and wondered how else to prepare.

My conversation with Mabry popped in to my head: that there was no right way to do this. Except I wanted so badly for it to work.

———

As I built up to my meeting with Carl seven years ago, my agenda had been stealth. It was sprinting. Faster. Go, go, go.

'I think we need more sessions,' my very first therapist said.

I snorted. 'Tell me about it. I'm keeping my phone on loud, okay? I know that's against the rules, but his brother says he'll call me as soon as he gets the all-clear from his mum. As soon as she says I'm allowed to come visit, I'm going. I might have to leg it.'

'How are you feeling?'

'HA!'

He waited. 'How are you feeling?'

'Like my guts are log flumes and the people riding the log flumes are in flames. I want to meet him. I want him to see me. There's a chance he won't want to see me back. If that happens, I'll probably puke up the log flumes. And the passengers.' I gripped the armrests of my chair. 'My dad is in the same hospital where my aunt died last year.'

For the first time, even my therapist looked shocked.

*'And I don't know how the fuck to tell my mum.'*

———

This morning I deliberately left home ultra-early, taking the longest way round that I could, spending the maximum time on public transport, keeping myself on the move.

My first bus was soundtracked by discordant notes: the horror-screech of brakes and engine. I switched to a train and let John know I was on my way. I told him what I was wearing. Remembered to ask if he could call me Georgina.

Nestling into the fabric of my fleece, I watched the snow-slush of last night's weather pass by, dank on the ground. The pens in my bag came from a male friend I'd once loved, who loved me well. The odd white hair on my trousers was an amulet of Mum's dog. The fleece was a gift from an uncle, my mother's only brother, in the early days of his widowerhood. It belonged to another aunt who had died when I was still a child.

Cancer. Stinking cancer.

———

By the time our hour was up, my phone had still not gone off. 'We'll have more sessions, okay?' the therapist told me, on his feet. 'We're not going to leave it like this.'

I thanked him. Swung the door open. Rushed through it and into the hallway.

Heard him call, 'Good luck,' from behind me. And: 'I'll see you next week, Georgina.'

———

We pulled in to a station. *I am meeting the man who gave me half my genes*, I wrote in my notebook, trying to trick myself again after reading a series of how-tos on method acting. A crowd of late-aged teens boarded, heading for college. The girl and boy nearest me were engrossed in discussion. Their subject was someone called Megan, who seemed to be a source of irritation. 'She just goes on and on,' said one, broadcasting to the carriage. 'Like, *hello*.'

'It's so fucking annoying. Deal with it.'

'Right? Megan can fuck off and die.'

'Ha ha ha ha ha.'

At the next stop, they were joined by another friend. She said hi, smiled and took the seat in front of them.

'*Hey*, Megan,' said the girl, her voice syrupy-sweet. 'How are you doing, my lovely?'

I turned to the window so no one could see my expression.

In snatches, I gathered that Megan's parents were going through a messy separation, steamrolling in tandem towards an angry divorce. Unsurprisingly, Megan was finding it tough.

'You've just got to push through these things,' quipped the boy.

'Yep,' his companion chimed in. 'Just *moooove* on.'

I glanced up. Megan was nodding.

Scrunching my eyes closed, I willed her to see what was happening, then tried to tune out the noise.

My phone filled my palm. I searched it for stories about other adults meeting their fathers for the first time. How should a person approach such a thing? The question, posed on a forum, had elicited reams of anecdotes.

'The less you expect the better,' said one.

'. . . don't beat yourself up on what you should or should not feel . . .' said another.

'Do it for yourself.'

We passed into a tunnel. A bright new flash of *I-can't-do-this* came over me. *My acting isn't good enough.*

Shrinking into the seat, I began to wilt.

Then, as we left the tunnel, a realisation.

*You're constantly acting*, it said. *Most people are.*

The word 'psychodrama' entered my head: the therapeutic strategy I'd heard about at Grendon prison. My fingers sought out articles through the screen. A form of drama therapy, that was it; re-enacting past situations in different roles and different ways; exploring and investigating significant moments, other realities.

Megan and her frenemies prepared to leave at the next station.

I watched them go. Held my tongue. Tried to appear calm.

*There we go, Georgie. Acting.*

The train moved on, towards midday. Madly, I searched for psychodramatic tips. Websites told me it would not work without all the participants fitting together. That every participant must be open. That a lengthy warm-up phase might be needed.

The plan came with risks, I could see that. Opening up to anything meant opening up to everything.

Love, loss, hate, hurt.

*The less you expect the better.*

———

On exiting my therapist's hallway I did as I had told him. I legged it. Clattered down the stairs. Plunged through the door to the street. Turned left, right, left. Remembered I was going to a station. My bag crunched against my thigh as I ran.

I was nearly at the end of that first street when my phone went off.

Michael was calling.

I answered, out of breath.

The first time I sat near Carl was at *Postman Pat*.

The second and final time would be at his funeral.

Shortly after my father's death, Michael started sending me Word documents: weekly instalments of text written just for me that described the life of the family I didn't know: past people, past homes, momentous events; from ancestors to boyhood through to the eighties, nineties and noughties. Grateful though I was for his efforts and openness, each week

I read the newest one it stung to see no mention of my mother.

By the time I came along – in Chapter 16 out of 20 – Carl was gravely ill and just a fortnight from his last breath. My name appeared then in conversations between Michael and his mother, Michael and his wife; debates around whether or not I ought to be informed of what was happening. Michael believed I should in spite of their fears about Carl's response. Unhappily, reluctantly, his mother agreed to ask my father if he wanted to see me there in intensive care.

My name reappeared in the next chapter, which covered a period two weeks on. This time, Michael referred to the morning I called to say I was coming, hoping to get the green light for my visit before I arrived at hospital. He described what had been happening for them. Looking at his words through my screen, I felt an intense disconnection. It was jarring to read what went on with this bunch of strangers who were my relatives.

In the days before my father's death, after Michael and I first spoke, he had asked my paternal grandmother again to raise the subject of me meeting Carl; to ask my dad if he would at last be willing to meet me. Michael wanted his mother to rush. Instead the woman seemed to drag her heels; seemed to go more slowly the harder he pressed.

The morning I rang he was waiting still; had been told to expect her call when she was ready. But the call, when it came, was to say Carl had died.

In that moment, Michael wrote, his first thought hadn't been of his brother. Instead he pictured me waiting to travel, anticipating this visit that could now never take place. It transpired that my paternal grandmother had not once asked Carl about me. Michael wrote bluntly about the mistakes his family had made, acknowledging that their behaviour had been selfish. Shameful. If his mother had consulted Carl, he could have said no to my visit, then at least I would have known where I stood. But by doing nothing when it counted, the family could simply tell themselves it was bad luck that I'd missed out.

What happened, Michael insisted, was not bad luck. It was a choice. My last chance had gone, he emphasised – as if the same realisation hadn't weighed me down ever since – and I, Georgina, Carl's daughter, could not have it back.

———

# 25
# REUNION

In Soho I ordered a thick hot chocolate. Surrounded by greenery and condensation, I stared into the just-wiped sheen of the table. My hand clumped into a fist under my chin.

I could feel myself slipping back to the hours just before I'd hoped to meet Carl. The questions I had formed.

*Did you ever think about me?*

Sip.

*Do you ever have regrets?*

Sip.

*What really happened with Caroline that night?*

Cup down.

*Are you okay?*

My lip was trembling.

As if there wasn't enough going on, by the time I'd finished my drink my period had started.

There was half an hour to go when I left the café, tamponed and dosed up on painkillers. My phone said I had 25 minutes to manage the walk in time.

Massaging the bloat of my stomach, I navigated through a section of town where I had lived with an ex-boyfriend. When I passed under the BT Tower, that 1960s totem of Fitzrovia, I looked up. The tower had been visible from my old home. As a result, for years, I'd felt like we were somehow friends. I gave the structure a wave. 'Hi, BT.'

The warm purple of its display screen shimmered and winked.

Reaching the outskirts of Regent's Park, my lungs felt tight and shallow. Ten minutes to go, and ice-cold rain was falling on my scalp. I stuffed my fingerless gloves into my pockets, and slowly repeated a mantra to the topiary, the leafless trees, the claggy dirt.

*I'm meeting my dad, I'm meeting my dad, I'm meeting my dad, I'm meeting my dad.*

The closer I got to our rendezvous point, the slower my walking became. Up ahead, I saw the small sign for the café, which directed visitors off the main path to reach it. I brought the scarf I was wearing right up to my ears and focused my attention on the ground.

When I reached the sign itself I turned.

I was 10 minutes early, yet a glance towards the café building told me a man was standing outside it. He was facing me.

*Shit.*

The metres between us lessened. Ten. Eight. Six. I looked up. The man observed me intently.

'John?' I asked.

'Georgina.'

We closed the gap.

*

I held out my hand. John opened his arms. We came together as a clumsy blend of handshake and hug, and pulled out again.

He smiled at me. I smiled back. His hair was fair, his eyes blue. I was struck by the realisation that our appearance was more alike than different. Leander had picked well.

'Fancy a coffee?' John's voice was soft and northern. I hadn't expected that.

Following him in, my bones felt steel-straight, as if I was relearning how to walk. Stepping inside, I expected to be enveloped by a bustling of tourists, parents, babies, friends, all enjoying time out at the park at lunchtime. Instead there was one man sitting at a bare table nursing a drink. A woman who wiped the coffee machine. A lot of cold, echoing space.

'I thought it might be busier,' I said.

John glanced back at me.

'This is . . .' I stared around and lowered my voice. 'It's not *quite* what I pictured.'

'It's all right,' said John. 'What would you like?'

'What would I like? Hm.' I stared at the board above our heads. 'Um . . . so there's . . . What do they have? Let's see . . .' I stared hard at the menu, fretting, unable to focus. The woman had stopped wiping and waited, held by my indecision. I turned back to John. 'Are you getting something?'

He ordered a coffee.

*It's only a drink*, I told myself. *You can do this.*

I chose a herbal tea and watched John reach for his wallet.

I said, 'I can pay.'

'No, I'll get this.'

'Okay.' I stepped back. 'Thank you.' As long as he collected the receipt I could pay him back tomorrow and—

'Here you go.' He passed me my drink, picked up his and surveyed the tables. No receipt requested. Should I ask on his behalf? Should we—

I stopped myself. My dad could buy me a tea. He could buy me a tea.

We went to a table near the only other customer. Settled in. John with his back to the wall, me facing him.

I took a breath. 'Thank you so much for coming,' I said, meaning it for both versions of John. 'I appreciate it.'

'Oh,' he said, 'I wanted to come. It was a wonderful thing to hear from you.'

I held my paper cup in front of my mouth. 'Were you waiting long?'

'Not at all. The park layout's a little confusing though, isn't it?' He shared a short story about how he'd got lost. Feeling to blame, I apologised. He gently let me know I didn't need to.

My mind clunked on, working on what to say next; how to guide us out of silence and awkwardness. But John took up the slack, asking after my journey. I answered without any detail and posed the same question. 'Whereabouts in the city did you come from?' I added, remembering he was London-based.

'I'm down from Sheffield.'

The line temporarily threw me. 'Is that where you live?'

He nodded, laugh lines crinkling.

For a moment I wondered if I had got it wrong. Then: *No, Georgie, we're pretending.* There would be deviations.

There had to be.

My mind let go. I needed to stay in the moment. With this man. Who could be my father.

As I sipped, John created a picture of Sheffield and his family: parents who were ordinary people. Kind.

'That's good,' I enthused. 'Kind is good. Kind is everything.'

'I'm lucky,' he said.

John revealed that he worked shifts in a music shop. The rest of the time he was a musician.

'What instrument?'

'The guitar.'

'No way! Bass guitar or real guitar?'

'Acoustic guitar.'

'Ah, okay.'

We got talking about music and gigs. It was then that he started to tell me how he had crossed paths with my mother: touring the country; strumming with his band in small county venues. 'I was in Bath that night when we met, playing at a pub.'

'Ah.' I could almost see it. 'Mum never told me that.'

'It was a bit of a hectic lifestyle. Different nights, different towns, never really sticking to one place.'

I nodded.

'How is your mum?'

'She's . . .' I wriggled in my seat to get comfortable. 'Yeah, she's all right. She's retired these days and lives on the coast with her dog. Spends a lot of time walking on the beach. She stayed in Somerset for a little bit after I was born, freelancing, odds and sods, then moved down to Dorset when I was quite young to be nearer my grandmother. I don't suppose you ever met Granny Codd.'

'No.'

'She's not around anymore unfortunately, but she was great. Basically my second parent. I spent a lot of time with her because Mum was working full-time at a paper to pay the bills and all that. Granny would be around in the mornings and when I came back from school.' I paused. 'She's left a pretty big gap behind her. Probably even bigger than either Mum or I really want to admit.'

'They sound like strong women.'

'Very. In their ways.'

John cocked his head. 'What does your mum think about you coming to meet me?'

I looked at my lap. 'She's not *hugely* thrilled, I don't think. Which I get. I mean, she asked a bit about you and then . . . got a little distant.'

'Right.'

'It's tough for her, I can see that.'

'I'm sure.'

'She'll come around, I think. It just takes some getting used to.'

There was a long pause.

'I'm really glad you wrote to me,' said John.

My shoulders rounded over. 'Yeah?'

'When your mum and I lost contact I . . .' He sighed. 'I know I could have tried harder, it's just . . . She seemed pretty happy with the arrangement. With keeping the distance, you know? And with Sheffield being so far away . . . She seemed like she was doing all the right things.'

I pursed my lips.

'So you have other kids now—' I began, expecting to hear more about the child he had mentioned in emails.

Instead he said no. No kids. 'Well, none apart from you.'

'Oh.' I caught myself. 'Okay. And how's that been?'

'Not having kids?'

I nodded.

'If you don't want a child that can be really important. And a good choice.'

'Mm.'

Our conversation drifted on, slowly mellowing. I started to lose track of the time. For a change – a change I could handle – John was asking questions of me as much as I was of him. We talked about how we'd both done at school. Talked about where we'd travelled. My writing. The shark book I had worked on for so long and which was now out in the world. In exchange I mined him for details of his personality. He was an obstacles man, he said. 'When something comes up, like a change or a new opportunity, I usually look for loads of reasons not to do it . . . Except not today.'

He asked if I wanted a sandwich. Though fairly concerned that my preference for egg mayo would spoil the air, John insisted I go for it. Again, he insisted on paying.

After that, he asked if I wanted to go to the zoo. Feeling cheerful, I agreed, suddenly grateful to Mum for suggesting it.

Suddenly looking forward to telling her what things were like there.

And to saying thank you. For all of it.

The conversation was easy as John and I walked through the rain and redeemed the two tickets I'd booked. Favourite songs, extended family, further education. Inside, at the giant statue of Guy the Gorilla, who had died of a heart attack in his early thirties – apparently without ever fathering a successor – the two of us stopped and looked on in admiration. 'I love animals,' John cooed.

'Cool! Me too!'

Metres later we were confronted by a sprawling map of options. Our next challenge arose.

'Where do you want to go?' asked John.

'Where do *you* want to go?'

'I really don't mind. This is your day. Whatever you want.'

'This is your day too,' I said.

We ended up heading for the penguins, where a talk was taking place.

The flightless birds torpedoed and bathed in the water, thrilled with the rain and the cold. For a few minutes, I half listened to the presenter. The rest of the zoo was calling. John picked up on my restlessness, and we broke away from the small group of other damp stragglers, their pushchairs shielded by plastic sheets; the bright hooded raincoats of toddlers all aglow.

Our eyes were next caught by the house for moths and butterflies, which promised a welcome burst of warm air.

Then on again.

To the lion pair snoozing away from the rain.

To the pond of sodden flamingos and pink pelicans.

To the macaws, shrieking hard in their cage.

There was plenty to comment on as we wended through, and I noticed that I had suspended both my discomfort about zoos, and my worries about John. Right then, I thought, we *felt* related.

(Seconds later I tested the thought again. It stuck.)

On our approach to the insect house, John confessed a phobia of spiders. I probed him to find out more, wondering if he was happy to continue – he said he was – then told him about my old phobia of fish; how that had spurred me on to try to find whale sharks, the biggest fish in the world. Walking a little ahead of him, I checked the display tanks for signs of spiders before he reached them himself.

Along the way we acquired a small boy. He was matching our pace. 'What's in here?' the boy asked me.

'I think it's supposed to be a stick insect?'

'Where?'

'No clue.'

We reached the next tank. 'GIANT SNAIL,' I said.

'I see it!' said the boy. He skipped ahead. 'What's in this one?'

'Gimme a second, I'm watching the snail.' I moved on. 'Another stick insect?'

'You're good with kids,' John commented, as our new leader urged us on to the fish tanks. 'You're a good people person.'

I came close to batting the compliment away. 'That's kind,' I said instead. 'Thanks.'

The kid overtook us, returning to his family.

Our day seemed to be going well so far. I wondered if we could sustain it. And where we should go from here.

In the atrium of the birdhouse, John asked if I'd had any father figures around me growing up. Matter-of-factly, I explained that I'd had two uncles with their own families, a colleague who worked with my mum that I really liked, some good schoolteachers here and there who probably wouldn't remember me now; that was it. We passed through plastic hangings to reach an open room of strutting birds. John said, 'I'm sorry to hear that. That must have been difficult.'

A small cluster of Victoria crowned pigeons crossed our path. Their bodies were as large as turkeys. Their heads burst outwards in blue feathered mohawks. I gazed in awe. Then, 'It was all right most of the time,' I said. 'Odd, isn't it? How not-odd odd can be?'

Leaving the birdhouse, hunting for primates (John was eager to find a creature like Guy), we entered another space shielded by plastic. On the other side, tiny monkeys leapt between ropes. They were fun to watch. Still, John wanted gorillas.

He asked a zookeeper for directions. She was detailed and clear on where we should go. 'Sounds great,' said John, with a thank-you.

I thanked her too.

We took a couple of steps away. 'Did you follow that?' he asked under his breath.

I admitted that I hadn't. 'I zoned out.'

He held the door open and let me walk through. 'I think you might get that from me.'

Jubilant feelings warmed my core as the two of us retraced our steps, in sight again of the penguins, pausing for giant tortoises, making headway. Finally we found the gorillas, and watched them get lairy as balls of lettuce were shoved through the bars towards them. 'I wonder if seeing this makes kids want to eat their greens,' said John, transfixed.

I turned to a small girl near us. 'Do you want to eat more lettuce now?'

She said no.

By that point, stepping out of that enclosure, we'd already covered a lot of ground. Yet there seemed much more to do and time was tight. When John suggested we find another round of hot drinks, part of me wanted to keep marching forward, making sure we didn't miss a thing. Another part was running on empty and needed a break. The third part said: *We're here for the man, not the zoo.* Besides, the tips of my fingers would not warm up. Slush-puddles soaked through my shoes.

I followed his lead.

We found the way to a large and cavernous café; quiet but not deserted. This time, John let me pay.

Again we sat facing each other, and found ourselves discussing justice and fairness. John said he had strong traits of both; that he found the traits exhausting. I listened, making sounds of agreement, feeling more and more like we were connected. As if part of me really had come from this person.

Then John moved the subject on to relationships:

specifically, relationships between the sexes. The chat led to my relationships. The now, the then, the men.

A story I'd spent years trying to forget pressed for freedom.

*Is it safe, though?*

*Yes. It's safe.*

'Okay. Well . . .'

John nodded at me to continue.

There was one relationship that bothered me, I confided. 'It was with a guy who had a tricky relationship with his father . . .'

I explained how the father had hit me once. In front of the boyfriend. Whacked me from behind as I leaned over a kitchen counter.

'It really hurt,' I told John. It was meant to hurt.

My boyfriend's brother had been in the room with us. 'That was weird,' he had declared.

'It *was* weird,' I told John now. 'Then I turned to face their father and said, "Don't you *ever* fucking touch me like that again." The man laughed so hard his face turned red. He looked like this angry ulcer about to pop. My boyfriend didn't say anything. Not a thing.'

'And you dumped him the next day,' John prompted.

'No . . .' My hand covered my eyes. 'Urgh.'

I took a breath.

'I stayed with him another few years. He told me he wanted to start a family with me; persuaded me he was serious. I proposed and he said yes. Then the dad heard about the wedding and intervened. Which also hurt.

'A few months after that, my fiancé left without warning. He said his parents told him love ought to be fun and easy-going. That I ought to be fun and easy-going. And that he didn't ever want to come back.'

Finally, I exhaled. The shame was out.

I peeped through my fingers.

John looked like he'd seen a monster.

'Let me tell you something,' he said, 'and this is very important.'

He came closer.

'Men are dicks.'

As he sat back, I erupted with laughter. 'You can't say that!'

'It's true.'

'But that's your whole gender!'

'Listen, I know what men are like. Any guy in his twenties and thirties, you've got to watch yourself.'

'There are good ones!'

'The minority. Look, I told you earlier that I'm an obstacles person. It's not just me. I work with a guy in the shop who's in his early thirties. His views on women are terrible. Women aren't human. For him and so many others like him, women are just obstacles getting in the way of what they really want, i.e. sex.'

'Lots of men grow out of it though, don't they?'

'Some. Not all.'

'Hm.'

'Some people expand their views the older they get. Others get smaller and narrower.'

I fiddled with my coffee cup. 'I find that hard to accept. I would rather see the best in people.'

'That's a beautiful impulse,' said John. 'But' – he pressed

his hands into each other – 'you can't be kind to everybody. You need to hold on to your sense of who you are.'

Hearing his words felt eerie, as if he knew me well beyond these few hours. I wondered how he had done that. I wondered what else he knew.

The conversation moved again: a discussion about the Left and the Right; about how, the older he grew, the more the Centre seemed to be the answer. That space of grey and uncertainty.

And then, looking into my eyes, he said, 'I've made such a mess of things.'

Immediately it was clear: he was not talking about politics.

I swallowed. 'Is it a mess?'

To me, at that moment, everything seemed okay. We were sitting there. We seemed to be liking each other's company. Both of us had been smiling, drinking warm drinks out of the cold. After everything, even the worst things, we could still have time at the zoo.

Yet John's expression looked lonely and forlorn. I watched him in silence, immersed. An audience of one.

'There are two storylines that explain why I wasn't around for you,' said John. 'Two pathways I could have taken. The first storyline is one I made myself believe for a long time. That storyline was about practicalities. It said that you and your mum were far away, that you were doing fine without me; that your mum was content and handling things and that was what she wanted. We lost contact, and I told myself that was okay. You didn't need me. That was that. That's the obstacles part of me, like I told you earlier.'

John paused. I could not look away. The inside of my head felt soft; in motion.

'The second storyline is one I didn't want to see or think about. In that storyline, the distance didn't matter. That wasn't what this was about. Instead I was scared. Really scared.

'I was afraid to be near you and your mum, and take that step to move closer. I told myself if I stayed on my own, I could only damage myself. But if I came to be with you and your mother, any damage of mine would damage you both. It was cowardly of me. And that was the truth. That story was the truth.'

The two of us were held up by each other's eyelines. A small trickle of sadness emerged in my throat. Deep, it came. From a place I had no name for.

My mouth stayed shut.

'I want to tell you, Georgina, that I deeply regret my decision to stay away. I wish I had been stronger than that. I wish I had decided just to go for it. To be with you and your mum, and be present. To have been your father.'

I kept myself there. Kept looking at him.

Imagining Carl.

'I'm sorry,' he said, in a voice that was solid and sure.

'I'm sorry.' The words were out.

They were kind. They were not demanding.

The silence held.

'You know—' My voice rasped.

I stopped.

Had to break eye contact.

Tried again.

'Before I met you today,' I said, 'I thought I might be angry. I thought I might have rageful and resentful feelings towards you . . . and I don't.'

My throat was closing.

'I understand what you're saying,' I said. 'That makes sense to me. I relate. If someone came up to me tomorrow and told me I was going to be a parent, I don't know what I'd do. And I'm grateful to you for taking the time to explain it so honestly . . .' I tried to make eye contact again and couldn't. 'I think it's probably good that you weren't around really, in a way. You weren't ready. But . . .' I tried to fill my lungs. 'It's been so hard.'

A sob came out.

I did not know who I was talking to anymore.

'When I wrote to you,' I said, 'I was feeling frustrated with my life, and who I was, and where I'd come from. I wanted to see what else I was made up of and make a new space for myself . . . It was really hard,' I repeated, crying. 'My mum had to work full-time. She did her best. She also struggled. I could see that as a child. My grandmother was there, I know, but she had her issues too. Everyone has their issues.' I sniffed. 'I'm very – I'm very grateful that you agreed to meet me today.'

'I missed out, Georgina.'

It took a while for the shock of the pain to subside. For my mind to merge back with the present. While the transition happened, John held the space. His actions and movements were meaningful. My gratitude was sincere.

And suddenly we were in some kind of aftermath. As hard as I tried, I couldn't keep track of the words. I think we were talking zoos again; other animals to see before the gates closed. I remember standing up. I remember both of us deciding that we needed to visit the bathroom.

Sat on the toilet, rubbing my eyes, the tiredness crashed against me. My plasticine brain was sloppy and wet. I wanted to hold it firmer; prop it up with the phrases I had from John. The sorry. Regret. True and false.

There was too much going on.

Outside the bathroom, a little less dazed, I stood at the place we'd agreed to meet, waiting for John to emerge. A couple with a pushchair and a toddler were by the corridor. The kid had a brilliant coat with a dinosaur hood. 'I want a coat like that,' I said. And, to its mother: 'Why do babies get the best clothes?'

She shrugged. 'It isn't fair, is it?'

They left. I turned away. Minutes passed. Four, five, six. There was no sign of John anymore. Now I was creating storylines. The one: that he was still on the toilet. The other: that he had fulfilled his mission and gone.

I noticed I was finding it hard to stand still.

I peered into the hallway. No sign of the man. Sidling up to a table, I rested against it, telling myself to picture the air going in and out of my nostrils.

*Okay*, I thought. *So that's it.* At least I'd had the chance to understand.

'Oh, you're *there!*' said John. 'I've been waiting in the wrong place.'

I jumped to my feet. 'No! No, I was here.'

Our steps fell into sync. We headed for the door we had entered through.

'I thought you'd left,' I twittered, as if I hadn't minded; as if it was only funny. 'Like, you'd said your piece and—'

'No!' said John. 'Goodness, no. Now where do you want to go next?'

———

'Do you think,' I had said to Michael, in his house, during our interview, 'if Caroline hadn't died, do you think Carl would have made a good father?'

Immediately he said no. 'I don't – He was too . . . He was too loose; he was too disorganised. He had no money. They were in debt. He drank. He spent what he didn't have. And he just – he didn't seem to have any life sense and any nous. He was good at certain things, but he wasn't prepared to face up to the normal everyday challenges that every-body faces.'

I cleared my throat. 'Do you think . . . I would have got on with him?'

'I don't know,' he said. 'It's hard to say.' He considered it more intently. 'I don't think so.'

My heartbeat flickered. *Did this mean I had not missed out?*

'As a parent you can't get away with just being charming,' Michael said. 'You've got to have something more to offer.'

To be there through the hard stuff too.

———

Closing time came up on us. By then my feet were blocks of ice. I didn't mind. While John led the way to the lemurs I checked my watch. In theory we had 40 minutes left. In practice, exhaustion was threatening to overtake me. Now our final hurdle loomed: the question of how to part ways.

As we passed through the gift shop, John asked which direction I was heading in. I told him south and gave him an out, not wanting him to feel obliged to stay. 'You'll probably be going east, I'm guessing.'

He glanced about him. 'I'll walk back through the park with you if that's okay?'

'That's very okay.'

Our last 15 minutes were light and heavy. John asked what TV shows I watched; I told him I didn't have a TV. He found that thrilling.

We talked about art and painting. 'The critic John Berger—'

'I've heard of him!' I said.

'—did this book called *Ways of Seeing*. It talks about how art is not complete without the person who sees it. Between you and the artwork there is a space, and that is where the art appears.'

'I love that!'

'Yeah, it's great.'

As the gates of Regent's Park came into view, I asked: 'What happens after we die?'

The man guffawed.

Together we talked about energy. We talked about the cosmos.

And then we reached the pavement by the roadside, in

earshot of the traffic on Euston Road. 'I keep going this way now,' I said.

John turned. 'I go this way, I think.'

He came back to face me. I hesitated, then opened my arms.

As John pulled me in to a hug, tears pooled in my eyes. I relaxed my head. Let it fall. Pulled tighter.

John pulled tighter too.

His touch said regret. And welcome. It said, *I am here. So are you.*

I stayed in that space for as long as I could. He waited a little while before he let go.

'I'd like to write to you,' I said as we moved apart. 'If that's okay?'

'I'd be delighted.'

'Thank you so much.'

'Thank you. Take *good* care.'

Now facing in different directions, we started to walk.

As I moved out of view, my insides swirled. Things kept shifting; my brain kept shifting.

'There are no dead ends,' John had told me, somewhere between the penguins and flamingos. 'Just events that take you on to the next thing.'

I staggered back into the centre of town. My shoulders loosened. Something had been taken off me. Something that had never been mine to hold.

I was ready to put it down now. Ready for rest.

# ACKNOWLEDGEMENTS

Big thanks to the people and groups who helped transform these words and experiences into something that can be held and read – whether supporting practically, emotionally, linguistically, financially, nutritionally, or by cheering from the sidelines.

*Editors:* Hazel Eriksson and Jo Thompson.

*Agent:* Ed Wilson.

*Project Editor:* Eve Hutchings.

*Copyeditor:* Holly Kyte.

*Interviewees:* Ash, Becca, Jeremy Davies, Robin Hadley, Frank L'Engle Williams, Sophie Lewis, Mario Liong, Winn Tam and Jordan Thierry.

*Spark*: the Most Honourable Bridie France, plus Chris Benderev and the team behind 'Classified Dad', *This American Life* (June 2022).

*First Readers:* Cailey Rizzo and Richard Lambert.

*General Support*: the Cousins Team, the Creative Writing Team, the Ex-Colleague Teams, the Undergraduate Team. In addition: Albie, Alex I., Amber M-B., Bea B., Beth D., Catherine K., Chelsey F., Chris, Christine S.,

# ACKNOWLEDGEMENTS

Clare B., Fanny C., Fliss Q., Fliss W., Gay P-W., Graham H., Holly, Ian F., Jackie N., Jamie S., Jeff M., Jez F., Jo L., Jon C., Josie A., Kay S., Liz B., Mabry, Malachi, Mangs, Nicola B., Paul, Polly at Tommy's, Rilke, Safia F., Sam R., Sarah, Tim H., Tom B., Tom L., Victoria B., Victoria S., Zach B. and Zakia U.

*Life Support:* Ben Marks, Eleanor Wasserberg, Katie Hunter and Marie Larford.

*Writing Support:* Arts Council England DYCP Fund, ArtHouse Jersey, CNF Club, the Hawthornden Foundation, the Society of Authors, Spread the Word and Team Write Club.

*Special Thanks:*

To Claire, a dream mentor;

To Leander, for a top referral service;

To John, whose company was a revelation (and who steadfastly refused to accept sandwich money);

To Nick, who has been there in various ways (including by my side at the *Postman Pat* interval, it turns out);

To Michael, whose openness helped ease a heavy time;

To Peter, who continues as Pops and remains ever ready for further larks;

To the intrepid dadvert respondents who shared their words, experience, humour, time and true feelings;

To the therapists, especially Rachel and Group (♥ you know who you are);

To Fraser, who appeared after the timeline of this book, at exactly the right moment. Thank you for leaving us both space to protect and provide for each other – and for mercifully steering clear of any discipline;

And to Mum, who by linking me with London Zoo unwittingly linked me to somewhere Carl liked – and wittingly gave me a stable home of pig-punctuated décor, pig-dogs, pig-out meals and (affectionate, maddening, mutual) pig-headedness. Thank you, thank you, thank you.

Written with loving memories of Norma, Jenny and Granny.

# RESOURCES

## Books

Katherine Angel, *Daddy Issues: Love and Hate in the Time of Patriarchy* (Verso, 2019)

Esther Dermott, *Intimate Fatherhood: A Sociological Analysis* (Routledge, 2008)

Robin Hadley, *How Is a Man Supposed to Be a Man? Male Childlessness – a Life Course Disrupted* (Berghahn Books, 2021)

Kathryn Harrison, *The Kiss: A Secret Life* (Fourth Estate, 1997)

Barbara Hobson (ed.), *Making Men into Fathers: Men, Masculinities and the Social Politics of Fatherhood* (Cambridge University Press, 2002)

Frank L'Engle Williams, *Fathers and Their Children in the First Three Years of Life: An Anthropological Perspective* (Texas A&M University Press, 2019)

Sophie Lewis, *Abolish the Family: A Manifesto for Care and Liberation* (Verso, 2022)

Sophie Lewis, *Full Surrogacy Now: Feminism Against Family* (Verso, 2019)

Mario Liong, *Chinese Fatherhood, Gender and Family: Father Mission* (Palgrave Macmillan, 2017)

Anna Machin, *The Life of Dad: The Making of the Modern Father* (Simon & Schuster, 2018)

Paul May, *Approaching Fatherhood: A Guide for Adoptive Dads and Others* (British Association for Adoption and Fostering, 2015 reprint)

Ross D. Parke, *Fatherhood (The Developing Child)*, (Harvard University Press, 1996)

## Documentaries

Joe Berlinger, *Conversations with a Killer: The Ted Bundy Tapes* (Netflix, 2019)

Jordan Thierry, *The Black Fatherhood Project* (Dream Chase Media, 2013)

## Audio

*A Bright Yellow Light*, BBC Radio 4 (produced by Amanda Hancox, 2019)

'It Takes a Village', *If These Ovaries Could Talk* [podcast] (Jaimie Kelton and Robin Hopkins, 2022)

'The Impact of Fathers on Our Love Life', *Love Maps: A Podcast about Love, Sex and Relationships* [podcast] (Jo Nicholl, 2020)

## Organisations

*Adoption UK* – '[connecting] people across the adoption community, [supporting] adopters and adoptees, and [working] with them to influence the decisions that affect their lives':

# RESOURCES

www.adoptionuk.org

*Al-Anon* – 'for anyone whose life is or has been affected by someone else's drinking':
www.al-anon.org.uk (UK)
www.al-anon.org.au (Australia)
www.al-anon.org.nz (NZ)
www.alanon.org.za (SA)

*Alcoholics Anonymous* – 'concerned solely with the personal recovery and continued sobriety of individual alcoholics who turn to the [AA] for help':
www.alcoholics-anonymous.org.uk (UK)
www.aa.org.au (Australia)
www.aa.org.nz (NZ)
www.aasouthafrica.org.za (SA)

*Become* – 'the [UK] national charity for children in care and care leavers':
www.becomecharity.org.uk

*Befrienders Worldwide* – 'our members and volunteers around the world provide confidential support to people in emotional crisis or distress, or those close to them':
www.befrienders.org

*Changing Minds NZ* – '[New Zealand] not-for-profit … [led by] people who have navigated their own lived experience journey through mental health and addiction':
www.changingminds.org.nz

*Cruse Bereavement Support* – '[helping] people through one of the most painful times in life – with [UK-based] bereavement support, information and campaigning':
www.cruse.org.uk

*DADS Network* – 'committed to promoting a fathering culture in Hong Kong':
www.dadsnetworkhk.org

*Families Need Fathers* – 'UK charity supporting dads, mums and grandparents to have personal contact and meaningful relationships with their children following parental separation':
www.fnf.org.uk

*Fatherhood Institute* – 'UK charity working to build a society that values, prepares, and supports men as involved fathers and caregivers':
www.fatherhoodinstitute.org

*Gingerbread* – 'the charity for single parent families . . . [providing] expert advice and practical support for single mums and dads in England and Wales':
www.gingerbread.org.uk

*Grief Centre* – '[supporting] every person, regardless of financial circumstance, through their individual loss and grief journey':
www.griefcentre.com.au (Australia)
www.griefcentre.org.nz (NZ)

*Helping Minds* – 'supporting mental health issues for families, young people & adults [in Australia]':
www.helpingminds.org.au

*Mind* – 'offering help whenever [people] might need it through . . . information, advice and local services':
www.mind.org.uk

*NAPAC* – The National Association for People Abused in Childhood . . . [providing] accessible direct support services to survivors and those who support them':
www.napac.org.uk

*Netcare Akeso* – 'person-centred mental healthcare [in South Africa] . . . using creative tools and skills for sustainable mental health and wellness':

www.netcare.co.za

*Pregnant Then Screwed* – '[seeking] legislative change that will foster greater parity between men and women, both in the home and the workplace':
www.pregnantthenscrewed.com

*Samaritans* – '[making] sure there's always someone there for anyone who needs someone':
www.samaritans.org (UK)
www.samaritans.org.au (Australia)
www.samaritans.org.nz (NZ)

*Stand Alone* – 'provides support to adults that are estranged from their family or a key family member. There are times when it's right to walk away':
www.standalone.org.uk

*Tommy's* – 'dedicated to finding causes and treatments to save babies' lives as well as providing trusted pregnancy and baby loss information and support':
www.tommys.org

# END NOTES

## 1. (DIS)EMBARKING

**14 'On average, children who experience . . .'** 'Single parents: facts and figures', Gingerbread, www.gingerbread.org.uk (updated September 2019, verified February 2024).

**14 'being born to an unmarried mother . . .'** H. M. Mikkonen et al., 'The lifelong socioeconomic disadvantage of single-mother background – the Helsinki Birth Cohort Study 1934–1944', *BMC Public Health*, 16: 817 (2016).

**14 'the well-fathered daughter . . .'** Linda Nielsen, 'How Dads Affect Their Daughters into Adulthood', Institute for Family Studies (3 June 2014).

**15 'Girls in homes without . . .'** Sarah Yang, 'Father absence linked to earlier puberty among certain girls', Berkeley News (17 September 2010).

**15 Lastly, full-blooded puberty . . .** 'Early or Delayed Puberty', NHS (page last reviewed September 2022, verified in February 2024).

## 3. STRATEGY

**32 On the more troubling end of the spectrum . . .** Joshua Rapp Learn, 'Mama Bears Use Humans To Keep Their Cubs Safe', *Smithsonian Magazine* (27 June 2016).

**34** **one leading site reported . . .** Kayla Kibbe, 'Why More Young Guys Are Embracing the Sugar Daddy Life', Inside Hook (11 December 2020).

**34** **As one 27-year-old summarised . . .** Georgette Culley, 'SWEET OR SICKLY? Inside a "Sugar Baby Summit" where girls learn how to meet sugar daddies and how to have kinky sex', *Sun* (16 April 2018).

**35** **'fathers are a biological necessity . . .'** Attributed to Margaret Mead in Harold A. Minden's *Two Hugs for Survival* (McClelland & Stewart Ltd, 1982).

**43** **'My reactions to my "broodiness" . . .'** Robin Hadley, *How Is a Man Supposed to Be a Man? Male Childlessness – a Life Course Disrupted* (Berghahn Books, 2021), p.1.

**44** **Up to a 23 per cent decline . . .** Becca Stanek, 'How Male Fertility Changes With Age', *Forbes Health* (updated 9 August 2023).

**44** **an increase in miscarriage rates . . .** Fertility Education Poster, 'Do you want to have KIDS in the future? 9 things you should know now', British Fertility Society (undated, verified February 2024).

**44** **In a 2009 British survey . . .** Hadley, *How Is a Man Supposed to Be a Man?* p.15.

## 5. NICE PEOPLE

**69** **'And we know . . .'** Anna Machin, *The Life of Dad: The Making of the Modern Father* (Simon & Schuster, 2018), p.39.

**70** **average age of children adopted . . .** 'What sort of children need adoptive families?' Adoption UK, www.adoptionuk.org (verified November 2023).

## 6. FIRST MEETING

**96** **'My father is an absence . . .'** Kathryn Harrison, *The Kiss* (Fourth Estate, 1997), pp.5, 51 and 67.

## 7. PUSH

**101  80 per cent of men . . .** Anna Machin, 'The 10%', annamachin. com (27 July 2017, verified February 2024).

**101  While 78 per cent of British women . . .** 'Conceptions in England and Wales: 2017' and 'Conceptions in England and Wales: 2021', Office for National Statistics (released 15 April 2019 and 30 March 2023 respectively).

**101  82 per cent of women by aged 40 . . .** Results presented by Gretchen Livingstone and D'Vera Cohn, 'Childlessness Up Among All Women; Down Among Women with Advanced Degrees', Pew Research Centre (25 June 2010).

**101  More recent figures for sub-Saharan Africa . . .** Florianne C. J. Verkroost and Christiaan W. S. Monden, 'Childlessness and Development in Sub-Saharan Africa: Is There Evidence for a U-shaped Pattern?' *European Journal of Population*, 38: 3 (10 March 2022), pp.319–52.

**102  a 'process [that] may increasingly leave men . . .'** Ibid.

**102  In Ghana infertility can provoke hostility . . .** Dorcas Ofosu-Budu, 'Infertility among married women in rural Ghana: Cultural Contexts and Individuals' Lived Experiences', *Dissertations in Social Sciences and Business Studies*, University of Eastern Finland (2021).

**102  In the US, men are less likely to . . .** Alivia Kaylor, 'Breaking the Stigma of Male Infertility to Promote Greater Health Equity', *HealthcareExecIntelligence* (27 March 2023).

**103  'whereby desires for recreational and luxurious opportunities . . .'** Verkroost and Monden, 'Childlessness and Development in Sub-Saharan Africa'.

## 8. LOST

**114  'Males accounted for three-quarters of suicides . . .'** 'Suicides in the UK: 2017 registrations', Office for National Statistics (2 September 2018).

## 9. DISTRACTIONS

**127 a 178 per cent increase in . . .** Gareth May, 'Why is incest porn so popular?', *VICE* (25 February 2015).

**128 20 most common female roles . . .** Jon Millward, *Deep Inside: A Study of 10,000 Porn Stars and Their Careers*, jonmillward.com (14 February 2013).

## 10. MIXED

**140 'We want to be able to say . . .'** Joe Berlinger, *Conversations with a Killer: The Ted Bundy Tapes* (Netflix, 2019).

## 11. FUNDAMENTALLY FLAWED

**152 'Fathers, even more than mothers . . .'** Ross D. Parke, *Fatherhood (The Developing Child)*, (Harvard University Press, 1996), p.146.

**152 'The most powerful predictor . . .'** Ibid., pp.145–6.

**152 'There is no doubt . . .'** Machin, *The Life of Dad*, p.x.

**152 *50 per cent of local households . . .*** Hannah Richardson, 'A million children growing up without fathers', BBC (10 June 2013).

**152 Dickens, who had 10 'legitimate' children . . .** Arifa Akbar, 'Why Dickens was not the family man history would have us believe', *Independent* (18 May 2020).

**159 'a social unit . . .'** Cambridge Dictionary Online, dictionary. cambridge.org (verified June 2023).

**160 'For a time, it all seemed . . .'** David Brooks, 'The Nuclear Family Was a Mistake', *Atlantic* (March 2020).

**160 'A father, historically, protects . . .'** Katherine Angel, *Daddy Issues: Love and Hate in the Time of Patriarchy* (Verso, 2019), pp.55 and 12.

**161 'the *natural* way clearly privileges . . .'** Sophie Lewis, *Full Surrogacy Now: Feminism Against Family* (Verso, 2019), pp.114 and 116.

**162 'I've noticed that a lot of people . . .'** Sophie Lewis, *Abolish the Family: A Manifesto for Care and Liberation* (Verso, 2022), p.4.

164 'Apparently Dad once . . .' Excerpts from 'Autoanalysis: Caren Alltsritch', later published in *Parapraxis Magazine* (December 2022).

165 **that one in five British families . . .** 'The Prevalence of Family Estrangement', Stand Alone and Ipsos MORI (2014).

165 **a separate poll in the US indicated . . .** Fern Schumer Chapman, 'Why So Many Families Are Living With Estrangement', *Psychology Today* (2 January 2023).

165 **'growing awareness of mental health . . .'** Maddy Savage, 'Family estrangement: Why adults are cutting off their parents', BBC Family Tree (1 December 2021).

## 13. HALF-NODS

193 **'a man or boy who . . .'** Cambridge Dictionary Online, dictionary.cambridge.org (verified March 2023).

## 14. MOTHER

196 **'My dad has a long commute . . .'** Quoted by Karen Alberg Grossman, '2018 FATHER OF THE YEAR AWARDS RAISES $1.25 MILLION FOR CHARITY', *Mr Magazine* (12 June 2018).

196 **a CEO who'd so bravely . . .** Karen Alberg Grossman, 'FATHER OF THE YEAR AWARDS LUNCHEON CELEBRATES WONDERFUL DADS', *Mr Magazine* (17 June 2019).

196 **In his acceptance speech, Bush . . .** 'As a matter of fact, I don't think I would've quit drinking had it not been for being a dad. You see what happened to me was alcohol was becoming a love and it was beginning to crowd out my affections for the most important love if you're a dad and that's loving your little girls. So for me, fatherhood meant sobriety from 1986 on,' George W. Bush. Speech quoted by Natasha Bertrand, 'George W. Bush named "Father of the Year"', Reuters (19 June 2015).

196 **between 2009 and 2019, the number of families . . .** 'Families and households in the UK: 2019', Office for National Statistics (15 November 2019).

197 **These days, 7 per cent of . . .** 'Economic activity and employment type for men and women by age of the youngest dependent child living with them in the UK: Table S', Office for National Statistics (2019).

197 **A UK government survey on . . .** 'Child sexual abuse in England and Wales: year ending March 2019', Office for National Statistics (14 January 2020).

197 **As author Peg Streep has said . . .** Interviewed by Sarah Boesveld, 'The curse of a mean mother', *Globe and Mail* (18 October 2009).

198 **According to the internet . . .** 'Sudden infant death syndrome (SIDS)', NHS (wording reviewed 21 October 2021, verified February 2024).

200 **NHS guidance failed to . . .** Anna Machin, 'In praise of fathers: the making of the modern dad', *Guardian* (19 June 2021).

203 **one in seven women experience . . .** Figures from Saba Mughal, Yusra Azhar and Waquar Siddiqui, 'Postpartum Depression', featured in the National Library of Medicine (updated 7 October 2022), and Amanda Ruggeri, 'Male postnatal depression: Why men struggle in silence', BBC Family Tree (6 June 2022).

203 **'I would tell my wife . . .'** Ruggeri, 'Male postnatal depression'.

203 **10 per cent of non-resident fathers . . .** Mona Chalabi, 'Dads that don't live with their children: how many stay in touch?' *Guardian* (20 November 2013).

## 15. FATHER'S DAY

208 **'More than *90 per cent* . . .'** Lucy Adams, 'Sex attack victims usually know attacker, says new study', BBC News (1 March 2018).

## 16. DAUGHTER

234 **A 2011 study described . . .** R. A. Foley and M. Mirazón Lahr, 'The evolution of the diversity of cultures', *Philosophical Transactions of the Royal Society B: Biological Sciences*, 366: 1567 (12 April 2011), pp.1080–9.

**238 lesbian mothers experienced unfair discrimination ...** Summary description from 'Our campaigns: Lesbian parents', Rights of Women; research from 'Lesbian Mothers on Trial: A Report on Lesbian Mothers and Child Custody' (1984).

**238 'no evidence that the development of children ...'** Charlotte J. Patterson, 'Children of Lesbian and Gay Parents', *Child Development*, 63: 5 (October 1992), pp.1025–42.

**238 'Empirical research has indicated ...'** Jeff Hearn, 'Men, fathers and the state: national and global relations', in *Making Men into Fathers: Men, Masculinities and the Social Politics of Fatherhood*, Barbara Hobson (ed.), (Cambridge University Press, 2002), p.263.

**239 a separate sociological study ...** Cited by Esther Dermott, *Intimate Fatherhood: A Sociological Analysis* (Routledge, 2008), p.124.

**239 'When mothers are around, fathers ...'** Findings from a 2014 study by Dr Ruth Feldman of Bar-Ilan University, reported in 'Are gay dads better than straight ones?' Jeremy Davies, Fatherhood Institute, and from a 2014 study by Pilyoung Kim of the University of Denver, reported in Machin, *The Life of Dad*, pp.122–3.

**239 76.4 per cent of them desired ...** Quoted by Hadley, *How Is a Man Supposed to Be a Man?* p.16.

**239 same-sex couples in the UK ...** Adoption and Children Act 2002, legislation.gov.uk.

**239 Read tales about the kiki 'ballroom scene' ...** See Anja Matthes and Sony Salzman, 'In the Kiki Ballroom Scene, Queer Kids of Color Can Be Themselves', *Atlantic* (7 November 2019).

## 18. ELEPHANT

**265 'Fathers are particularly important ...'** Parke, *Fatherhood*, p.150.

**270 3.2 per cent and 9 per cent of adoptions ...** Lesley Ashmall and Mario Cacciottolo, 'I sent my adopted son back into care', BBC (31 January 2017).

272 'It's like eating an elephant...' Paul May, *Approaching Father-hood: A Guide for Adoptive Dads and Others* (British Association for Adoption and Fostering, 2005), p.71.

## 19. STATUS QUO

287 'Children need their fathers...' Parke, *Fatherhood,* p.257.

288 Nearly 2 million single parents... 'Single parents: facts and figures', Gingerbread (using references from September 2019, verified February 2024).

288 'On average, those who ...' Sumi Rabindrakumar of Gingerbread, supported by Álvaro Martínez-Pérez, Winona Shaw, Nathan Hughes and Phil Mike Jones, 'Family Portrait: Single parent families and transitions over time', University of Sheffield (2019).

289 'They're such different things ...' Ash interviewed by Jaimie Kelton and Robin Hopkins, 'It Takes a Village', *If These Ovaries Could Talk* (21 February 2022).

290 Of the 95,000 kids with ... 'Divorces in England and Wales, children of divorced couples: historical data, 2013 edition', Office for National Statistics (23 November 2015).

294 'Among the Paraiyan ...' Frank L'Engle Williams, *Fathers and Their Children in the First Three Years of Life: An Anthropological Perspective* (Texas A&M University Press, 2019), p.48.

295 fathers who experienced couvade symptoms ... Parke, *Fatherhood,* p.21.

297 'It doesn't change the fact...' Nadim Ednan-Laperouse speaking to Emily Buchanan, *A Bright Yellow Light*, BBC Radio 4 (produced by Amanda Hancox, 2019).

301 As one sociologist put it ... Helena Bergman and Barbara Hobson, 'Compulsory fatherhood: the coding of fatherhood in the Swedish welfare state', *Making Men into Fathers*, Hobson (ed.), p.95.

## 20. NOT SURE

**305** 'Becoming a father is not a single event . . .' Parke, *Fatherhood*, p.17.

**312** statutory parental leave . . . Press release, 'Five-day statutory paternity leave to take effect on January 18', government of the Hong Kong Special Administrative Region (11 January 2019).

## 21. FINE

**317** 'Through almost every studied culture . . .' J. Neil Tift, 'What are the three primary roles of a father?' Continued (2 March 2020).

**324** 'Just because we have the equipment . . .' '100 Women 2016: Parents who regret having children', BBC News (6 December 2016).

**324** 'Any absence is a wound . . .' Jo Nicholl, 'The Impact of Fathers on Our Love Life', episode 5, *Love Maps: A Podcast about Love, Sex and Relationships* (25 June 2020).

## 22. ESCAPE

**327** 'People who are short on relatives . . .' Elif Batuman, 'Japan's Rent-a-Family Industry', *New Yorker* (23 April 2018).

**328** 'painted the father as a heroic figure . . .' David Robson, 'Ikumen: How Japan's "hunky dads" are changing parenting', BBC (27 November 2018).

**329** 'In a significant minority . . .' Parke, *Fatherhood*, p.8.

**329** 'Are the men of the African Aka tribe . . .' Joanna Moorhead, 'Are the men of the African Aka tribe the best fathers in the world?' *Guardian* (15 June 2005).

**330** 'a relatively rare form of fathering . . .' Machin, *The Life of Dad*, pp.54–6.

**331** after the Second World War, children . . . Ilona Oster, 'A new role for fathers? The German case' in *Making Men into Fathers*, Hobson (ed.), p.151.

331 **almost a quarter of children** ... Adrienne Burgess, 'Dads Through the Ages: A History', DAD.info (undated).

334 **'concerns about discriminatory ...'** HM Chief Inspectorate of Prisons, 'Report on a scrutiny visit to HMP Grendon, 2 and 9–10 March 2021' (2021).

334 **'Hi, I'm Adam ...'** ' "Hi, I'm Adam, I killed my daughter": inside Grendon prison', Channel 4 News (15 July 2014).

334 **'Surveys, however, have revealed ...'** 'Imprisoned Fathers', Families Need Fathers (10 August 2014; accessed June 2023).

335 **an estimated 312,000 children** ... Sarah Kincaid, Manon Roberts and Professor Eddie Kane, 'Children of Prisoners: Fixing a broken system', Crest Advisory and the Centre for Health and Justice (February 2019).

335 **almost 2.4 per cent** ... Population of under-18s in England and Wales estimated as 12,653,507 in 'Estimates of the population for the UK, England, Wales, Scotland and Northern Ireland: Mid-2019', Office for National Statistics, www.ons.gov.uk (2019).

335 **65 per cent of sons** ... Kincaid et al., 'Children of Prisoners'.

337 **'It is up to extended relatives ...'** Jordan Thierry, *The Black Fatherhood Project* (Dream Chase Media, 2013).

339 ***Do you not think*** ... Quoted in email. Original source unknown.

341 **'Mums can choose to pay ...'** Jasper Hamill, 'RENT-A-DAD: Father's Day "Daddy on Demand" service launched by "sugar daddy" dating website Arrangement.com', *Sun* (16 June 2017).

341 **'Rent A Dad': available to** ... Jeff Yablon, rent-a-dad.nyc (verified June 2023).

## 24. CARL

367 **'The less you expect ...'** 'Some advice on meeting my father for the first time?' Quora (verified June 2023).